FRANCOPHONE LITERATURES: AN INTRODUCTORY SURVEY

Belinda Jack

OXFORD UNIVERSITY PRESS

*This book has been printed digitally and produced in a standard specification
in order to ensure its continuing availability*

OXFORD
UNIVERSITY PRESS

Great Clarendon Street, Oxford OX2 6DP

Oxford University Press is a department of the University of Oxford.
It furthers the University's objective of excellence in research, scholarship,
and education by publishing worldwide in

Oxford New York

Auckland Bangkok Buenos Aires Cape Town Chennai
Dar es Salaam Delhi Hong Kong Istanbul Karachi Kolkata
Kuala Lumpur Madrid Melbourne Mexico City Mumbai Nairobi
São Paulo Shanghai Singapore Taipei Tokyo Toronto

Oxford is a registered trade mark of Oxford University Press
in the UK and in certain other countries

Published in the United States
by Oxford University Press Inc., New York

© Belinda Jack 1996

The moral rights of the author have been asserted
Database right Oxford University Press (maker)

Reprinted 2002

ISBN 0-19-871506-4

For Allan

Acknowledgements

Colleagues with specialist knowledge of various areas generously agreed to read drafts of a number of sections and their help has undoubtedly made this a better book than it would otherwise have been. Peter Hawkins read Part I, Bridget Jones, Part II, Alexander Hargreaves, Part III, and Christopher Rolfe, Chapter 12. Colleagues at Christ Church allowed me to rehearse arguments and articulate various problems informally. I am indebted to them, and to the College's Governing Body for providing me with equipment and funding for travel and attendance at various conferences.

The new European Humanities Research Centre in Oxford has been a very exciting base from which to work during the last year. I would like to thank the Director, Dr Ian Maclean, and the British Academy for the Post-Doctoral Fellowship which I hold at the Centre. The British Academy also provided me with the means to travel to both Quebec and the West Indies. These trips were invaluable also from the point of view of collecting material and in less tangible ways, subtly changing my understanding. Meeting with various writers, most particularly with Jean Bernabé (in Martinique) and Amin Maalouf (at the Maison Française d'Oxford), and corresponding with other writers, is also something which has made a great difference.

Heartfelt thanks go to my family and friends for continuing to take a real interest in my academic concerns, and to the younger members for encouraging me even though the nature of my activity remains somewhat mysterious. As I write, all that my children have seen is an awful lot of paper. Those who have looked after them, particularly Susie Ess, have also made this enterprise possible. I would like them to know how much I appreciate their devotion and kindness.

Contents

INTRODUCTION

1. Nationalisms, Nomenclature, and the Genesis of the Discipline(s)

French literature is generally proposed as a relatively unproblematic and valid subject or discipline. This is in spite of debates about, for example, the nature of the canon, and the status of regional literatures and their relationship to the canon (not to mention debates about the validity of studying literary production independently from other forms of cultural production). The institutionalization of the study of national literatures and their displacement of the classics as the principal 'humane' discipline occurred at a particular historical moment; the growth of empire and the rise of national literary disciplines happened simultaneously. It is only recently that the existence of francophone (and for that matter anglophone, lusophone, and hispanophone) literatures, which can no longer be unproblematically annexed to the mainstream European parent literature, has been fully acknowledged. Furthermore the nature of the relationship between the European literature and literatures in the European language (or a language closely related to it) is, increasingly, analysed not to reveal the latter as imitative or an extension of the European parent literature, but rather as fundamentally subversive, a rebellious child which obliges the parent to redefine his or her identity in relation to the next generation.

That the writing of France's European neighbours Belgium and Switzerland displayed particular local colour or certain local con-

In footnotes, for book references the place of publication is Paris unless otherwise stated.

cerns was, of course, recognized early on, as were differences between French and French-Canadian texts. The European countries were by the nineteenth century independent nation states and Canada became a Dominion in 1867 with considerable autonomy (although the colonial nature of French Canada's relationship with anglophone Canada also has to be considered). This relative independence from France, however, in many ways separates the literary histories of these countries from those, most obviously, of the former colonies proper.

Institutions and groups in Belgium, Switzerland, and French Canada (but also small literary groups in certain colonial areas, for example, Martinique, Guadeloupe, French Guiana, and La Réunion in the Indian Ocean) were themselves concerned to promote and map national (loosely defined) literary traditions when questions of nationalism dominated political, cultural, and intellectual life. But in spite of concern to assert difference and varying degrees of literary distinctiveness, texts deemed worthy of recognition by the French tended to be assimilated into French literature. On the whole, of course, the major literary influences in the areas mentioned were those of metropolitan France and most writers participated in more or less orthodox ways in the major French literary movements of their time, often delayed by a decade or two (Romanticism, Parnassianism, Symbolism, and later and in more innovative ways, Surrealism, for example). Writing by Africans, on the other hand, which emerged much later than in other areas, was initially subsumed under 'colonial literature', a branch of the colonial sciences, a composite of disciplines informing the colonial project.

It is now recognized that a plurality of literatures written in the French language (or languages) exists, even if the status of these literatures falls short of the autonomy of certain literatures written in English or Spanish; American and Australian literatures were the first to assert, and be widely recognized as having, literary traditions of their own. More recently American (and indeed Australian critics) have initiated and largely fired a lively debate concerning the post-colonial. Drawing frequently on writers associated with 'French' theory (Michel Foucault, Jacques Derrida, Jean Baudrillard, Jean-François Lyotard, Louis Althusser, Michel Pêcheux, most particularly), they have explored the relationships between the post-modern, post-structuralist, and post-colonial, for example. Theorists concerned, broadly speaking, with the post-colonial, including Edward Saïd, Gayatri Spivak, Henry Louis Gates Jr., Homi K. Bhabha, and Jan Mohammed (among a growing number) have become immensely influential within the American Academy. A post-colonial theoretical canon is emerging, evidence of a new discipline.[1] There is no comparable francophone academy within which a comparable francophone discipline might emerge. Although French centres for the study of francophone literatures have been established (the Centre d'études francophones at the Université de Paris XIII, most importantly), France's relationship with the francophone world, in large part her former colonies, remains a complex one which will be discussed further. Thus while academic discussion which might be described as concerned with francophone post-colonialism (the term 'post-colonial' has interestingly not been prominent within the French debate) takes place worldwide, there is no obvious centre on which the debate might be focused. The lack of consensus concerning nomenclature is symptomatic of the dissolution of the debate, and militates against the genesis of a more homogenous discipline. Thus the literatures discussed here are known by their national appellations (Cameroonian, Belgian, Mauritian, etc.), but also under a wide range of rubrics and in different groupings: Negro, Neo-African, Negro-African, French-Canadian or Quebec (the difference is a significant one), Negritude, West Indian, Black, Third World, Post-European, and so on. New appellations emerge all the time. For example, in his recent essay 'Le Chaos-monde, l'oral et l'écrit', the West Indian writer Édouard Glissant opposes the literary production of the West (l'Occident) to 'les littératures commes les nôtres—les littératures du sud et les littératures des pays antillais'.[2] Within the francophone debate new nomenclature becomes ever more diverse; within the anglophone debate, American post-colonial studies, not without a degree of irony, is rapidly gaining hegemony.

The vitality and institutional power of the American debate has encouraged some francophone writers, particularly those from the West Indies for whom America is a close presence, to ally themselves in effect with the American Academy. Édouard Glissant has been Professor at the Université de Bâton Rouge in Louisiana and

[1] Publications such as *Colonial Discourse and Post-Colonial Theory: A Reader* (Hemel Hempstead, 1993) are also evidence of a new discipline.

[2] Edouard Glissant, 'Le Chaos-monde, l'oral et l'écrit', *Écrire la 'parole de nuit': La Nouvelle littérature antillaise*, ed. Ralph Ludwig (1994), 111–29 (p. 116).

Maryse Condé increasingly publishes her critical work (and translations of her fictional writing) in America.[3] The influential essay-manifesto *Éloge de la Créolité*, published by Gallimard (1989), by three prominent young francophone West Indian intellectuals, Jean Bernabé, Patrick Chamoiseau, and Raphaël Confiant, was translated by M. B. Taleb-Khyar in 1990 and published first in the journal *Callaloo: A Journal of African American and African Arts and Letters* (University of Charlottesville, 1990), although later published by Gallimard in a bilingual edition (1993).

2. French Colonial Activity

The history of French exploration, missionary and trading activity, and colonization, and the dispersion and adoption of the French language across the globe is, of course, different from that of English, Spanish, or Portuguese (the three most important European colonial languages). During the last five hundred years France has won and lost what can be regarded as two colonial empires: one in the Americas, the Indian Ocean and the Indian subcontinent, in the sixteenth, seventeenth, and eighteenth centuries respectively; the other, in Africa, Indo-China, and Oceania, during the nineteenth and early twentieth centuries, when the territories of the first empire had largely been lost to Great Britain as a result of France's defeats for the most part in Europe but also overseas.

In North America, the French presence became significant with the arrival of explorers, trappers, and missionaries in the seventeenth century, although Jacques Cartier had, of course, been sent by François I in 1534. Cartier discovered the St Lawrence and explored as far as Hochelaga (Montreal). Quebec was founded by Samuel de Champlain in 1608. René Robert Cavelier de La Salle claimed the Mississippi basin for France in 1682 and it was, of course, in honour of Louis XIV that it was named Louisiana. Colonization in North America was relatively slow and the number of settlers relatively small.

French colonial forces in the Caribbean region arrived in the seventeenth century. A colony was also founded on the South American mainland (French Guiana). African slaves worked the

[3] See e.g. 'Order, Disorder, Freedom and the West Indian Writer', *Yale French Studies*, 83/2 (1993), 121–36.

sugar plantations which constituted the main source of income in the various territories. The ratio of African slave to white settler was more than ten to one.

In the Indian Ocean, colonies were established in the Île Bourbon (later La Réunion), the Île de France (later Mauritius), the Seychelles, and parts of Madagascar in the seventeenth and eighteenth centuries. In the Indian subcontinent trading posts were established along the coast at Pondicherry, most importantly, Chandernagor, and Mahé, from the mid-eighteenth century onwards. By the mid-eighteenth century a French Protectorate had been established over much of the subcontinent largely through the efforts of the remarkable Joseph François Dupleix.

From the middle of the eighteenth century France began to lose hold of her first empire but during the first half of the nineteenth was well on her way to establishing a second. In the Americas most was lost to Britain in the wake of the Seven Years War (1756–63) and during the Napoleonic Wars (1803–15). All that remained were small territories in the Caribbean region and the Indian Ocean.

The expansion of a second empire began with the conquest of Algeria in 1830. From Senegal in West Africa French forces pushed into the African interior. Cochin-China (southern Vietnam) was taken in 1859 and a few years later Cambodia became a French Protectorate. Tahiti, in the Pacific Ocean, also became a French Protectorate (in 1842) and New Caledonia was annexed in 1853.

These considerable colonial gains were built on under the Third Republic when, under the leadership of Jules Ferry, France gained further protectorates: Tunisia, Annam, Tonkin (which together with Cochin-China makes up Vietnam), Laos (in 1893), and Morocco (1912). Madagascar had been annexed in 1896. In sub-Saharan Africa still more significant gains were made and by the beginning of this century most of Western and Central Africa had been grouped into two vast French administrative areas, Afrique Occidentale Française (AOF), and Afrique Équitoriale Française (AEF).

3. French Language(s) Worldwide

An essentially military account of France's colonial history fails to reveal the differences in the significance of the French language in the various colonial areas and, intimately bound up with this, the differences in the literary histories of the francophone areas. The presence and concentration of French settlers, the length of time the French held control, and the nature of the indigenous linguistic situation, to a large extent explain the differences in the nature and importance of francophone literary activity in the former French empire.

Some one and a half million settlers populated France's overseas territories when the French empire was at its height. The number of people under French control at this point was somewhere around seventy million. The ratio of colonizer to colonized varied dramatically from area to area. Where the French colonial policy was one of sustained settlement the area would be one of the *colonies de peuplement*. Otherwise what was envisaged was that the area be rather one of the *colonies d'exploitation*. In the end it was only Algeria which became the former although there were larger numbers of French settlers in the other North African territories than elsewhere in Africa.

Estimates vary but it is generally agreed that there were some sixty thousand French-speakers in North America in the mid-eighteenth century who were then cut off from France by the Treaty of Paris in 1763 which ceded New France (with the exception of New Orleans) to Britain. Today more than a quarter of Canadians are French-speaking.

French survived into the nineteenth century in Louisiana and the size of the French-speaking community was enlarged by the arrival of Acadians deported by the British in 1755 and by refugees from Saint-Domingue (Santo Dominico until 1844 when it became the Dominican Republic) during the revolution in Haiti. Today educational programmes encourage French-language learning as part of a wider pedagogical plan to revive regional and ethnic cultures. There are also between two and three million French-speakers in the North Eastern United States, immigrants from Quebec and Acadia.

Although Creoles (each area in the Caribbean and Indian Ocean has its own particular Creole) are the languages of everyday communication both publicly and privately, French remains the administrative, business, and educational language. In what are now French Overseas Departments (Martinique, Guadeloupe, French Guiana, La Réunion), French is spoken by almost everyone. In Haiti French is spoken only by a small minority. On Mauritius, French is spoken by half the population. Mauritius is one of the most linguistically rich Creole islands: English, French, a number of Indian languages, and Chinese are all spoken by sizeable groups.

In North Africa, Arabic has offered a practical alternative to French in the former colonies and protectorates, and Arabic replaced French in the schools after independence, though some had been bilingual all along. Berber languages are also spoken by significant minorities. The educational and employment possibilities for North Africans in France has, however, encouraged acquisition of the language. More importantly, French is increasingly seen as a means of maintaining intellectual and political communication with the non-Arab world. French therefore has an ambiguous, if not paradoxical status. Before independence French was, of course, regarded as the language of colonial oppression. Since independence, however, Arabic has increasingly been regarded by some as the language of tradition and a new oppressive conformism; French is thus proposed by some intellectuals as the language of liberation.

Although French arrived with the missionaries in the Lebanon in the mid-nineteenth century, it was not until later, with the adoption of the French Mandate, that it became important. A large percentage of the present population (roughly half) is bilingual, although Arabic is the official language. During the last two decades, from the beginning of the war in the Lebanon, until its recent end, the likely future of French-speaking has been hard to assess.

As in North Africa French became a significant presence in Africa with the arrival of the French colonial forces in the nineteenth century. Although the teaching of French was seen as the most fundamental aspect of the assimilation of Africans, French schooling was most successfully implemented in and around major cities, particularly along the coasts. Since independence, attempts have been made to institute African languages to replace French as the language of power: administration, politics, business, and education. The vast number of African languages, their lack of recognition worldwide, and the difficulties of standardizing languages which have been little written, have militated against the complete rejection of the French language in the former French, and of course Belgian, colonies. Again estimates vary considerably, but it is likely that only 15 per cent of the relevant populations in sub-Saharan Africa (in the former French colonies and territories) are French-speaking.

In addition to the areas considered above, French remains important in most of the areas penetrated by French colonial activity. In those places which remain French territories (Polynesia, New Caledonia and its dependencies) the French educational system guarantees the survival of French. In Pondicherry (transferred from French to Indian administration in 1954) French remains an important second language as is the case on the Indo-Chinese peninsula.

In other parts of the world, particularly during the nineteenth century, French was the language of social distinction (for the Russian aristocracy, for example, for diplomacy, and in prestigious Turkish schools). Today English has largely taken over as the influential second language, although in South America, Poland, and Romania, French is learnt by a significant number of schoolchildren. French organizations, particularly the Alliance Française, work to teach French in a large number of overseas countries.

4. Decolonization and France's Relationship with the Francophone World

Most overseas territories of France became independent during the period between the end of the Second World War and the early 1960s when other European powers similarly altered their relationship with their former colonies. Although the engineers of French colonial policy were advocating, by the beginning of the century, *association* in place of the original *assimilation*—that is, retaining separate cultural identity while working together for mutual gain— rather than the complete substitution of French culture in place of the indigenous culture, attitudes to decolonization were very much informed by the earlier philosophy. This residual unwillingness to abandon the *mission civilisatrice*, combined with France's loss of national consciousness and pride in that identity as a function of the German Occupation of 1940–4, further encouraged politicians to resist decolonization in an attempt to boost the nation's mood by making something of France's presence overseas. On the other hand France's relative weakness at the end of the war, and the rising power and influence of the United States (and a number of American anti-colonial politicians in particular) encouraged an increasing anti-colonial discourse in France, often stimulated by Marxist ideas which were informing events in different areas worldwide. Left-wing Christian associations, that grouped around the journal *Esprit*, for example, argued for reform rather than the complete abandoning of the colonial venture. Even contributors to a journal such as Sartre's *Les Temps modernes* rarely argued for outright decolonization.

Syria and Lebanon, relatively recent French territories (over which they had gained a Mandate in 1920), were the first to gain independence, in 1945. But at the Brazzaville conference a year earlier, de Gaulle had made it clear that his vision for the future of the French overseas territories did not embrace independence. De Gaulle refused to recognize Ho Chi Minh's declaration of independence for Vietnam in 1945. War broke out a year later when he left office, and was to run until 1954.

Under the Fourth Republic the empire became the Union Française. Three associations with France were possible: that of *département français d'outre-mer* (DOM), that of *territoire d'outre-mer* (TOM) and that of *état associé*. Long-established territories such as Martinique and La Réunion became *départements*, as did Algeria with its large settler community. In sub-Saharan Africa and Madagascar the colonies became *territoires*. Protectorates, such as Indo-China, Morocco, and Tunisia became *états*. But these changes were little more than changes of nomenclature and administration and in 1954 the French were defeated at Dien Bien Phu. A few months later, in November of the same year, the Algerian War broke out and raged for eight long and particularly bloody years. By the end most French intellectuals were arguing in favour of decolonization. Morocco and Tunisia became independent in 1956, and the relatively moderate demands of leaders such as Léopold Sédar Senghor were met without conflict. The Union Française was replaced by a transitional Association, with independence envisaged a few years later. Guinea chose to opt for independence immediately and the other sub-Saharan African territories and Madagascar followed two years later. These dramatic changes were bracketed by the Algerian War which finally ended in 1962. *Coopération*—criticized by some as neocolonial interference—which is the official policy instituted after the empire had been fully dismantled, is based on economic and cultural aid.

5. Francophone Literary History

Literary historical shifts in perspective crudely reflect these political changes. It was not until after the Second World War that some literary manuals, anthologies, and pedagogical texts first distinguished between French literature and other writing in French.

Léon-Gontran Damas, a West Indian, but publishing in Paris, produced his anthology, *Poètes d'expression française* in 1947 and Senghor's anthology was entitled *Anthologie de la nouvelle poésie nègre et malgache de langue française* (1948).

These are two examples among a number. Then in 1960, Maurice Bémol published an *Essai sur l'orientation des littératures de langue française au XXe siècle*. This was a strikingly new title, suggesting that in some ways autonomous literatures, which could no longer be annexed satisfactorily to French literature, had appeared. The author makes explicit reference to his concern to examine 'les problèmes posés par l'existence des littératures françaises hors de France' and the 'degré d'autonomie de ces littératures', the importance of 'éléments locaux dans la formation de l'originalité des auteurs et dans la puissance des orientations qui en émanent', etc., but no mention whatsoever is made of any works of African, West Indian, or Indian Ocean origin! Where mention of authors from these regions is made in other comparable publications, there is a common tendency to misspell names. In the 1968 edition of Antoine Adam *et al.*, *Littérature française* (Larousse), ii. *XIXe et XXe siècles*, in a small section entitled 'La Littérature française dans le monde', there is reference to 'un Soumbène Ousmane', 'un Maximilien Quenom' (both misspelt: Sembène, Quenum).[4] The depersonalization effected by the use of the repeated indefinite article combined with the lack of concern for correct or consistent orthography suggests a lack of seriousness, if not contempt.

Texts had, of course, been written in French in numerous areas of the world several decades before any of these manuals were published and it is revealing to explore, briefly, the kinds of literatures to which these texts were seen to belong and what the ramifications of various appellations might be. In considering a number of examples, what quickly becomes clear is the degree to which texts which were 'up for grabs' (which were not obviously part of French literature however vaguely defined) were likely to be annexed by literatures which display an incestuous relationship (one which should be proscribed as being too close) between two sets of criteria, those of definition of the 'area', and those that are *evaluative*.

For example, the first texts by Africans writing in French were

---

[4] For a fuller account, see Dorothy S. Blair, 'État et Statut de la critique française de la littérature négro-africaine d'expression française', *Œuvres et critiques*, iii, 2/IV, l, numéro double, 'Littérature africaine et antillaise' (1979), 39–52.

quickly annexed by colonial literature, a branch of the colonial sciences. This discipline had all but a monopoly on texts about Africa. It was colonial writers who made it their business to monitor and promote, in a systematic way, writing by Africans. Roland Lebel, one of the most vociferous promoters of colonial writing, made very clear what he believed its ontology should be. Works of colonial literature, 'revêtiront un intérêt ethnographique et traduiront la psychologie des races; dans le domaine colonial, cette curiosité naturelle prend une signification plus précise: c'est l'expression du besoin de la connaissance intime du pays et de ses habitants, utile à notre domination.'⁵ Where the significance of the writing was seen to transcend the colonial context, the text would be claimed for French literature. Prefaces are often revealing paratexts which demonstrate, despite the recognition of difference, the degree to which the reader is encouraged to approach the text as a contribution to French literature. For example, Robert Boudry, in an informative introduction to a text by the Malagasy writer Jean-Joseph Rabearivelo, which describes in some detail the particularities of the Malagasy form of the *hain teny*, for example, concludes:

Devenu français de culture et d'expression, il restait malgache d'inspiration et de sentiment. Il ne pouvait pas servir par-delà le tombeau cette terre qui l'avait porté, et sur laquelle, quelque jour sans doute, un *tsangambato*, l'une de ces pierres commémoratives qui s'élèvent, hautes et frustes, sur les mamelons chauves, rappellera au voyageur le nom du poète qui fut le chantre de l'Imérina, et introduisit le premier un nom malgache dans la littérature française.⁶

In some francophone areas, most importantly French Canada, Switzerland, Belgium, and Haiti, but also in Martinique and Guadeloupe, debates about the nature of nationalism and its relationship with literary production took place during the nineteenth century. In Haiti *Le Républicain* (1837) was an important focus for nationalist concerns as was the *Revue bèlge*, founded in 1836. In Switzerland, titles such as Albert Richard's *Les Helvétiennes* (1827) and Juste Olivier's *Poèmes suisses* (1830) testify to the relation between literature and nationalism.

---

⁵ Roland Lebel, *L'Afrique occidentale dans la littérature française depuis 1870* (1925), 225.

⁶ Jean-Joseph Rabearivelo, *Vieilles chansons des pays d'Imérina* (Tananarive, 1939), 23.

In French Canada, historical and linguistic circumstance, in particular the ever-present threat of (the) English, had encouraged discussion of what constituted a national literature very early on and this alliance remained strong until the second half of this century. The artistic and aesthetic consequences of this were not, however, altogether stimulating. A very narrow allegiance grew up between the forces of nationalism and the literary establishment. For example, when Anne Hébert published (in abridged form and at her own expense) 'Le Torrent', now recognized as one of the great (liberationist) works of Quebec literature, it represented a radical departure from a long-standing tradition of realism in French-Canadian writing. The 'literature of the land' (*littérature du terroir*) was, when 'Le Torrent' was first published, firmly entrenched as a literary canon. It proclaimed the crucial role of the land for the survival of the French-Canadian 'race' and tended to uphold rural, traditional, conservative, Catholic—in short, contemporary nationalist—values. 'Le Torrent' did not conform to this mode of writing, indeed it is frequently cited by literary historians as the text that transgressed, subverted, and finally liberated French-Canadian writing. It was not, however, well received when first published. In a typical review in *La Revue de l'Université Laval*, Bertrand Lombard wrote: 'Le plus grave, c'est que les personnages de Mademoiselle Hébert ne sont pas *de notre terroir* et appartiennent, par la tristesse de leur destin, aux absurdités existentialistes.'[7]

6.   France's Literary Control

Many of the appellations referred to above—colonial, Negro-African, French-Canadian—now belong largely to literary history. They have been replaced by national appellations—Senegalese, Malagasy, Quebecois (although, of course, Quebec is not—yet!—an independent nation)—but also by the umbrella term 'francophone literatures' (the colonial associations of the umbrella are unfortunate if not wholly inappropriate).

Paris, capital of the French nation is, of course, the centre of the francophone world and remains the powerful locus of French-language publishing despite the emergence of important publishing

---

[7] Bertrand Lombard in *La Revue de l'Université Laval* (Quebec, 1951), quoted by René Lacôte, *Anne Hébert* (1969), 62–3; emphasis mine.

houses in many francophone areas. A number of publishers in Quebec, for example, have long been and are becoming increasingly influential, not only publishing French-Canadian writers but attracting authors from all over the French-speaking world. An early and in many ways revolutionary text, Ahmadou Kourouma's *Les Soleils des indépendances*, was first published in Montreal in 1968. Rather than 'respecting' the norms of the colonial language, the French of the text is often literal translation from the Malinke, as in the title of the novel which means 'the era of independence'. That there had been an expectation that francophone writers respect the colonial language is made very clear in a review of René Maran's *Batouala* in *L'Afrique* (1922):

M. Maran a pris soin de truffer son style d'une abondante terminologie petit nègre, voire même tout à fait nègre. Cette précaution n'ajoute rien de pittoresque, tant il est vrai que l'exotisme ne réside pas dans le vocabulaire, mais dans la peinture vivante [. . .] Le vocabulaire nègre de M. Maran est dangereux, il souligne l'incertitude et la pauvreté de son vocabulaire français.[8]

The assumptions underwriting the reviewer's perspective are clear: that the author must be seeking to participate in the established conventions of the picturesque or exotic, and that he should wish to exhibit the degree to which he has been successfully assimilated by writing a correct French. The reviewer's contention that there is something dangerous about Maran's project is consistent with the text's banning in Africa by 1928. What is revealed here is the degree to which the subversion of *la langue* (the tongue) is read as subversive of a *national* language, related to, if not synonymous with, the subversion of the nation and its interests. That the subversions of Kourouma's text should have attracted the attention of a Canadian (and indeed Quebec) publisher, rather than a French publisher, is not surprising at that moment in the history of *la francophonie*.

In spite of the growing importance of various centres of publishing outside France, and universities which support teaching and research in the area of francophone literatures (most importantly in Africa and North America, especially Quebec), Paris remains the powerful centre. Nor should the fact that the ideology of

---

[8] J. Ladreit de Lacharrière, 'Batouala', *L'Afrique française* (1922), 36–7 (p. 36). For a discussion of reactions to *Batouala* in the French press, see R. Fayolle, 'Batouala et l'accueil de la critique', *Actes du Colloque sur la critique et réception de la littérature française* (1978), 23–9.

francophonie is bound up with French interests in the francophone world, particularly in Africa, be underestimated. French cultural centres in Africa, and the state-sponsored journal *Notre Librairie*, also support and promote, and of course influence, the production and consumption of African literature.[9]

A large number of organizations have also been established to promote the French language and to strengthen the worldwide francophone community. The oldest, the Alliance Française, was set up in 1883 to improve the international standing of French (and France). AUPELF, the Association des universités partiellement ou entièrement de langue française—the infelicities of the name are symptomatic of the complexities of the organization—was founded in 1961 to encourage communication between academics and universities. ADELF, the Association des écrivains de langue française, grew out of what had originally been the Société des écrivains coloniaux, founded in 1926. FIDELF, the Fédération internationale des écrivains de langue française, founded in Montreal in 1982, testifies to a Quebec desire not only to create its own market for the production and consumption of French-Canadian writing, but also to attract francophone writers to participate in the French-Canadian literary scene. A further and significant indication of France's continuing concern to protect and promote French is the relatively recent creation of the Haut Conseil de la francophonie, made up of experts whose role is to advise how to defend—and encourage use of—French. The more narrowly political and economic equivalent to these organizations—despite its name—is ACCT, the Agence de coopération culturelle et technique, established to promote trade and technical co-operation between some thirty states. Because of the complexities of Quebec's constitutional position the first Summit did not take place until 1986, in Paris, a decade and a half after the organization had been established. The second summit took place in Montreal in 1987, and the third in Africa. This sequence reflects the hierarchy of political and economic power of the major blocs which make up the francophone world. The consequences of this particular balance of power are many and complex.

The significance of Western participation in African literature (and more specifically the French in francophone Africa) is stated in

---

[9] The CLEF guides are, e.g., concerned to include in their bibliographies works which are *disponibles*. This means, in effect, that works published in France are more likely to be listed than works published elsewhere.

extreme terms by Christopher Miller in his essay 'Theories of Africans', published in an important volume, *'Race', Writing and Difference*, the first work thoroughly to explore some of the ideas of literary theory in their relation to African literature. 'Knowledge— particularly Western knowledge of Africa', Miller argues,

far from being simply *lux et veritas*, can most often be revealed as a corrosive project of appropriation, wherein the Western reader projects desires onto the Other. Once the African text has surrendered its meaning, a treaty is signed, written by the Western critic who thereby influences not only reception of the present work but also publication of future African works, still largely published in Paris. This interpretive tie between reader and text is also a bond of enslavement.[10]

Miller's words raise numerous questions which will be discussed later. To propose a universal Western critic, and to suggest that the critic's task is simply one of interpreting and fixing meaning is, of course, to simplify. But Miller raises a number of points which need to be considered in relation to particular texts and groups of texts.

7. Francophone Linguistic and Formal Subversion

To define a literature as 'francophone' is to draw attention to its language. In many cases the term is used in conjunction with national appellations, such as 'Francophone Cameroonian', 'Francophone Belgian'. To describe it in this way draws attention not only to the constituent texts' *national* status, but also to the lack of consonance between language and national identity. Cameroonian literature is also constituted by texts written in African languages; Belgian literature is also written in Flemish. A seemingly obvious but much ignored *donné* of the francophone linguistic and cultural space, is that it is at least a bilingual, and more often a multilingual, space. The consequences of this are far-reaching and historically determined in ways which Tzvetan Todorov has explored:

Dans un passé pas très éloigné, tout ce qui pouvait se rapprocher de ce que nous appelons aujourd'hui dialogisme, était perçu comme une tare. Inutile

---

[10] Christopher Miller, 'Theories of Africans: The Question of Literary Anthropology', *'Race', Writing, and Difference*, ed. Henry Louis Gates Jr. (Chicago, 1985 (1986 edn.)), 281–300 (p. 284).

de rappeler ici les invectives de Gobineau contre les races mixtes, ou celles de Barrès contre les déracinés. Je citerai, plutôt comme une curiosité, cette phrase plus récente de Malraux qui s'appuie, du reste, sur une autre autorité: 'Le colonel Lawrence disait par expérience que tout homme qui appartient réellement à deux cultures . . . perdait son âme.' [. . .] Malgré leur présence ou même leur fréquence, aujourd'hui ces attitudes me paraissent appartenir, historiquement, au passé; elles sont consonantes au grand moment patriotique des États bourgeois, qui n'est certes pas révolu, mais dont on peut néanmoins entrevoir la fin, ne serait-ce que sur le plan idéologique. Qui de nos jours ne préférerait se réclamer du dialogue, de la pluralité des cultures, de la tolérance pour la voix des autres?[11]

The 'great patriotic moment' of which Todorov speaks is also the moment at which 'national' literatures emerged. It is also the high point of colonialism. The great movements of people, one of the far-reaching consequences of colonialism and post-colonialism, have brought about an extraordinary mixing. The multiculturalism which results is a challenge. As Julia Kristeva argues, 'A l'heure où la France devient le *meltingpot* de la Méditerranée, une question se pose, qui est la pierre de touche de la morale pour le XXIe siècle: comment vivre avec les autres, sans les rejeter et sans les absorber, si nous ne nous reconnaissons pas "étrangers à nous-mêmes"?'[12]

The complexities of the linguistic and cultural spaces in which francophone texts are written, published, criticized, and read, are thus necessarily bound up in, and in part constitutive of, the complexities and ferment of contemporary literary, cultural, and social theory, described, for example, in terms of the threat to cultural coherence in Jean-François Lyotard's stimulating and controversial book *La Condition postmoderne: rapport sur le savoir* (1979). Todorov's call for acceptance of difference and otherness becomes something closer to philosophical necessity in the polemic of critics who challenge the certainties imposed by Western critics on the non-Western world. It is members of the post-colonial third-world intelligentsia who have done much to shape the political conscience of literary theory (most recently of deconstruction) and to contribute a new urgency and complexity to the feminist debate. Some of the most important francophone theorists (among a growing number) are: Frantz Fanon, Aimé Césaire, Léopold Sédar Senghor, Léon Gontran-Damas, Léonard Sainville, Étienne Léro, René

---

[11] Tzvetan Todorov, 'Bilinguisme, dialogisme et schizophrénie', *Du bilinguisme*, ed. Abdelkebir Khatibi (1985), 11–26 (pp. 12–13).

[12] Julia Kristeva, *Étrangers à nous-mêmes* (1988), back cover.

Depestre, Malcolm de Chazal, Albert Memmi, Abdelkebir Khatibi, Tahar Ben Jelloun, Edouard Glissant, Mbwill a Mpaang Ngal, Assia Djebar, Maryse Condé, Awa Thiam, Catherine N'Diaye. The contributions of these writers are informed by (and inform) disciplines and ideologies as different as psychoanalysis, Marxism, Surrealism, Negritude, post-colonialism, post-modernism, post-structuralism, the new historicism, deconstruction, *Antillanité*, *Créolité*, and diverse forms of feminism. Negritude is one of the most difficult to define and is examined in the chapter devoted to sub-Saharan Africa.

The organization of the present book is intended to expose the tensions between the francophone, on the one hand, and the national, regional, or other affiliations (to an ideology, Negritude, or feminism, for example, a religion or politics, Marxism most obviously, or a particular group, immigrant writers' groups, for example), on the other. Whilst the title relies on the term 'francophone', the book is divided under the headings of geographic areas and, in most cases, nations.

The term 'francophone' was first coined by the geographer Onésime Reclus at the end of the nineteenth century and used to designate both a socio-linguistic and geopolitical phenomenon: to describe French-speaking populations and to describe a French-speaking bloc. It was not until the 1960s that it was used again in a special issue of the journal *Esprit* entitled 'Français dans le monde' (November 1962). For many the term describes an ideology, a neo-colonial French desire to retain links with the former French colonies and to deny or weaken national autonomy. For others, most obviously French-Canadians, it is an ideology which promotes French in a climate in which there is considerable fear that the number of French-speakers will rapidly decline. In other contexts, the North African, for example, French is seen most obviously as a crucial means of international communication in a society in which different forms of censorship interfere with the free expression of ideas.

To write in the French (or a French) language is to participate in *la francophonie*, if the term is taken to mean the use of the French (or a recognizably French) language by a writer who is not French, or by a writer who believes his or her identity is not French (even if he or she has become a French national). To describe a literary text as 'francophone' is to distinguish it from a 'French' text and therefore to emphasize a certain difference. Part of the purpose of this book is to identify the francophone (or non-French, anti-French, or supra-French) aspects of the francophone literary text.

The etymology of the term 'francophone' refers, of course, to spoken language: when the term was first coined relatively little had been written in the relevant areas. The *literary* designation needs, however, to be stressed, however linguistically impure it may be to propose francophone literatures. Another way of looking at this is to see the francophone *literary* project as inherently subversive. Until recently many of the texts examined in this book were read almost exclusively 'abroad'. The context from which the text emerged was exotic or at least foreign. One of the many consequences of this was that, crudely speaking, texts were read as mimetic representations. Readings thus privileged sociological, anthropological, racial, or geographical difference (often identified in terms of theme), as opposed to linguistic (new practices, the direct translation of foreign idioms, for example) or formal difference (for example the subversion or adaptation of French literary typologies, Exoticism, or Surrealism, respectively). Thus a further concern of the present book when treating certain texts is to focus on the language of the francophone text in both the French sense of *langue* (tongue) and *langage* (system) and to analyse the relationship between these two; in particular to ask whether the francophone text, in many instances, stages a dramatic confrontation between *langue* and *langage*. Within the francophone debate one of the most powerful statements on language which privileges the first sense and one of the most frequently quoted is Frantz Fanon's: 'Parler, c'est être à même d'employer une certaine syntaxe, posséder la morphologie de telle ou telle langue, mais c'est surtout assumer une culture, supporter le poids d'une civilisation.'[13]

But this is only one of a wide range of differing attitudes to language and the degree to which the francophone writer is free fundamentally to shape that language. At the beginning of his essay 'Writing "Race" and the Difference it Makes', Henry Louis Gates Jr. uses a quotation from Mikhail Bakhtin's *Discourse in the Novel* as an epigraph:

Language, for the individual consciousness, lies on the borderline between oneself and the other. The word in language is half someone else's. It becomes 'one's own' only when the speaker populates it with his own intention, his own accent, when he appropriates the word, adapting it to

---

[13] Frantz Fanon, *Peau noire masques blancs* (1952), 13.

his own semantic and expressive intention. Prior to this moment of appropriation, the word does not exist in a neutral and impersonal language (it is not, after all, out of a dictionary that a speaker gets his words), but rather it exists in other people's mouths, in other people's intentions: it is from there that one must take the word and make it one's own.[14]

It is the potential for the transformation of French to allow for the articulation of difference that the North African writer Nabil Farès stresses in an article in a special issue of *La Quinzaine littéraire* associated with the 1985 Salon du livre entitled 'Écrire les langues françaises'. Having listed a large number of major francophone writers, Farès maintains:

On le voit, la liste est longue, écrivains, traducteurs, ou essayistes qui par leur pratique de la communication active ont installé la francophonie dans un autre lieu que celui où elle fut à l'origine, pauvre doctrine de la ségrégation coloniale. Désormais la francophonie, en dépit d'attitudes encore 'racistement' présentes, est cet espace des œuvres et analyses où entrent en communication les différents domaines de la pluralité culturelle et humaine.

Further denying the fixity of the French language (despite institutional attempts to fix language, Farés defines language in terms of practice), he writes, 'C'est à un espace de l'étrangeté dans la langue et de la langue que la francophonie doit son développement: la littérature dite francophone dépasse en son mouvement les multiples étroitesses réductrices.'[15] In the same publication the West Indian writer Maryse Condé claimed: 'Je n'y crois à la francophonie [. . .] Communauté de locuteurs fondée sur les mots qu'ils utilisent quand on sait que les mots n'ont aucun sens. Hormis celui que leur insufflent l'imagination et la sensibilité de l'écrivain.'[16] This is revealing about the difficulties inherent in the use of the term 'francophone'. Because of its associations with a French attempt (and one considered by many to be neocolonial in many respects) to nurture a worldwide French-speaking community (analogous in some ways to the British Commonwealth), writers such as Condé dissociate themselves from it. Yet her understanding of language and the potential for what is in effect the denationalization of the

---

[14] Henry Louis Gates Jr., 'Writing "Race" and the Difference it Makes', *'Race', Writing and Difference*, 1–20 (p. 1).
[15] Nabil Farès, 'En d'autres lieux', *La Quinzaine Littéraire*, 436 (16–31 March 1985), 24.
[16] Maryse Condé, 'Au-delà des langues et des couleurs', ibid. 36.

French language, is very close to Farès's position which he associates with *la francophonie*. In other words, for Condé the term is primarily descriptive of a community (the French-speaking world) and its relationship with a parent community (France), whereas for Farès it is descriptive of a subversive linguistic usage and one which denationalizes French.

8.   Language(s), Literatures, and the Grouping of Texts

The geographic dispersion of French has encouraged linguistic variation. Even within the metropole itself the unity of the French language is problematic. Attempts by the Académie française to eliminate regional differences in order to maintain a linguistic order (closely associated, many would argue, with a political order) have been largely successful. Overseas however, 'other' French languages have developed. Regionalisms, archaisms, transpositions and borrowings from other languages, and new syntactic forms, all contribute in varying degrees to other French languages; *belgicismes*, *helvétismes*, *quebécismes*, *haïtianismes* are all carefully catalogued by the French. Academics in French Canada, in particular, approach the matter from a quite different perspective and are interested in the nature of *québécois* as a distinct language with its own lexis, grammar, and morphology. Where French is a second language as opposed to a mother tongue, considerable 'interference' takes place. The inclusion of new words, nouns in particular, is immediately striking. Flora and fauna, and foodstuffs unknown in France are named in other languages. More subversive of French is the creation, in Canadian French, of verbal expressions formed from nouns: *droiter* for *tournèr à droite*, *grêver* for *faire grève*. Another linguistic practice which subverts rather than expands French involves the mixing of registers which (otherwise) belong in a strict hierarchy. Whether as a literary technique or a mimetic representation, examples of this practice can be found in both African and Quebec texts.

In Quebec a linguistic continuum exists, marked at one end by a 'standard' French, and at the other by Joual. Spoken in working-class areas of Montreal, such as Hochelaga, Joual is incomprehensible to the French-speaker. Its name derives from the corrupt pronunciation of the French, *cheval*. Some linguists regard Joual as a nascent French Creole. The product of both an urban/industrial environment and contact with English, Joual has been claimed by some writers as the language of an authentic Quebec literature. This is the subject of fierce debate. A 'standard' *québécois* has also been described by linguists and institutionalized in grammars and dictionaries used in Quebec schools.

In Africa the linguistic context is quite different and much more complex. French is very rarely the mother tongue. The degree to which an African first language colours the French varies from place to place. Every aspect of language can be affected in particular: pronunciation, syntax, vocabulary, intonation, rhythm, accent. The extraordinary project of an *Inventaire des particularités lexicales du français en Afrique noire*, published in 1983, testifies to the richness of French African languages.

Linguistic complexity, *diglossie* (a context in which two languages exist alongside one another), *polyglossie* (a context in which more than two languages exist): these phenomena are inherent in the francophone. By dividing the present study into the given sections, texts are grouped according to the linguistic spaces (crudely divided) from which most emanate (writing in exile is the obvious exception here).

Each part of the book follows a more or less chronological order as, very roughly, do the chapters. Different ways in which the literature under discussion might be approached are discussed early in each chapter. Similarly the decision to approach individual francophone literatures from a national perspective (as in most sections here) is often questioned. Questions of nationhood, genre (relationships with oral traditions and other artistic media), and the distinctness of writing by women, for example, are often discussed with reference to the literature under consideration. The aim is to minimize the surreptitious influence of organizational decisions by foregrounding them and suggesting other ways in which the material treated might be discussed. Different itineraries are possible, each offering a different perspective from different 'heights', others taking shortcuts which avoid altogether texts which, taking another route, would emerge as central. The purpose is to offer one way in (while stressing the consequences of having opted for that way) to sizeable, complex, exciting, but often neglected literatures. There has been no attempt to be in any sense comprehensive. Priority has been given to those authors and texts which are generally proposed as major. This also explains why, although mention is made of works published in the 1990s, more is made of texts published up until the 1980s. Equally it is only literatures of a substantial size which have been included. The business of this book is not to propose a new canon of authors or texts, still less to propose new literatures, but to contribute to the debate concerning the problems and paradoxes of the francophone literary text and its literatures, whilst at the same time introducing them. It is unlikely that the range of texts mentioned in this book will be easily available to readers. For this reason I refer, where possible without prejudicing the ideas of this book, to extracts reproduced in more readily accessible reference works so that readers can refer, if not to the full context, at least to a wider one.

French-speakers have access (although the degree to which this is the case is an important subject of debate) to these texts which are still, unfortunately, outside the most widely recognized canons or syllabuses. These texts are assumed to be marginal. Gayatri Spivak has pointed out that marginalia are the essential notes about the text made in the margin. The marginal may generate the important debate. Francophone texts were deemed unimportant (to use an etymologically less complex term), and still are by many, because their literary merit, their linguistic complexity and formal innovation, their political and philosophical urgency, their often complex intertextual relationships with canonical texts of the French tradition which they frequently parody, subvert, or deconstruct, have often been overlooked. It is frequently only their sociological difference that has been identified. Still more often the assumption is made—by those who have not read these texts—that they can only be of so-called sociological interest. It is hoped that this book will allow readers to identify which particular texts and literatures they may want to go on to explore more thoroughly than space allows here. Readers are also referred, at the end of each part, to the growing number of excellent studies which will guide further investigation. In these Guides to Further Reading, and in the Bibliography, the place of publication is Paris, unless stated otherwise.

PART I EUROPE AND NORTH AMERICA

1

BELGIUM

BELGIUM is as artificial a country as any, made up of three distinct areas. Two of the three, Wallonia and Flanders, were united in 1830, with Brussels as the capital. In 1920 the German-speaking cantons in the east were also added. A monarchy, a parliament, and a constitution were adopted. Most areas of Belgium are at least bilingual. In the north, Flemish and Dutch are spoken; in the east, French and German. In Brussels all three languages are spoken and a dialect—in which a written literature also exists—*la brusselaire*. The practical difficulties of Belgian multilingualism have allowed for the increasing use of English, particularly in international organizations and businesses.

The relatively recent date of the country's birth, the complexities and artificiality of its being, the multiplicities of multilingualism, no doubt account at least in part for a certain lack of confidence and an attitude of profound intellectual and political scepticism. Belgian writers tend to look beyond their own country both for a literary tradition into which to be grafted and for an audience; or their identity tends to be defined not in terms of their status as Belgians, but rather in their opposition and refusal of French assimilation. In either case, however, most francophone writers publish in Paris as there are few major literary publishing houses in Belgium and a Parisian readership is often more readily accessible than an audience at home; most Flemish writers, correspondingly, are published in Amsterdam.

Many francophone Belgian writers are not concerned to belong to a Belgian tradition but this does not, of course, mean that their writing will necessarily be straightforwardly French. To deny the Belgian dimension of the writings of Michaux, Norge, Beck, or Rolin—all writers born in Belgium but who now hold dual nationality—would be mistaken. *Extra-territorialité* is an important feature of francophone Belgian writing, as it is of so many other francophone literatures.

It was a cultural event, a performance of *La Muette de Portici* at the Théâtre de la monnaie in Brussels which, according to popular memory, prompted the Belgian revolution. Spectators ran into the streets and proclaimed their 'amour sacré de la patrie'. Whether or not this event was the major catalyst, there is no doubt that it encouraged action. The Dutch occupation was brought to an end and the following year the nine provinces of the southern Netherlands were given independence. From then on Belgium was to be governed by a constitutional monarchy. The middle classes had control and French was instituted as the official language throughout the country. It was only at the very end of the century, in 1898, that official publications were published in both Flemish and French.

With Belgian nationalism at its height, writers were preoccupied with the notion of an autonomous Belgian literature. What was envisaged was a literature in which the multiplicities of Belgian culture—particularly the mix of Flemish and French—would be synthesized. What was written were *romans de mœurs*, patriotic poetry, and historical drama. None of this touched on social conditions, particularly the severe deprivation suffered by much of the population. In 1866 more than half the population was illiterate.

Charles De Coster is generally regarded as Belgium's first major writer. *La Légende et les Aventures héroïques, joyeuses et glorieuses d'Ulenspiegel et de Lamme Goedzak au pays de Flandre et ailleurs* (1867) is a 'bible nationale', encouraging both territorial and spiritual liberation.

In the last quarter of the nineteenth century the influence of the Parnassian movement in France was felt. *La Jeune Belgique* (1881–97) advocated art for art's sake yet, at the same time, declared 'soyons nous'. Independence, autonomy, and authenticity were the requirements, but they were to be advocated in writing which did not engage with contemporary social, historical, or political realities. Distancing itself from official, academic writing, *La Jeune Belgique* was an important forum for young writers such as Iwan Gilkin and Albert Giraud and provoked important intellectual debate.

Edmond Picard's intentions were very different, yet in many ways complementary. A socialist, Picard advocated a writing which engaged with contemporary realities. His attempts to encourage a 'monodrame', a theatre which would be the vehicle of an appropriate ideology, failed.

The last quarter of the nineteenth century was also the time at which symbolism was a dominant intellectual movement. *La Wallonie*, founded by Albert Mockel in 1886, brought together a group of writers (including, of course, French writers such as Moréas, Pierre Louÿs, André Gide, Mallarmé, Verlaine) who were concerned to defend the unity of the francophone world. Five Belgian writers in particular, all associated with the symbolist movement, are among Belgium's most important writers of the nineteenth century.

Maurice Maeterlinck (1862–1949) is one of the the best-known Belgian writers. Debussy set many of his poems to music, further drawing him to public notice. *Serres chaudes* (1889), his most famous collection, is symbolist and mythological.

His plays, in particular *Les Sept Princesses* (1891), *Pelléas et Mélisande* (1893), *Alladine et Palomides* (1894), *Intérieur* (1894), and *La Mort de Tintagiles* (1894) encapsulate and introduced to a wide public, francophone symbolism. *Intérieur*, in which a deceptive calm surrounds a family threatened by tragedy, is perhaps the most celebrated. *Monna Vanna* (1902) is set during the Italian Renaissance; *L'Oiseau Bleu* (1908) is an extravaganza for children. During the 1980s, which saw a new interest in him, comparisons with Samuel Beckett and Marguerite Duras were made, pointing to his modernity. In the plays he wrote at the end of his life he included Flemish songs and round dances.

The œuvre of Charles van Lerberghe is more coherent than that of Maeterlinck. *Entrevisions* (1898) and *La Chanson d'Ève* (1904) explore the unknown and the invisible. Émile Verhaeren (1855–1916) is equally symbolist although more laboured than van Lerberghe. Max Elskamp (1862–1931) is less orthodox. His *Œuvres complètes* are considered a francophone Flemish *livre des merveilles*. Highly original and only partially symbolist, Elskamp's poetry is marked by an idiosyncratic lexis constituted in significant part by archaisms and neologisms.

Georges Rodenbach (1855–98) was born in Tournai but spent most of his relatively short life in Paris. He wrote melancholy *fin-de-siècle* poems: *Tristesse* (1879), *La Mer élégante* (1881), *La Règne du silence* (1891). Most significantly, in terms of his status as a francophone Belgian writer, Rodenbach's novel, *Bruges-la-morte*

(1892), is a highly atmospheric revelation of both that place and the author.

Although *La Wallonie* was the most important journal of the last quarter of the nineteenth century, other significant periodicals did appear, most notably *L'Art libre* (1871), *L'Artiste* (1875), and *L'Actualité* (1876). Texts by major French authors of the period, Zola and Huysmans, for example, were introduced to a Belgian public by means of these journals.

Reminiscent of Zola's fiction, *Un Mâle* (1881) by Camille Lemonnier (1844–1913), is a realist novel. Although contemporary reviewers treated Lemmonier with a degree of derision—*La Jeune Belgique* described him as a 'macaque flamboyant'—his writing was to suggest new possibilities for younger writers. Georges Eekhoud (1854–1927), in *Kees Doorik* and *Kermesses* and *Dernières Kermesses*, as in Lemonnier's *Un Mâle*, has as his heroes men without refinement, 'natures'. Their supposed lack of civilization is, however, thrown into perspective by the inadequacies and brutalities of the bourgeois society which exploits such men as the heroes of Eekhoud's fiction. It is the lives of peasants and workers which concern Eekhoud in the titles mentioned. In *Le Cycle Patibulaire* it is all those who live on the margins of society.

Also identifiable as working within a proletariat/socialist realist tradition is Neel Doff (1858–1941), whose text, *Jours de famine et de détresse* is one of the most outspoken condemnations of contemporary Belgian social injustice. It was in the middle of the nineteenth century that the Belgian Labour Party had been founded (1855). Strikes by miners, textile workers, and weavers were violently suppressed.

At the beginning of this century a greater diversity of writing emerged. What had been a dominant form of naturalistic writing gave way to forms of regionalism. The writer Hubert Krains (1862–1934), typically, celebrated life in his native Hesbaye in such novels as *Pain noir* (1904). Reacting against what became the popular mode of writing, Christian Beck (father of Béatrix Beck), who denied *l'âme belge* and argued for the homogeneity of francophone literatures, also produced a journal, *Antée*, to publicize his ideas.

Other new journals appeared, representing and further encouraging diversity of writing. *Belgique artistique et littéraire* was founded in 1905 and explored the relationship between literature and politics. Two Catholic periodicals, *L'Art et la vie* and *Durendal* represented Catholic and relatively conservative literary views. Also principally preoccupied with the past were *Le Thyrse* (1899), which published texts by André Baillon, and *La Revue nationale* directed by Robert Merget.

During and in the years immediately after the First World War, however, the mood was to change dramatically. Emblematic of a new vigour and desire for fundamental change was *Résurrection* (1917–18) founded by Clément Pansaers. Advocating art as the force to be directed against the destruction of the bourgeoisie, the journal was banned by the Germans during the Occupation.

In 1920 the Belgian Communist party was founded and during the early years of the decade writing was no longer the monopoly of a small group. Workers such as Constant Malva, a miner, Jean Tousseul, and Francis André, an agricultural worker, began to write. At the same point the visual arts became more adventurous. René Magritte emerged as a powerful new painter. The review *Sept Arts* represented a diverse range of arts, including cinema. Other journals, very different from those of the first two decades of the century, emerged. *Ça ira* was concerned primarily with literary matters. *L'Avant-poste* expressed the interests of a group of writers and painters working towards an aesthetic which would later manifest itself as Belgian surrealism. Among the most important of a number of journals which emerged at this point (*Le Libre Essor, Les Cahiers mosans, Les Cahiers du Nord, Haro!*), was *Signaux de France et de Belgique*, originally *Le Disque vert*. The aim of the journal was to establish Belgian literature as a national literature recognized internationally. Writers from Belgium, France, and elsewhere contributed: André Salmon, Jean Cocteau, André Malraux, Blaise Cendrars. From 1924 onwards the issues were devoted to particular writers or subjects: Charlot, Freud, Lautréamont.

Like *Sept Arts* which was attacked as too moderate, *Au grand jour* (1927) and *Distances* (1928) were influential forums for groups of artists including Magritte, E. L. T. Messens, the poet and musician, the poet Camille Goemans, and the musician André Souris. It was the last who, with Paul Mouge, published *Correspondance* (1924), a Surrealist manifesto. Initially they worked in partnership with the Parisian Surrealists, but later broke away, like so many francophone groups initially swept along in the Surrealist current but later seeing their affiliation as a form of assimilation because of the French Surrealists' reluctance to see the difference between the French and the francophone Surrealist enterprise.

After the war the journal *Cobra*, and later *Mauvais temps* published by the the group Rupture, founded by Achille Chavée, A. Lorent, and M. Perfondry, promoted a revolutionary surrealism. Dadaism and *pataphysique* were promoted by Christian Dotremont, initiator of the movement (the journal lasted eight issues). The achievement of Dotremont has only recently been fully explored, initiated by a major exhibition, 'Dotrémont peintre de l'écriture', at the Centre Wallonie-Bruxelles in Paris. His major texts begin with *Lettre d'amour* (1949) and end with *J'écris donc je crée* (1975), a series of twenty-five 'logogrammes'. Almost all his texts belong in relationship with the visual production of the artists associated with the Cobra movement.

During the 1930s the range of Belgian novels extended considerably. Charles Plisnier (1896–1952), whose novel *Faux Passeports* won the Prix Goncourt in 1937, was the force behind the *Manifeste du groupe du lundi* which was signed by some twenty writers and which denounced regionalism and denied, to a great extent, a difference between Belgian and French writing. They argued that 'les hasards de l'histoire, le voisinage, les relations spirituelles, le caractère [. . .] universel et attractif de la culture française ont réduit au minimum entre les littératures des deux pays les nuances de la sensibilité.'[1] Plisnier adopted extreme positions, at different points revolutionary Marxist and revolutionary Catholic. His novels chronicle the lives within the provincial bourgeois family (*Mariages*, 1936; *Meurtres*, 1939–41; *Mères*, 1946–8). Similar, although still more sociological, are the novels of Constant Burniaux (1892–1975): *Les Sœurs de notre solitude* (1958), *L'Odeur du matin* (1967), *D'Humour et d'amour* (1968), *Kalloo, le village imaginée* (1973). He also wrote *récits* and fantastic tales.

It is a concern to document contemporary economic and social reality that dominates the writing of Albert Ayguesparse (born 1900): *La Main morte* (1938), *L'Heure de la vérité* (1947), *Une génération pour rien* (1954). Like Hélène Burniaux, he has also written tales of the fantastic (*Selon toute vraisemblance* (1962). The *fantastique quotidien* (fantastic amid the ordinary) characterizes much of the writing of Franz Hellens (1881–1972). Gabrielle Rolin, a novelist and critic (for *Le Monde* among other papers), first wrote under the pseudonym Elizabeth Trévor. Her texts are within the tradition of

---

[1] J.-P. de Beaumarchais, Daniel Conty, Alain Rey (eds.), *Dictionnaire des littératures de langue française* (Bordas, 1984), p. 218.

the psychological novel (*Le Secret des autres*, 1960; *Le Mot de la fin*, 1972).

Social documentation becomes, in the work of Edmond Kinde, the angry young man of his generation, violent denunciation of social injustice (*Le Couteau de l'orage*, 1978; *Les Ornières de l'été*, 1957; *Le Temps des apôtres*, 1967).

Well-known as a Belgian literary historian and critic, Robert Montal (born 1927) has also written a number of classical novels (*La Traque*, 1970; *Le Jeu du prince et du printemps*, 1966). Also highly individual in terms of his contribution to francophone Belgian writing, is Georges Simenon (born 1903), whose style was much admired by Gide, for example. He wrote a very large number of detective stories in which detail accounts for much of their appeal. Simenon has been hugely successful commercially.

Daniel Gillès (born 1917) has also made a highly distinctive contribution to francophone Belgian literature. Influenced by the gigantic scale of such novelists as Jules Romains, Martin du Gard, Dante, Tolstoy, Belgium is often the milieu or origin for his characters (*Mort la douce*, 1952; *Jetons de présence*, 1954). *La Termitière* (1960) is one of a very small number of Belgian novels the locus of which is the Belgian Congo.

Dominique Rolin is also a case apart. Born in Brussels in 1913, Rolin is often considered one of Belgium's most important modern novelists. Author of some twenty works in forty years, her œuvre divides into a number of phases. The novels of the early 1940s, up to *Deux Sœurs* (1946), like almost all her later writing, is above all concerned with the family, but in her early novels the settings are somewhat Gothic and literary references somewhat laboured. A greater simplicity of plot and style (neonaturalism), marks out the novels of the 1950s from those of the earlier period. *Le Lit* (1960) stands apart from the rest of her writing. She has described the text and the experience which gave rise to it as 'une fracture dans ma vie': the death of her husband. From *Le Lit* on, Rolin's texts became more stylistically complex, more autobiographical, and increasingly concerned with their own intertextuality: certain scenes recur in a number of texts and suggest the obsessional (see, for example, *Dulle Griet*, 1977; *L'Infini chez soi*, 1980; *Le Gâteau des morts*, 1982). In the later texts characters are often identified by their initials alone, or simply by pronouns (*pro-noms*) or designated in terms of their relationship within the family. Although the phases briefly described above are different, they are marked above all by Rolin's central concern: the family and more generally genealogy, in all its mysteriousness.

Among the early francophone Belgian women writers, Marie Gevers (1883–1975) and Madeleine Bourdouxhe (born 1906) choose the *milieu* of the Flemish rural poor (*La Ligne de vie, Paix sur les champs*), and the working class (*La Femme de Giles*, 1937), respectively. Gevers also celebrates nature (*Plaisirs des météores*, 1938; *Madame Orpha ou la Sérénade de mai*, 1933). The writing of Renée Brock (1912–80), most particularly the poems of *L'Amande amère* (1960), conveys a sense of women's conciousness of the world.

Béatrix Beck (born 1914) is one of the most influential francophone Belgian women writers. She was a member of the Jeunesses Communistes and throughout the Occupation risked arrest. She qualified as a barrister and worked principally for minors. Her first work, *Barny*, was published in 1948. *Léon Moron, prêtre* won the Prix Goncourt in 1952. Her later writing includes *La Décharge* (1979) and *Devancer la nuit* (1980). Like Franz Hellens, cited above, Maud Frère (1923–79) explores the consciousness of the child and adolescent (*L'Herbe à moi*, 1957; *La Grenouille*, 1957; *Les Jumeaux millénaires*, 1962). She has also written for children.

Suzanne Lilar, born in Flanders in 1901, is an outstanding francophone woman writer. Her work has excited international acclaim and has been translated into numerous languages (including Japanese). Her *Journal de l'analogiste* (1954) won the admiration of André Breton and Julien Gracq. *La Confession anonyme* (1960), republished in her name, was made into a highly acclaimed film by André Delvaux (*Benvenuta*, 1983). Lilar has worked mainly within three genres: theatre, the novel, and the essay. Throughout her writing (associated no doubt with her bilingualism), there is a concern for origins and for coincidence, that is to say for patterns matching. Her writing also explores gender (and androgyny), eroticism (and its relationship with mysticism), and love, and the relationship between the sexes. *La Confession anonyme* proposes corporal love as 'une catégorie méconnue et comme interdite du sacré'—*A propos de Sartre et de l'amour* (1967) is a critique of Sartrean puritanism with regard to sexuality and love. Her autobiographical text, *Une enfance gantoise* (1976) is a fascinating account of childhood experience told by a woman in her seventies.

In addition to those dramatists already mentioned, francophone Belgian theatre is represented principally by two playwrights: Fernand Crommelynck and Michel de Ghelderode. Crommelynck, whose early work shows the influence of Verhaeren and Maeterlinck, is principally a dramatist. *Le Sculpteur de masques* (1908), one of his first plays, in verse, was performed first in Moscow. He later wrote a prose version which was performed in Paris in 1911, his début in that city. It was not until after the war, however, which put a temporary stop to his career, that he found real success with *Le Cocu magnifique* (1920) in Paris, which was to be performed around the world (Geneva, Brussels, Rome, London, Turin, Milan, Berlin, Budapest, Oslo, Buenos Aires). In 1930 *Tripes d'or*, which like the earlier play is a tragedy which flirts with the tragicomic, was also well received. Here it is greed which is the destructive agent. Hormidas eats his gold in an attempt to guard it against theft and in the end dies. During the 1930s Crommelynck worked increasingly in the cinema, producing a version of *Le Cocu magnifique* with Jean-Louis Barrault (1946). His later work for the stage includes *Une Femme qu'a le cœur trop petit* (1934) and the masterful *Chaud et froid ou l'idée de Monsieur Doit* (1934) where the tragicomic again asserts itself. Here the human foible that generates the drama and the emotion, is jealousy and its destructive unreasonableness. In addition to other plays which are generally deemed lesser, Crommelynck wrote poems and an interesting novel, *Monsieur Larose est-il l'assassin?* (1950). He died in 1970 leaving various unfinished manuscripts.

Michel de Ghelderode is author of some eighty plays, around a hundred short stories, and a large number of poems, articles, and letters which are of considerable literary-critical interest. *La Balade du Grand Macabre* (1934), *Mademoiselle Jaïre* (1934), and *La Farce des Ténébreux* (1936), are arguably the plays which represent de Ghelderode's greatest achievement. Death (and sometimes the death wish), is central to them all, eroticism and sexual inhibition more or less so. All his plays are concerned with big questions and each related in some way to the question of the business of human life. 'D'où vient l'homme? Où va-t-il?', asks one of his characters. The reply emphasizes both a desire to cut through philosophical pretension and to suggest the driving force of erotic desire: 'D'un trou dans un autre'. While immensely successful on the Parisian stage, de Ghelderode's writing draws on Flemish popular culture and is equally well received at home.

Minor dramatists include Herman Closson (1901–82), author of *Le Cavalier seul, William ou la Comédie de l'aventure, Halewijn* (1972), fantastic, mythological plays which draw to some extent on local legends. Secretary of the Académie royale de langue et de littérature françaises, Georges Sion has also written a number of plays (*Le Voyageur de Forceloup*, 1952; *La Matronne d'Éphèse*, 1943; *La Malle de Paméla*, 1955). Jean Mogin's mystical plays (including *À chacun selon sa faim*) have been highly acclaimed both in Belgium and abroad. Irony and humour are also important to his art.

Although there is immense range in the œuvre of Jean Sigrid (born 1920), the enigma of human destiny recurs as central to most of his work (*Les Beaux Gestes, L'Homme à la branche, Pitié pour Violette, La Grande Volière, Les Cavaliers, L'Espadon*).

Félixa Wart-Blondiau, editor of *Le Peuple* and a militant socialist and femininst, wrote a number of plays which, while obviously promoting certain political and social attitudes, are also complex and subtle.

Belgium has a reputation for being a country in which poetry is the most important genre. Numerous anthologies (Liliane Wouters (ed.), *Panorama de la poésie française de Belgique*, 1976, is one of the best) bear witness to the vitality and variety of francophone Belgian poetry. Festivals, more numerous and better supported than in any other francophone region, Knokke-le-Zout, les Midis de Poésie, la Maison Internationale de la Poésie, also encourage both poets and their readership. But it is also the case that the reputation of Maeterlinck or Verhaeren, both at home and abroad, has not been matched by any poet since.

Maeterlinck became interested in Belgian folk songs and Jacques Brel, who describes himself not as a poet but as a *marchand de chansons* has very much enriched contemporary Belgian song in *Le Plat Pays, Il neige sur Liège, Les Flamandes, Bruxelles* (*Œuvre intégrale*, 1982).

The relative weakness of Belgian cultural nationalism is visible in the lack of consensus concerning the canon of francophone Belgian writing. There is very little sense of which poets, particularly, constitute Belgium's major voices. This is further complicated by the volume of poetry published, much of it at the author's own expense. Publication in Paris and participation in major poetry festivals do mark poets out from the majority, in most cases in ways which are critically justifiable.

During the first half of the century Albert Ayguesparse's poetry, beginning with *Derniers feux à terre* (1931) and *La Mer à boire* (1937), became less concerned with poetic ideologies and increasingly pre-occupied with a relatively small number of themes: happiness and unhappiness and their relationship with time, the solace of nature and the impossibility of finding permanent emotional stability. His later collections include *Encre couleur de sang* (1957) and *Les Armes de la guérison* (1974).

One of Belgium's most prolific and popular poets, Géo Norge, published his first collection, *27 Poèmes incertains* in 1923. It is generally with his collection *Râpes* (1949), however, that most critics identify the beginning of his important creative period. Certain recurrent antitheses are central to much of his poetry: the sacred and the profane, the serious and the light-hearted, good and evil, powerlessness and the powerful, past and present. Antithesis is also the guiding principle in terms of register, the juxtaposition of the colloquial and the formal, and rhetoric, in terms of succinctness and verbosity, for example. His collected *Œuvres poétiques* (1923–73) were first published in 1978. Published a little later, Géo Libbrecht's œuvre is more complex and varied but the revelatory power of poetic language is always central (*Mon orgue de barbarie*, 1957; *Balle perdue*, 1964; *Passage à gué* and *Minotaure*, 1975).

André Miguel's poetry is essentially lyrical, concerned with the self and its relationship with nature (*Infus d'amour*, 1952; *Toisons*, 1959; *Boule androgyne*, 1972; *Corps du jour*, 1974). Equally preoccupied with the self, but here the self as the object of disgust and hatred, André Gascht's poetry is violent and psychologically preoccupied. Gascht is also a critic. More varied is the poetry of Jean Tordeur, although always bound up with questions about the relationship between action and contemplation (*Éveil*, 1941; *Prière de l'attente*, 1947; *La Corde*, 1949; *Le Vif*, 1955; *Conservateur des charges*, 1964).

The same diversity visible in the poetry of those already mentioned is evident in women's poetry of the post-war period. The quantity of writing is considerable and combined with its range constitutes one of the most marked literary developments of the middle of the century. Many of the women involved in this poetic explosion are often also critics and *animatrices* of various kinds. Jeanine Moulin, for example, has published a number of important collections of poetry, beginning with *Feux sans oie* (1957) and *Rue chair et pain* (1961), and critical studies including work on Marceline Desbordes-Valmore, Christine de Pisan, Fernand Crommelynck, Nerval, and Apollinaire. She has also been a central figure in the 'Midis de la Poésie' festivals. Like much of Moulin's poetry, Andrée Sodenkamp's texts are obviously concerned with women's experience (*Femmes de longs matins*, 1965; *La Fête*, 1973).

More fully integrated into an international scene are Lucienne Desnoues and Claire Lejeune. Desnoues, who was encouraged by Colette, Supervielle, and Giono, writes a celebratory poetry which rejoices in people, the world—and language. For Lejeune, a major figure in the *Cahiers Internationaux du Symbolisme*, poetry is a quest (*La Gangue et le feu*, 1963; *Le Pourpre, Le Geste*, 1966; *Le Dernier Testament*, 1969; *Elle*, 1969; *Mémoire de rien*, 1972).

Liliane Wouters is probably Belgium's best-known woman poet. She has published collections of poetry, plays, and critical texts including anthologies. Her own writings (beginning with *La Marche forcée*, 1954) are violent linguistic grapplings for fulfilled desire. Her *Panorama de la poésie française de Belgique* (1976) forms a very useful introduction to the subject. She does, however, have reservations as to the validity of the 'subject' her anthology proposes. In her introduction she cites Magritte: 'Les groupements d'artistes parce qu'ils sont "wallons" ou parce qu'ils seraient par exemple "végétariens" ne m'intéressent en aucune façon (quoique des artistes "végétariens" auraient une petite superiorité sur les artistes "wallons").'[2] Magritte's attitude contrasts with those contemporary writers who celebrate their 'belgitude'. Also part of the contemporary scene are those who advocate a more local, regional (as opposed to national) belonging. Different languages, and dialects which reflect these regional differences, are also exploited: those of Namur, Borinage, Liège, Gaume, the Ardennes. There are also those who are only concerned with the reception of their work as French poetry, looking exclusively to Paris for reactions to their work.

Various groups represent different literary positions: Le Groupe du Roman, the Atelier de l'Agneau at Liège, and those associated with *Phantomas* and *Temps mêlés*. These two journals represent a continuing form of Belgian surrealism (closely defined). Other journals include *Marginales, La Revue générale, Le Journal des poètes, Papyrus, Cahiers du grif, Clés pour le spectacle*. Most importantly perhaps, in terms of stimulating the contemporary literary scene, the Théatre poème in Brussels, directed by Monique Dorsel, brings together Belgian and other writers for readings, debates and performance art.

The vitality and experimentation evident in the poetry of the 1960s and 1970s is also visible in the novel from the 1960s onwards. Although writers such as Jean-Pierre Otte (*Julienne et la rivière*, 1977) are clearly within the tradition of a naturalist rural novel, the rela-

---

[2] Liliane Wouters, *Panorama de la poésie française de Belgique* (Brussels, 1976), 8.

tionship between man and nature is not the central concern. Hubert
Nyssen, a poet and critic as well as novelist, also emphasizes the
importance of the relationship between man and nature and this is
bound up with a suspicion about the modern. On the whole, however, the regional and traditional *roman de la terre* gave way, during
the 1960s, to more exploratory writing.

An extreme example is provided by Marcel Moreau's violent,
often erotic texts. *L'ivre livre* (1974) is autobiographical. His other
notable works include *Quintes* (1962), *Bannière de Bave* (1966), *La
Terre infestée d'hommes* (1966), *Écrits du fond de l'amour* (1968), *Julie ou
la dissolution* (1971), *La Pensée mongole*, an essay (1972), *À dos de Dieu*
(1980).

Very different are the *romans engagés* of Pierre Mertens who has
travelled widely and whose novels are concerned with both national
and international events. Mertens is highly conscious of Belgian
writing's tradition of anti-academicism: 'Depuis quelques années, il
n'est peut-être plus un pays d'Europe occidentale où l'opposition du
non-conformisme intellectuel à l'académisme soit pareillement
radicalisée. Si l'académie n'avait pas existé, les Belges l'auraient
inventée.'[3] In his short stories (*Le Niveau de la mer*, 1970; *Nécrologies*,
1975; *Ombres au tableau*, 1982) and in his novels (*La Fête des anciens*,
1971; *Les Bons offices*, 1974; *Terre d'asile*, 1978; and *Perdre*, 1983, a
rewriting of *Salammbô*), Mertens is concerned with broad canvases,
with history (*La Fête* concerns the lives of three generations of men),
politics (his second novel describes the international revolutionary
climate of the 1960s), the displacement of people(s) (particularly
in *Terre d'asile*), and with his own country and its capital city in
particular.

Equally wide-ranging but less ideologically preoccupied is
Bosquet de Thoran's *Le Songe de Constantin* (1973). A meditation on
human history, the seriousness of *Le songe* contrasts with the ludic
qualities of *Le Musée* which takes place in a space which is at once
museum and theatre and in which children are the protagonists.

It was Raymond Queneau and Louis-René des Fôrets who
brought François Weyergans to the attention of Gallimard who
published *Le Pitre* in 1973. Deceptively circumscribed and tentative,
Berlin mercredi followed in 1979, a fragmentary text which captures
a man's thoughts as he travels in a train.

---

[3] Quoted in J.-L. Joubert *et al.* (eds.), *Les Littératures francophones depuis 1945*
(1986), 279.

More conventional are the writings of Henry Bauchau (*La Déchirure*, *Le Régiment noir*, 1972) and Paul Aloïse Bock (*Le Sucre filé*, 1976, and *Le Pénitent*, 1981). Both authors are concerned to explore questions of identity, and in the case of the second this is highly personal and closely bound up with childhood experience in particular.

Formally more innovatory and overtly modern, if not post-modern, are the texts which make up Jacques Crikillon's *Supra-Coronada* (1980). Prose fragments, the texts describe solitary wanderings in empty urban and sub-urban cityscapes (of the mind?). Ruins and rubbish suggest that this is a post-civilization landscape, the era which follows and contrasts with a period of order.

While Huguette de Broqueville and Vera Feyder have both written important novels (Feyder's *La Derelitta*, 1977, was awarded the Prix Rossel), Anne-Marie La Fère is widely regarded as Belgium's most important francophone woman writer. *Le Semainier* (1982) is a landmark in Belgian writing for a number of reasons. Formally exciting, it dramatizes questions concerning representation and its relationship with genre, and men and women's access to powerful means of representation. The text is made up of documentary fragments and letters with instructions for delivery (which belonged to the fictional heroine who has committed suicide before the text begins), and commentaries on these provided by the lawyer charged with putting the heroine's affairs in order. The heroine was director of a theatre in Brussels (the Théatre réseau?), thus introducing the potential for further exploration of representation. Amid all the ambiguities of the text are questions about our sense of belonging, both in terms of place and other people. This is something which La Fère has found problematic, as she describes in her *Confessions d'une Belge honteuse*: 'Ma honte, c'est de m'être fait passer pour Française en un temps où l'impérialisme culturel français était très fort.'[4]

Supporting and promoting contemporary Belgian women writers and artists, the *Cahiers du Grif* (Groupe de recherches et d'informations féministes) animated by Jacqueline Aubenas, Marie Denie, Françoise Colin (among a large number), are primarily concerned with cultural politics in the broadest sense.

Very little resistance poetry emerged in Belgium during the Second World War, unlike in France. Among the few examples is some of the poetry of Marcel Thiry whose publications appeared over a

---

[4] Quoted ibid. 289.

long period (1924–75). His collected poetry was published under the title *Toi qui palis au nom de Vancouver*. It was only then, in the 1970s, that his work gained wide recognition. As in Goffin's poetry, features of modern life are important: modern means of transport, the car, the train, the rocket, in particular. Apollinaire was an important influence, and earlier, symbolism (in *Le Cœur et les sens*, 1919, for example). His guiding concern, however, transcends the objects of his poetic world, and is bound up with his concern to 'changer une émotion en durée'. His poetry, in particular *Statue de la fatigue* (1934), *La Mer de la tranquillité* (1938), and *Usine à penser les choses tristes* (1956), asserts the power of language to deny the abyss of nothingness. As secretary of the Académie royale de la langue et de la littérature françaises de Belgique and as founder of the Rassemblement Wallon, Thiry demonstrated his commitment to the variety of languages, in the French sense of *langues*, that is, his belief in the importance of linguistic *differences*, as well as his concern, as a poet, for language.

One of the most celebrated Belgian surrealists, Achille Chavée, was a central figure in the group Rupture (which published the journal *Mauvais temps* in 1935). Always politically involved, Chavée published poems and aphorisms. His most important collection is perhaps *De vie et morts naturelles* (1965).

During the second half of the century and particularly since the 1960s, the range of francophone Belgian poetry has been comparable to much of what has been written in France. One of the most interesting poets not already mentioned is Werner Lambersy, author of *Silenciaire* (1971) and *La Diagonale du fou* (1982), which continue, to some extent, the fragmentary, revelatory work of Queneau. Jacques Crickillon's *L'Ombre du prince* (1971) is in the lyrical tradition of such poets as Saint-John Perse. Jacques Izoard's poetry (beginning with *Les Sources de feu brûlent le feu contraire*, 1962) is reminiscent of the work of Char and Reverdy. His poems are concise and enigmatic, often filled with small everyday objects, like those to be found in Francis Ponge's *Le Parti pris des choses*. Although not numerous, a number of francophone Belgian playwrights have contributed to the contemporary literary and cultural scene: René Kalisky, Louvet, Jacques de Decker, and Pascal Vrebos. The plays of Louvet, like those of Kalisky, explore historical events. The theatre of Kalisky, a Polish Jew, explores the relationship between historical happenings and identity, particularly the identity of the atheist Jew; also the political complexities of the Palestinian/Israeli conflict, and other major moments in European history such as the rise of Fascism (*Jim le téméraire*, 1972). Kalisky's plays also focus on the repetitions of history and the multiple patterns which connect peoples of different times and places. In *Dave au bord de la mer* (1979) the conflict between the biblical Saul and David is paralleled by the conflict between Israel and Palestine.

Jacques de Decker, in addition to translating plays from other languages (English, German, and Dutch), has written a number of remarkable plays (*Petit Matin; Jeu d'intérieur; Epiphanie*) in which the characters' insatiable desires are almost always in some way violent, perverted, and socially subversive.

William Cliff's poetry, including *Homo sum* (1973), *Écrasez-le* (1976), *Marcher au charbon* (1978), is in many ways emblematic of much contemporary francophone Belgian writing. Parodying the marginalized status of the Walloon writer, his texts also satirize 'great' literature. Described by Claude Roy as the 'Buster Keaton de la versification', Cliff's texts are post-modern in their playful pastiche.

Belgian literature is heterogeneous in part because of the diversity of allegiances which the country's writers display. Some reject, while others are highly conscious of, tradition. Some proclaim their 'belgitude', while others define themselves in terms of a regional identity. Many participate in Parisian literary debates and many move there. Those that remain committed to the Belgian literary sphere often define their position paradoxically. In a revealingly entitled article, 'La Belgique malgré tout', J. Sojcher expressed a typical attitude. His concern was 'Faire l'éloge d'un pays aux allures de non-patrie, de non-État, où l'on peut se sentir de non-nationalité tout en vivant dans le confort d'une nation démocratique.'[5]

---

[5] Quoted in *Dictionnaire des littératures de langue française*, 223.

2

SWITZERLAND

'LA Littérature romande existe-t-elle?' Jacques Mercanton denies it: 'une littérature se définit par la langue dans laquelle elle est écrite. Or il n'y a point de langue romande. Ainsi donc le terme *littérature romande*, même si on en fait emploi assez souvent, n'a aucune signification.'[1] Yet as Bertil Gallant argues:

La littérature romande existe, non par des idées ou par un style qui seraient caractéristique de ces écrivains—décèle-t-on des traits typiques ici ou là? on pourra en débattre à l'infini—mais parce qu'une communauté romande, divisée de surcroît en communautés plus petites, les Cantons, suisse par les mœurs et française de langue, s'est montrée assez vigoureuse, assez unie en ce domaine particulier, pour susciter, indépendamment de Paris, une littérature.[2]

What is crucial, according to Gallant, is the existence of a *community* of writers and readers. What matters is:

La durée, l'intensité, la qualité, l'originalité d'une *relation* entre ceux qui écrivent et ceux qui lisent sur un territoire donné. Entre Genève et Fribourg, entre Porrentruy et Sierre, entre La Chaux-de-Fonds et le Léman, les circonstances, certaines volontés, les écoles en leur diversité, la manière de publier, l'esprit de la critique et le goût de la population ont consolidé au cours des années une vie des lettres qui possède sa propre échelle de valeurs.[3]

There is little doubt which writers of this century meet the criteria for inclusion within *la littérature romande*: Ramuz most obviously, Charles-Albert Cingria, Monique Saint-Hélier, Catherine Colomb, Gustave Roud, Corinna Bille.

[1] Quoted by Bertil Galland, *La Littérature de la Suisse Romande expliquée en un quart d'heure* (Geneva, 1986), 11.
[2] Ibid. 14.   [3] Ibid.

Ramuz himself, in a famous letter to his French publisher, succinctly expresses the major difficulty with which the francophone Swiss writer is faced:

C'est bien le sort en gros de mon pays d'être à la fois trop semblable et trop différent, trop proche et pas assez,—d'être trop français ou pas assez; car ou bien on l'ignore, ou bien, quand on le connaît, on ne sait plus trop qu'en faire. On n'a aucun intérêt à aller le découvrir, parce qu'il n'est pas une île lointaine et qu'ainsi il n'a rien qui pique la curiosité; et pourtant quand, pour une raison ou pour une autre, il devient présent et se manifeste, alors manifestement il inquiète: il inquiète par exemple les critiques littéraires 'français' s'il se mêle d'écrire son français.[4]

It is in part the absence of obvious difference that explains the incorporation of so many Swiss writers into the French tradition: Jean-Jacques Rousseau, Mme de Staël, Benjamin Constant, Blaise Cendrars, Philippe Jaccottet, Albert Cohen. Swiss critics have been similarly assimilated: Jean Starobinski, Jean Rousset, Marcel Raymond, Albert Béguin. In terms of the writers' own allegiance, it is to a region rather than the nation, that they express their belonging. Although French-speakers are a minority within the Helvetic Federation (19% French-speaking; 69.3% German-speaking; 9.5% Italian; 0.9% Romansh), the regions or cantons enjoy considerable autonomy. Four are French-speaking, the Pays de Vaud, Geneva, Neuchâtel, and the Jura which gained cantonal status in 1978 and which was previously part of Berne. The former became the twenty-third canton of Switzerland. The Valais and Fribourg are in the majority French-speaking.

The Swiss cantons, sovereign states, have distinct histories and cultural and literary traditions. Francophone Swiss literature is thus constituted by a number of literatures. Religious differences are often marked. Fribourg, which before the Revolution was part of the old Confederation, contributed writing marked by Catholic and conservative values. The landscape of Le Valais is evoked not only in writing by those from the region but also by the *vaudois*, Ferdinand Ramuz, and Rousseau, for example, originally from Geneva. Catholic values are also important in much of the writing from Le Valais, but in subtler ways than much of the writing from Fribourg. Writers from Geneva are often concerned with the city's urbanism, independence, and, early on, its Protestantism. The Pays de Vaud and Neuchâtel were also influenced by Protestantism.

---

[4] Quoted in J.-L. Joubert et al., *Les Littératures francophones depuis 1945* (1986), 296.

The regional distinctness of much francophone Swiss writing has to be set against the force of influence of the language and culture of France. In the eighteenth century the various *patois romands*, like most French provincial patois, suffered from the growing importance of French. Towards the middle of the century French replaced local patois in Geneva and by the end of the century in Lausanne. In the country patois continued to be spoken even within public education until the beginning of the nineteenth century. Patois is still spoken in rural areas today and is now learnt by some for politico-cultural reasons.

In addition to the linguistic influence of France, and important commercial and military exchanges, Switzerland, most particularly, Geneva, the Pays de Vaud, and Neuchâtel, was profoundly affected by the influx of Protestant Huguenots. The revocation of the Edict of Nantes in 1685 brought French immigration into Switzerland to its culmination.

The origins of Swiss writing go back to the Middle Ages. Oton de Granson (1340–97) wrote poems within the courtly lyrical tradition. All that remains of the *Chronique*, the earliest significant prose text, written by the canons of the Chapter of Neuchâtel are a few fragments, most was destroyed in a fire in the nineteenth century. The sections which remain include the opening sections of an account of the Battle of Saint-Jacques in 1444, and a description of the arrival of Charles le Temeraire at Granson.

Towards the end of the fifteenth century Jan Bagnyon emerged as the first novelist of the Pays de Vaud. *Fierabras-le-Géant* was published under this and other titles in Geneva, Paris, and Lyon in numerous editions over a fifty-year period. It is a life of Charlemagne and the first Kings of France. A number of plays written during the fifteenth century in the Pays du Vaud still exist: *La Dispute de l'Âme et du Corps* (1427), *Mystère de la Passion* (1453). In addition to religious mystery plays, a certain number of *soties*, concerned with contemporary events, also survive. Three chroniclers also made an important contribution to early francophone Swiss writing: François Bonivard (1493–1570; *Chroniques de Genève*), Jeanne de Jussie (1503–61), Pierre de Pierrefleur (*Mémoires*). The first was only published in 1831 as Calvin had disliked both the language and certain sections of the work which chronicles events up until 1530, the years leading up to the Reformation. The language draws on local idiom and the style is often familiar and spontaneous. Very little survives of Pierre de Pierrefleur's *Mémoires* but what does remain provides evidence of a concern for linguistic difference, for a language *du pays* which he describes as 'gros et rude'. Rather than describing it as French, he describes it as 'gaulois', adding, 'car nous autres, Helvetteriens, ne sommes ni ne fûmes oncques sujets à France'.[5]

The Reformation marked profoundly Neuchâtel, Lausanne, and, above all, Geneva. These were to become the three centres of francophone Protestant writing, a writing concerned above all with religious truth, conveyed in a clear and simple language. Guillaume Farel (1489–1565) was the central figure of the Reformation in Suisse Romande. His treatises, unlike his sermons for which he was famous, are written in a turgid style (*Sommaire*, 1524; *Du vrai visage de la Croix*, 1530).

On his return from Ferrare, Calvin passed through Geneva and was persuaded by Farel to participate in the religious and social reformation of the city. Calvin's *Religionis Christianae Institutio* had probably been completed in 1535 before his arrival in Geneva, and his contribution was therefore one of putting into practice ideas and policies which had previously been expounded principally in theory.

Calvin's first biographer, Théodore de Bèze (1519–1605), was also an important early influence and innovator in the arts. In 1550 he directed a student production of *l'Abraham sacrifiant* for which he also wrote an important preface in which he explores the linguistic and formal developments which are necessary for religious theatre. The classical, profane tradition, he argues, is not sufficiently flexible to convey the breadth and depth of biblical material which went beyond the experiences of classical tragedy. Less elevated and controlled, the language of his theatre is closer to everyday speech and to the discourse of the humanist reformers. Bèze also translated the Psalms (1551–62) and this may explain the poetic, psalmic qualities which permeate his *Chrestiennes Méditations* (published in 1581) where rhetoric and rich figurative language combine in a new prose genre.

In terms of literary writing, the Reformation brought a change in the language and style of prose. Abstract questions, logical argument, and the clear exposition of difficult ideas encouraged writing which drew on a wider range of expression and rhetorical form, such as the dialectical, for example.

---

[5] J.-P. de Beaumarchais, D. Conty, A. Rey (eds.), *Dictionnaire des Littératures de langue française* (3 vols.; Bordas, 1984), 2233.

During the eighteenth century Voltaire came to Switzerland, and Swiss writers Rousseau and Mme de Staël contributed to an intellectual life which was never more cosmopolitan. In Geneva, Voltaire attracted an interesting group of writers: Jacob Vernet (one of the editors of the *Bibliothèque italique* and author of *Vérité de la réligion chrétienne*), the editors Gabriel and Philibert Cramer, Charlotte Pictet who was to marry the novelist Samuel de Constant (*Le Mari sentimental*, 1786). In addition to acting as the focus of much literary debate, Voltaire also did much to stimulate theatre in Geneva.

It was in this same city that Rousseau was born, but his reputation with his fellow *genevois* was not altogether straightforward. His *Lettre à d'Alembert* articulated public opinion about the theatre. *La Nouvelle Héloïse*, however, was considered pernicious and banned by the Conseil. The *Contrat social* and *Émile* were publicly burned. But Rousseau had his supporters and a wider debate was thus stimulated principally concerned with the State Constitution. The spokesman for the government was Jean Robert Tronchin (1710–93), whose *Lettres de la campagne* constitute an elegant defence of the Constitution in which the principles which underpin it are also lucidly analysed. Rousseau's response, written from his exile in the Jura, *Lettres écrites de la montagne* (1764) further stimulated public debate. It is very much as a *genevois* that Rousseau contributed to francophone Swiss writing. His writings constitute a written account of the particularities of the religious, political, and moral life of Geneva. The Swiss landscape and lakescapes, in *La Nouvelle Héloïse* (1761) and *Rêveries du promeneur solitaire* (1782) are both magnificent descriptions of the beauty of Switzerland and intimately bound up with the idea of 'landscapes of the mind', landscapes as models for particular ways of understanding (Swiss) people and their world.

Significant groups of writers also formed in and around Neuchâtel. At Colombier, Mme de Charrière (1740–1805), originally from Holland, attracted, notably, Benjamin Constant (1767–1830) and Henri David de Chaillet, editor of the influential *Journal hélvétique ou Mercure suisse*. Mme de Charrière's novels are essentially *romans de mœurs* in which the manners and personalities of contemporary *suisses romandes* are skilfully, sometimes maliciously, conveyed.

A concern to distinguish francophone Swiss poetry from French poetry is visible in the title of Philippe Bridel's *Poésies hélvétiennes* (1782). Editor of *Étrennes helvétiennes* and later *Conservateur suisse*, he also wrote *Les Tombeaux* (1799).

More influential still was the contribution of Mme de Staël (1766–1817). Her father was from Geneva and her mother, *vaudoise*. Her education, faith, and morality are profoundly bound up with the country of her birth. Her interest in Rousseau (*Lettres sur Jean-Jacques Rousseau*, 1788, was her first publication), further accounts for the sense of her belonging to a Swiss tradition which her writings did much to encourage. Her concern was above all for the freedom of the individual, the prerequisite for full human development and happiness. The public, political corollary of this was an antipathy for Napoleonic politics which undermined the freedom of the individual. *De l'Allemagne* (1810) was her most influential work in which she expounded a philosophy influenced above all by August Wilhelm Schlegel. She attracted a group of writers around her, in Paris and Coppet, including her cousin Mme Necker de Saussure, who translated Schlegel's *Cours de littérature dramatique*, Charles Victor de Bonstetten (*L'Homme du Midi et l'Homme du Nord*, 1824), Jean-Claude Léonard Simonde de Sismondi (*La Littérature du midi de l'Europe*, 1813).

The eighteenth century was thus a period of considerable intellectual activity in Switzerland, activity which was both cosmopolitan and conscious of Switzerland's place in Europe and the world whilst at the same time developing a sense of Switzerland's difference and the differences between both Swiss cities (particularly Geneva) and the constitutive *cantons*.

At the beginning of the nineteenth century Alexandre Vinet, a theologian and teacher, was an influential figure expounding and developing the liberal ideas of the previous century. He argued, for example, for the separation of Church and State. His writings explore theological and social questions, and he also wrote notable works on French literature. His *Chrestomathie française* (1829–30) was widely read. Both the landscape and the local speech of the Geneva region are important in the work of Rodolphe Toepffer, son of the painter, Adam Toepffer.

One of the most important nineteenth-century writers in terms of Swiss literary history is Henri Frédéric Amiel (1821–81). His major work, *Journal intime*, covers the years from 1847 until his death. He also wrote literary-critical studies, *Il Pensieroso* (1858) and *Jour à jour* (1880). He was one of the earlier writers to express a desire for an autonomous *littérature romande* which he envisaged developing alongside a *littérature savoyarde*.

Two young poets whose lives were cut short were Frédéric Monneron (1813–37) and Henri Durand (1818–42). The range of Monneron's poems is more limited than that of Durand. The former's poems are dominated by death and are abstract and philosophical. Durand's, by contrast, are happy, concerned with friendship, the family and place, particularly the *Alpes vaudoises* and areas of the Leman. The œuvre of Juste Olivier (1807–76) was written over a much longer period. He also acted as the figurehead of a group to which the younger poets belonged and it was he who founded the *Revue suisse* (1838–61), the group's journal. During the radical revolution of 1846 Olivier moved to Paris, having sold the *Revue* to a *neuchâtelois* publisher. Olivier was concerned to create an authentic *vaudois* poetry. *Le Canton de Vaud* explores the canton's history and cultural distinctiveness.

Olivier was one of a number of writers to whom Eugène Rambert (1830–86) devoted biographies (*Alexandre Vinet, histoire de sa vie et de ses ouvrages*, 1875; *Alexandre Calame*, 1884). He also wrote a *Journal d'un neutre* during the war (1870–1).

Numerous writers belong to what might be described as a cosmopolitan Swiss tradition. Although born and domiciled in Florence, Marc Monnier (1829–85) was later to become, in 1871, Professor of Comparative Literature at Geneva. Poet (*Lucioles*, 1853; *Amours permises*, 1861; *Nouvelles napolitaines*, 1879), and satirist (*Comédies de Marionettes*, 1871), Monnier's critical writing is also important: *Genève et ses poètes* (1874), *Histoire générale de la littérature moderne: la Renaissance* (1884), *La Réforme* (1885). He also translated Goethe's *Faust*, for example. Victor Cherbuliez (1829–99) studied in Paris and Germany. Although his writings are often compared to those of George Sand, his social, political, and moral concerns are those of an essentially Swiss tradition. A *romancier idéaliste*, the characters of his novels often serve to test or illustrate a particular manner of being. His first novel, *Le Comte Costia* (1863) was published in the *Revue des deux mondes* and met with such success that all his subsequent novels were also published by the journal.

Edouard Rod also spent considerable lengths of time away from Switzerland. His early novels show the influence of Zola (*Palmyre Veulard*, 1881; *La Femme d'Henri Vanneau*, 1885). Two rustic novels, *l'Eau courante* (1902) and *l'Incendie* (1906) take place in the Nyon region, where he was born. These two intensely local novels are often regarded as archetypes of the *roman romand*. Rod also contributed to the *Revue des deux mondes*, supported *La Semaine littéraire*, and encouraged Ramuz early on before he had been recognized as an outstanding young writer.

Charles Gaspard Vallette (1865–1911) was another contributor to *La Semaine littéraire*. He was also editor of *La Suisse* and wrote substantial works of literary history, essays, and shorter prose works, often satirical (*Jean-Jacques Rousseau, Genevois*, 1911; *Croquis de route*, 1903; *Promenades dans le passé*, 1906; *Reflets de Rome*, 1909; *Croquis genevois*, 1912, posthumous).

Like his father, Marc Monnier, Philippe Monnier (1864–1911) made an important contribution to francophone Swiss writing. His publications include essays (*Le Quattrocento*, 1901, 2 vols.; *Venise au XVIIIe siècle*, 1907), short stories, portraits (*Causeries genevoises*, 1902) and two novels (*Le Livre de Blaise*, 1904; *Mon Village*, 1909). In these, local speech, schoolboy slang, and classical French are humorously mixed.

Author first of poetry (*La Néva*, 1890; *Lassitudes*, 1891), Louis Dumur (1863–1933) was also one of the founders of *Mercure de France* (1890). His early novels are romantic (*Albert*, 1890; *La Nébuleuse*, 1895), whereas his later novels (*Pauline et la Liberté de l'amour*, 1896; *Nach Paris*, 1919; *Le Boucher de Verdun*, 1921) are concerned with contemporary social and political problems. In his numerous articles and reviews, Dumur was an outspoken critic of many Swiss political positions. He always maintained, however, that a francophone Swiss cultural and literary tradition existed and should be encouraged.

This was precisely the ambition of a group of young writers, at the beginning of this century, founders of *La Voile latine* in 1904. Cingria, Gonzague de Reynold, Ramuz, and Henri Spiess argued for a 'retour aux sources', a return to their traditions, a quest for 'l'âme et le corps' of their country. When *La Voile* ceased publication in 1910, as a result of fundamental differences of opinion among the group, *Les Feuillets*, edited by Robert de Traz, appeared for two years (1911–13). In 1914, however, the considerably more influential journal *Cahiers vaudois* was founded. Among the important supporters of the *Cahiers* were René Morax, poet and dramatist, Edmond Gilliard, poet and essayist, Paul Budry (who was to have more influence on later generations than on his own), and Ramuz. Once again their ambition, expressed in the 'Raison d'être' of the first issue, was to give expression to an authentic local experience, that of the *pays romand*. The language would be new, simple, and transparent.

Individually many members of the group made contributions in a wide range of artistic and cultural activity. René Morax was the founder of the Théâtre de Jora in Mézières (Vaud) in 1908. His great interest, even before the opening of the theatre, had been in popular traditional performance art. The theatre closed during the First World War. When it reopened, performances included *Davel* (1923), a play about a heroic figure who fought for the liberty of the Vaud, and *La Servante d'Evolène* (1937), based on a story from the Valais.

The range of Edmond Gilliard's literary output is considerable. His essays (*Alchimie verbale*, 1926; *De pouvoir des vaudois*, 1926, a cultural manifesto; *La Croix qui tourne*, 1929; *La Dramatique du moi*, 1936–40; *Reconnaissance filiale*, 1943; *Journal*, 1945–52; *De Rousseau à Jean-Jacques*, 1950; *Outre-journal*, 1953). He also published two collections of poetry, *La Passion de la mère et du fils* (1928) and *Hymne terrestre* (1958).

More cosmopolitan, and fascinated by the modern, Charles-Albert Cingria published much of his writing in the *Nouvelle Revue française*. A great traveller abroad and walker in Switzerland, Cingria was also a scholar of the Middle Ages (*La Reine Berthe*, 1927; *La Civilisation de Saint-Gall*, 1929).

More single-mindedly concerned with the past and contemporary reality of Switzerland, Gonzague de Reynold (1880–1970) published a number of historical works including *Cités et pays suisses* (1914–20), *Histoire littéraire de la Suisse au XVIIIe siècle* (1909–12), *Contes et légendes de la Suisse héroique* (1914). He was also cofounder of the Nouvelle Société helvétique, a member of the Swiss delegation to the United Nations, and passionately interested in the nature of Europe and its political and cultural future (*La Formation de l'Europe*, 1944–57).

Charles Ferdinand Ramuz is arguably one of francophone Switzerland's most important writers. Born in Cully in the Vaud in 1878, Ramuz's œuvre divides into a number of phases. The first, which embraces novels such as *Aline* (1905), *Les Circonstances de la vie* (1907), *Jean-Luc persécuté* (1909), and *La Vie de Samuel Belet* (1911) is the least significant. *Raison d'être* (1914) marks the beginning of a series of more substantial novels in which metaphysical concerns become increasingly important. The naïvety and simplicity of the first phase gives way to writing in which the relationship between the individual and the group, between the contemporary moment and history, and these pairs and *place* become increasingly developed. It was at this point that Ramuz collaborated in the founding of the *Cahiers vaudois*, an important forum for discussion. *La Guerre dans le Haut pays* (1915) is a historical novel which was rearranged by Ramuz and Igor Stravinsky (*L'Histoire du soldat*).

Ramuz's writing at the end of the second decade of the century is marked by the influence of the Old Testament. The texts concern ordinary social contexts assailed by supernatural events (*Le Règne de l'esprit malin* and *La Guérison des maladies*, both 1917). *Les Signes parmi nous* (1918) is an apocalyptic novel.

The end of the war marks yet another phase in Ramuz's writing, dominated above all by celebration (*Salutation paysanne*, 1920; *Chant du Rhône*, 1920; *Passage du poète*, 1923). Landscapes, and most importantly mountainscapes, gradually assume a central place in Ramuz's texts. The two great texts are *La Grande peur dans la montagne* (1926) and *Derborence* (1934). Mystical, lyrical, and noble, Ramuz transformed the *roman rustique* into a major genre.

The intellectual life of francophone Switzerland during the first two decades of the century was also stimulated by activity in the other arts. Ernest Ansermet (1883–1969), the composer and conductor, was the animator and director of the magnificent production of *L'Histoire du soldat* (1918), in which Ramuz, Igor Stravinsky, and the designer, René Auberjonois, collaborated.

The tension between belonging and seeking to discover and develop an identity within Switzerland, and the desire to move out beyond the country, is a tension visible to different degrees in most francophone Swiss writing. It is the second tendency that dominates the life and writings of Blaise Cendrars (1887–1961), indefatigable traveller and seeker of the new. In Denis de Rougement's work the question of identity and allegiance is central. He argues for the necessity of a unified country, but also for the integration of Switzerland, within Europe and the world. His writings range from *L'Amour et l'Occident*, published in 1939, to *L'Avenir est notre affaire*, published in 1977.

During the second half of this century there is a growing sense that a writer's allegiance is first and foremost to a region of Switzerland; literary history identifies francophone Swiss writers of the second half of the twentieth century in terms of their native canton. This is, as with the relationship between any text and category, more or less appropriate depending on the œuvre in question. The Valais region is important in much of Maurice Chappaz's writing. Born in Martigny in 1916, his first work, *Les Grandes Journées de printemps* (1944), written in *vers libres* is a celebration of nature. *Le*

Testament du haut Rhône (1953) and *Tendres Campagnes* (1966) are written in a prose which draws on local expressions and a local imagery. There is also a sadness, characteristic of much of the writing associated with the Valais in, for example, *Le Valais au gosier de grive* (1960) and *Chant de la grande Dixence* (1965). In 1968 he published his most remarkable text, *Le Match Valais-Judée*. Different languages, patois, military jargon, the discourse of contemporary social science, are mixed in an extraordinary Baroque piece in which the action centres on a debate, organized by God, in which numerous historical figures participate on the occasion of the Church's celebration of the second millennium of its existence. The complexities of *Le Match* and equally the highly poetic and linguistically difficult *La Haute Route* (1974) may explain why Chappaz is little known outside Switzerland. His pamphlet *Les Maquereaux des cimes blanches* (1976) is a politico-poetic pamphlet, which denounces land speculation and the mismanagement of the environment.

The writings of Corinna Bille (1912–79), Chappaz's wife, are also shot through with a sense of the importance of place. Love of nature is a powerful source of creativity and energy in many of her texts (*Printemps*, 1939; *Florilège alpestre*, 1953; *Le Pays secret*, 1962; *Finges, forêt du Rhône*, 1975). The sense of the interrelation between people and nature permeates her novels and short stories. The catalyst for the drama of much of her early writing is the moment of change, experienced but not fully understood by the individual, adolescence for example (*Théoda*, 1944; *Journal de Cécilia*, 1971). In her later writings, which include stories for children, a sense of the fantastic and surreal threatens to disturb and disrupt the neo-realistic order (*Les Invités de Moscou*, 1977; *Cent Petites Histoires cruelles*, 1973; *Petites Histoires d'amour*, 1978). There is a lightness and humour in her later work which was less important earlier on.

Although Georges Borgeaud left Switzerland for Paris relatively early in his writing career, the dynamic created between exile and home has been, as for so many francophone writers living in exile, fundamentally important to his writing. *Le Préau* (1952) which tells of his childhood in the Vaud and Valais regions, won the Prix des Critiques. In 1974 his novel *Le Voyage à l'étranger*, which explores the relationship between exile and self-discovery, won the Prix Théophraste-Renaudot. *La Vaisselle des Evèques* (1959) is a love-story. *Italiques* (1969) is a collection of prose pieces, inspired by travel in Italy.

Like Chappaz's early work, much of Germain Claviens's *Lettres à l'imaginaire* (1974) is also concerned with rural life. The Valais region is equally central to Maurice Zermatten's texts. Considered by many to be the most important writer from the Valais region, he won the Prix Schiller in 1960. His novels are concerned with the *valais* way of life, its customs, traditions, faith (*La Colère de Dieu*, 1940; *Contes des hauts pays du Rhône*, 1940; *Le Cœur inutile*, 1943; *Le Jardin des oliviers*, 1951). Zermatten's essays have also been highly influential (*Chapelles valaisannes*, 1941; *Connaissance de Ramuz*, 1947).

Fribourg, a region in which Catholicism and conservatism dominate, has produced few notable francophone writers. In addition to Gonzague de Reynold, however, Alexis Peiry (1905–68) contributed an important text, *L'Or du pauvre* (1968), published posthumously, the first part of his memoirs which recount peasant life in the Gruyère region, told with a frank simplicity.

The Vaud region of Switzerland has produced a very significant percentage of francophone Swiss writers. Although profoundly influenced by Ramuz, Charles François Landry (1909–73) has written mainly about Provence where he lived for many years (*Diego*, 1938; *Baragne*, 1940; *Le Mas Méjac*, 1943; *La Devinaize*, 1951). He also published essays and autobiographical texts. Like Landry, Benjamin Vallotton also lived in the South of France and his later works take place in Provence. The heroes of some earlier works (*Le sergent Battaillard*, 1907; *Ce que pense Potterat*, 1915) are popular Swiss archetypes.

Both Cathérine Colomb (1899–1965) and Alice Rivaz (born in 1910) have contributed to a *vaudoise* tradition and both have written novels remarkable for their formal innovation. Colomb published her first novel in 1934 (*Pile ou face*). Like her later novels, *Chateaux en enfance* (1945), *Les Esprits de la terre* (1953), *Le Temps des anges* (1962), narrative discontinuity and subversion of the integrity of autonomous 'characters' suggest parallels with the French *nouveau roman*. Within the Swiss tradition, however, Cingria has clearly been an important influence. Alice Rivaz's writing is more obviously concerned with a woman's experience, particularly in her largely autobiographical texts, *Comptez vos jours* (1966), and *L'Alphabet du matin* (1969). The relationship between environment, on both a small tangible scale (that which is sensorily immediate) and on a larger scale (landscape), and the child's vision of things, is brilliantly explored.

Anne Cunéo (born 1936), writes as a woman and one who believes that women's freedom is a prerequisite of self-knowledge (*Mortelle Maladie*, 1969; *Poussière du reveil*, 1972). Comparable in some ways to Cathérine Colomb's writings, Yves Velan's texts display some of the formal aspects of the *nouveau roman* (*La Statue de Condillac retouchée*, 1973; *Onir*, 1974). Early on Velan took part in the intellectual activities of the *Rencontre* group and, for a time, argued for literary *engagement*.

Jacques Mercanton is one of the most eminent and respected francophone Swiss writers and critics. His fictional texts explore the complexities of human consciousness (*Thomas l'incrédule*, 1942; *L'été des sept dormants*, 1974). The first was awarded the Prix Rambert two years after its publication. As a literary critic Mercanton has published in a wide range of periodicals, most importantly, *Labyrinthe* and *Gazette littéraire*. *Poètes de l'univers* (1947) and *Le Siècle des grandes ombres* (1981) are two of his major critical texts.

Whilst many francophone Swiss writers have worked independently and without expressing a clearly defined literary or cultural credo, others have grouped around periodicals and attempted to exert more pressure collectively. During the 1950s, for example, the journal *Rencontre* (1950–3) acted as the focus for a group of younger writers who sought both social and literary change. The more overtly political dimension of *Rencontre* gave way, in the two periodicals which came after, *Pays du lac* and *Écriture*, to a greater preoccupation with aesthetics. One of the young writers associated with this group was Jacques Chessex. Early poetry (*Le Jour proche*, 1954) was later followed by, in particular, *Portrait des vaudois* (1967) which defies easy generic description. A compendium of texts (stories, both lived and imagined, careful descriptions, autobiographical accounts), what emerges is a sense of collective *vaudois* identity. *Carabas* (1971), on the other hand, explores individual identity in all its chaos (evoked through fantastic imagery) and indecipherability. Later texts, *Le Séjour des morts* (1977) and *Où vont mourir les oiseaux* (1980) are suffused with the presence of ugliness, violence, death. Chessex's novel *L'Ogre* won the Prix Goncourt.

Philippe Jaccottet is one of the best-known francophone Swiss writers outside the country. His œuvre is considerable, composed of poetry (including *L'Effraie et autres poésies*, 1953; *La Lumière d'hiver*, 1977), descriptions of landscapes, and a series of autobiographical texts (*Les Semaisons, carnets 1954–62*, 1963; *Carnets 1954–67*, 1971; *Journées, carnets 1968–75*, 1977). Jaccottet has also published numerous articles about Swiss and French writers in particular, published in, for example, the *Nouvelle Revue française* and the *Gazette de Lausanne*.

The theatrical tradition in the Vaud has not been particularly strong, but Henri Deblu (born in 1924) has made an interesting contribution with his plays *Force de la loi* (1959) and *Le Procès de la truie* (1962).

The Neuchâtel region of Switzerland has produced artists of international renown, Le Corbusier and Cendrars are two of the very best known. More obviously inspired by the landscape of the place of his birth, Guy de Pourtalès (1881–1940) draws on his childhood experience growing up an the banks of Lakes Leman and Neuchâtel. Lyrical and idealistic, *La Pêche miraculeuse* (1937) was awarded the Prix du roman de l'Académie française.

The Jura region is sung in the poetry of Monique Saint-Hélier (1895–1955). Memory and remembering are both themes and mechanisms stimulating narrative development in her novels and short stories (*Les Rois mages*, 1927; *La Cage aux rêves*, 1932; *Bois-Mort*, 1934; *Le Cavalier de paille*, 1936; *L'Arrosoir rouge*, 1955), admired by Rilke and Hesse. Anne-Lise Graberty, a much younger writer (born in 1949), in her text, *Pour mourir en février* (1970), explores an adolescent's revolt against the stultifying, moralistic attitudes of her family.

Human psychology remains more obscure and inexplicable in Saint-Hélier's writings than in those of Dorette Berthoud (1888–1975). The scope of *Vers le silence* (1948) is wide, charting the development of a society. She has also written historical studies (*César d'Ivernois ou le Poète enjoué*, 1932; *La Seconde Mme Benjamin Constant*, 1943).

Among the writers from the Neuchâtel region who left the area definitively to live elsewhere, and for whom the region has not, apparently, been a particularly important source of inspiration are Arthur Nicolet, Cilette Ofaire, Georges Piroué.

The Jura is today a single autonomous canton and this change of status stimulated a period of cultural, linguistic, and literary self-consciousness. First manifest after the Second World War, the sense of political difference reveals itself in the literary sphere in the 1960s in works such as Jean-Pierre Monnier's *Enquête d'une littérature* (1963), *Écrire en Suisse romande* (1979), and *L'Âge ingrat du roman* (1967), which offers ways in to his text *L'Arbre un jour* (1971). In all his writing (*L'Amour difficile*, 1953; *La Clarté de la nuit*, 1956), place, the Jura, is fundamentally important. The last is the story of a clergyman whose faith wavers, a relatively common subject explored in a number of francophone Swiss writings.

Also influential in terms of literary–critical debate in the Jura is Pierre Olivier Walzer's *Anthologie jurassienne* (1964), published by the Société jurassienne d'émulation. More *engagé*, Alexandre Voisard's poems were chanted at separatist movement meetings. *Liberté à l'aube* (1967) became immensely popular. Influenced by Surrealism and the poetry of the French Resistance, the Jura and Ajoie, where he was born, root his poetry in a particular place and identify it politically with a specific political and cultural movement.

Throughout the twentieth century, Geneva has been an immensely important cultural centre within francophone Switzerland both in the sense of extending its earlier role, and in terms of providing a centre for intellectual thought on an international level. The University of Geneva has been extremely influential in linguistics (Ferdinand de Saussure's contribution most famously). In terms of literary criticism, the École de Genève, with Georges Poulet (*La Conscience critique*, 1971) at its centre, became famous for a thematic approach to the literary text. Other critics associated with the School include Marcel Raymond (1897–1981; *De Baudelaire au surréalisme*, 1933; *Vérité et Poésie*, 1964), Jean Starobinski (born 1920; *Jean-Jacques Rousseau: la Transparence et l'Obstacle*, 1957). Other intellectuals include the writer and art historian Daniel Baud-Bovy (1870–1958), the local historian Paul Chaponnière (1883-1956), François Fosca (1881–1965), and the writer Georges Haldas (born 1917).

During the 1950s, Charles Mouchet (1920–79), Vahé Godel (born 1931), Albert Py (born 1923), formed the group Jeune Poésie, hoping to innovate, and open poetic horizons.

During the second half of this century, writers living in or closely associated with Geneva have written in most genres and about myriad subjects. Questions concerning the nature of human identity, of the power of language to describe the world and human experience of it, questions of religious faith and doubt, have all been written into francophone literature. Pierre Francis Scheenberger (born 1918) explores unexpected 'correspondances' within a neo-realistic narrative. Not dissimilar is the writing of Georges Ottino (born 1925). Other notable writers include Jean-Claude Fontanet (born 1925), Anne-Marie Burger (born 1928) and Yvette Z'Graggen (born 1920).

In the 1960s and 1970s theatre flourished in Geneva. Walter

Weideli (born 1927) made arguably the most significant contribution with *Un Temps de colère et d'amour* (1927), a play about the life of Jacques Necker. Contemporary Swiss film has also privileged Geneva as an important locus in, for example, Alain Tanner's *Jonas* (1967) and *Charles mort ou vif* (1969). These films explore the meaning and significance of the city, its energy, order, and efficiency and what these characteristics have to do with the people who live in it.

Contemporary Swiss cinema, like much contemporary writing, is preoccupied with questions of identity and the relationship between identity and our sense of belonging in a place. In an increasingly international world, Swiss nationalism, and suspicion of spurious internationalism, remains strong. Ramuz expressed this typically Swiss position in one of his many letters to his publishers:

Je vous réponds [. . .] parce que vous êtes internationaliste, je crois bien, et que je suis nationaliste. [. . .] J'aime que les littératures, comme les nations, comme les individus, rivalisent. La véritable littérature internationale est la somme des littératures nationales. Voilà tout. Cette somme, je puis dire, ne va pas sans conflit, luttes, déchirements, dissonances, éclipses réciproques. Il y a des apôtres de la fausse paix: la littérature internationale est une guerre qui ne finit jamais.[6]

---

[6] Letter to Gallimard; reproduced in Marianne Ghirelli, *Ramuz: Qui êtes-vous?* (Lyons, 1988), pp. 205–7.

3

QUEBEC AND FRENCH CANADA

Say it in French
la phrase prend ses détours
elle évite l'affrontement
remet à plus tard se perd
dans les inextricables parenthèses
les renvois

good god
la langue ne sent pas
le passage des mots
tu ralentis tu parles
d'un ton presque neutre
tu en prends ton parti

say it in French
chour
n'importe quand viens-y voir
dis-tu les yeux dans les siens
chacun cherchant le mot que tu désires
au lieu des points de suspension.[1]

The confrontation between English and French in Quebec (and French-Speaking Canada in general) is one of many appositions or antagonisms dramatized in Quebec texts: between Quebec and anglophone Canada, between Quebec and the United States, between Quebec and France, between secular or Protestant Quebec and Catholicism. Other tensions, between provincialism and cosmopolitanism, between 'folk art' and 'high art', between art and

---

[1] Michel Beaulieu, 'Say it in French', *Kaléidoscope*, quoted in J.-L. Joubert. Joubert et al. (eds.), *Les Littératures francophones depuis 1945* (1986), 369.

action, between democratic politics and direct action, also constitute much of the context of Québécois writing.[2]

An emphasis on language (in both the French senses of *langue*,
tongue, and *langage*, linguistic system) has also been a feature of
much contemporary writing in Quebec. Not only is the difficulty of
writing exemplified, in microcosmic form, by varied rhetorical devices ranging from aposiopesis to typographical peculiarities (to take
two very different examples), but also by bilingual or multilingual
texts, and experimentation with form sometimes similar to the strategies of the *nouveau roman*, for example. A well-known example of
a multilingual text is Bernard Tanguay's 'Ah l'amour!':

> in your belly, babe, I'm a sweet dish.
> ich women's liebe dich!
> come on Fräulein
> cruise-moi [chat me up],
> colle-moi,
> mets-moi su'l'dos,
> fais couler l'eau,
> flatte-moi l'bedon pis sors le chat![3]

Celebrating language(s) and playfully self-conscious in terms of register, these features of contemporary writing testify to a continuing
and widespread malaise about language, and one which has long
historical roots. A shift can, however, be read between a concern
with language (in the sense of *langue*) to a concern with language in
all its aspects. This shift can also be described as a move from a
desire to find an appropriate language (tongue) in which to write a
national literature, to a desire to find a language consonant with
québecité. Often this shift is equally visible in a move away from the
social and political towards the intimate and psychological.

The French first settled the area at the very beginning of the
seventeenth century (1604 in the Bay of Fundy; 1608 at Quebec). A
century and a half later New France had established itself as a

---

[2] The terms 'French-Canadian' and 'Québécois' are both ambiguous. The
former is often (but not always) used to distinguish between the French-speaking
community of Quebec and the French-speaking community outside the Province.
The latter is sometimes (but again not always) used to designate only the people of
Quebec city. I use the term *Québécois* to designate the French-speaking people of
the Province of Quebec and the Quebec diaspora.

[3] Bernard Tanguay, 'Ah l'amour!', 'Cinq poèmes entre 71 et 76', *La Barre du jour*
(Sept.–Oct. 1976), quoted in Joubert *et al.*, *Les Littératures francophones*, 354.

distinct region. Its remoteness, and France's neglect of her colony, encouraged self-reliance and an independent spirit. Conflicts between the French and the British encouraged a concept of national identity frequently based on difference (linguistic, religious, etc.). The Catholic Church stamped the colony with its distinctive character too. The Jesuits were active from the early years, the Ursulines arrived in 1642. When the province was ceded to the British more than a hundred years later, it was the clergy (often the most educated members of the community) to whom the population turned for leadership.

But Parkman's well-known description of New France, 'that priest-ridden province' fails to acknowledge a degree of lawlessness, and the people's spirit which often manifested itself in singing, drinking, and dancing, generally much to the clergy's disapproval. The homogeneity of the group militated against disintegration. Although originally there were linguistic and ethnic differences between the groups—the settlers were from the North and West of France, from Saintonge and Vendée through Brittany, Normandy, and the Paris region to Picardy—these were quickly disregarded.

Potential religious conflict was prevented by Richelieu's decree of 1627 that no Huguenots or Jews should emigrate to the colony. After a large influx of immigrants during the period 1663–73, the rate of immigration slowed down to a trickle. Thus the homogeneity of the population was further strengthened by the fact that at the time of the Conquest (termed 'la Cession' in French, and the difference reveals an interesting disparity of perspective), almost the entire people was third-generation North American. After ten years of half-hearted attempts to integrate the French-speaking community, the Quebec Act was decreed, acknowledging the strength of the community:

Whereas the provisions . . . have been found, upon Experience to be inapplicable to the State and Circumstances of the said Province (Quebec), the Inhabitants whereof amounted, at the Conquest, to above sixty-five thousand Persons professing the Religion of the Church of *Rome*, and enjoying an established form of constitution and System of Laws, by which their Persons and Property had been protected, governed, and ordered, for a long service of years, from the first Establishment of the said Province of Canada; the same are hereby revoked, annulled, and made void.

(The Quebec Act, Clause IV, 1 May 1775)[4]

---

[4] Quoted by Cedric May, *Breaking the Silence: The Literature of Quebec* (Birmingham, 1985), 23.

When the painter Paul-Émile Borduas published his famous manifesto *Refus global* in 1948 he referred to Quebec as a colony. In many ways it was a fitting description. The two relatively wealthy groups, the merchant class and farmers, were ousted by London and New York traders, and made members of the English élite or sank into subsistence farming respectively. Influential educational institutions remained intact, however, allowing for continued resistance: the colleges and classical seminaries established in the nineteenth century continued to educate the liberal professionals, lawyers, doctors, priests, teachers, and civil servants. There was a brief but bloody rebellion in 1837–8 and a sudden artistic flurry in the subsequent years. François-Xavier Garneau's *Histoire du Canada* was written in response to Lord Durham's Report of 1839, in which the latter had written some of the most quoted lines in French-Canadian history:

> I entertain no doubt as to the national character which must be given to Lower Canada; it must be that of the British Empire. I know of no national distinction marking and continuing a more hopeless inferiority . . . There can hardly be conceived a nationality more destitute of all that can envigorate and elevate a people, than that which is exhibited by the descendants of the French in Lower Canada, owing to their retaining their peculiar language and manners. They are a people with no history and no literature.[5]

Abbé Henri-Raymond Casgrain, a central figure in the literary world in the second half of the nineteenth century, referred to Garneau's *Histoire* thus: 'Ce livre était une révélation pour nous. Cette clarté lumineuse qui se levait tout à coup sur un sol vierge [. . .] nous en découvrait les richesses et la puissante végétation, les monuments et les souvenirs.'[6] Casgrain's own ambition, described in the manifesto of his journal, *Les Soirées canadiennes*, was 'soustraire nos belles légendes à un oubli dont elles sont plus que jamais menacées, de perpétuer aussi les souvenirs conservés dans la mémoire de nos vieux narrateurs'.[7] This reactionary patriotism was reflected in the work of most writers of the period, in the rallying verses of poets such as Octave Crémazie, Louis Fréchette, and Pamphile Lemay, and in the prose writing of P.-J.-O. Chauveau,

---

[5] Lord Durham's *Report*, quoted ibid. 25.
[6] Abbé Henri-Raymond Casgrain, quoted ibid. 26.
[7] Casgrain, quoted ibid.

P. A. de Gaspé (sen.), Patrice Lacombe, Antoine Gérin-Lajoie, and J.-C. Taché.

Before the Second World War Quebec had further declined into a nation of struggling farmers, using out-of-date methods, and a growing poor urban proletariat. Emigration was an increasingly attractive alternative. The war brought employment and prosperity but simultaneously a growing awareness of Quebec's relationship with the outside world, in particular the degree of economic power wielded by the United States. The repressive control exercised by Provincial Premier Maurice Duplessis prevented the *Québécois* from acting in response to their growing unease. Dissatisfaction was, however, expressed both influentially and violently by Paul-Émile Borduas and his fifteen co-signatories, authors of the post-surrealist manifesto, *Refus global* (1948). A *succès de scandale* in Duplessis's tightly controlled society of the time, the manifesto is now referred to often as the single event marking the beginning of 'modern' Quebec. Sade and Lautréamont were the liberators cited in the text and religion and the Church, progress, capitalism, and all artistic institutions were cited as the impediments to liberation and true creativity. Profoundly influenced by Dada and surrealism, the text introduced the idea of the avant-garde into Quebec artistic production.

In the wake of *Refus global*, Gaston Miron and others founded Les Éditions de l'Hexagone, a press which was to play a crucial role in the promotion of modern Quebec poetry and journals. Amongst the most notable poets published were Jean-Guy Pilon, Fernand Ouelette, and Paul-Marie Lapointe.

Founded in 1959, *Liberté* brought together a group of Montreal intellectuals some of whom were also associated with the Hexagone group. Although relatively apolitical at the outset, it became, during the course of the Quiet Revolution in the 1960s, increasingly neonationalist and secular.

When Duplessis died in 1959, and his party was defeated by the Liberals in 1960, the way was clear for dramatic change. It was around this time that the word '*Québécois*' came to mean the people of the province and not just the population of Quebec City. This represented a profound psychological change, as Jean Bouthillette writes:

Le réflexe nationaliste, à travers notre Histoire, témoigne de notre instinct le plus profond et le plus sûr: l'instinct ontologique de la liberté. [. . .] A l'heure de la décolonisation du monde, cet instinct nous rend universels d'emblée. C'est lui qui, dans l'intuition d'un nom—puisque tout a commencé dans un nom—retrouve dans toute sa réalité notre véritable identité, un nom qui lève toute ambiguïté, un nom clair et transparent, précis et dur, un nom qui nous reconstitue concrètement dans notre souveraineté et nous réconcilie avec nous-mêmes: Québécois.[8]

But at the same time as the national obsession was cured, so the dreams of a French Canada receded. French-Canadians outside Quebec became members overnight of the 'Quebec diaspora'. Bouthillette described such a person as a stranger to himself because, no longer conscious of belonging to a group, he becomes a foreigner in his own country.[9]

The educational reforms of 1964 and the withdrawal of the Catholic Church from areas in which it had previously been influential: education, politics, medicine, trade-unionism, and business, further encouraged radical change. The Parti Pris group associated with the political and cultural journal of the same name, sought to identify not the superficial injustices (Duplessis's corruption, for example), but the fundamental problems deeply rooted in Quebec's social and political structures. Drawing on and developing the ideas of writers associated with decolonization, most particularly Jean-Paul Sartre, Frantz Fanon, Albert Memmi, Jacques Berque, Aimé Césaire, and Léopold Sédar Senghor, their programme for writing was closely bound up with their vision of Quebec writing as a colonial literature:

L'aliénation dont nous souffrons, et qui existe à tous les niveaux, vient de ce que nous sommes colonisés et exploités:—au niveau politique, nous n'avons qu'un gouvernement provincial [. . .]
—au niveau économique, la presque totalité de nos richesses naturelles et de notre industrie est dans les mains d'étrangers. [. . .]
—au niveau culturel, la dégénérescence de notre langue et l'abâtardissement de notre peuple témoignent de notre aliénation; 'l'élite' intellectuelle clérico-bourgeoise soutient de l'intérieur le pouvoir de ceux qui nous colonisent et nous exploitent en entretenant les mythes humanistes ou religieux qui perpétuent et justifient notre soumission.[10]

The use of an 'international French', it was argued, would fail to allow Quebec writers to recognize their colonized status. Joual was

---

[8] Jean Bouthillette, *Le Canadien Français et son double: essai* (Montreal, 1972), 95–6. [9] Ibid. 32.
[10] Laurent Girouard, 'Notre littérature de colonie', *Parti pris*, 1/3 (Dec. 1963), 30.

thus promoted as the true language of Quebec literature. In the December 1963 issue the idea of a French-Canadian, as opposed to Quebec literature, was firmly rejected. The poets Gaston Miron, Paul Chamberland, and Gérald Godin, and the novelists, Jacques Renaud, André Major, and Laurent Girouard, were some of those associated with the Parti Pris group.

Miron's own poetic productivity was no doubt adversely affected by his running of l'Hexagone (*Deux sangs*, his only early volume, was published in 1953). *L'Homme rapaillé* (1970), published by the Presses Universitaires de Montréal, is widely regarded as a major collection and includes a number of important essays. Often compared with Pablo Neruda and Aimé Césaire, his poetry is about both social justice and nationalism (loosely defined).

The creation of the Parti Québécois in 1968 was the tangible sign of a fundamental change of political attitude. The cultural corollaries were predictable and considerable: a narrower nationalism gave way to experimentation with language and form (vernacular theatre and film became increasingly important). One of the most immediate descriptions of the difference between Canadian writing in French—that of the *ancien régime* of New France—and Quebec writing, is G.-André Vachon's:

J'appelle ÉCRITURE CANADIENNE la somme des textes, réalisés sous l'Ancien Régime, qui tentent de conjurer, en français, l'improbabilité d'une installation humaine, en Amérique septentrionale [. . .]
J'appelle ÉCRITURE QUÉBÉCOISE les textes qui, depuis plus d'un siècle se nourissent, et naissent, d'un doute réel quant à la possibilité d'une installation française en Amérique britannique du Nord.[11]

These are texts which proclaim their *québécité*. French-Canadian writing, on the other hand, describes a difference and the difference is external to the writing, all the more so because there is no national language unique to French Canada. Difference is, however, the focus of a number of early texts, Joseph Quesnel's *L'Anglomanie ou le dîner à l'anglaise* (written in 1803 but unpublished until 1932–3), for example, which is a parody of a French-Canadian seigneur's aping (under the influence of his son-in-law) of English ways. Philippe Aubert de Gaspé's *Les Anciens Canadiens* dramatizes the relationship between two former schoolfriends, a Scot and a *canadien* who meet again during the siege of Quebec City in 1759. In works such as

---

[11] Quoted by G.-André Vachon, 'Naissance d'une écriture', *Études françaises*, 9/3 (Aug. 1973), 191–6 (p. 194).

these, difference is discussed and described but is not written into the fabric of the text, does not constitute an element of its *literariness*. The reason Michel Tremblay's *Les Belles-Sœurs* is often cited as the seminal text of modern Quebec literature is because difference arises out of various subversive moves, most importantly the use of Joual which celebrates its status as a bastardized French which, rather than describing the dispossessed status of the play's characters, is a language (tongue) which perfectly represents them. Transvesticism is an important feature of much of his theatre where the etymology of the word 'travesty' is teased out to suggest other kinds of imitation and misrepresentation. For Joual-speakers (or all non-French speakers of French), to speak the language of France is one such travesty. French has, however, been the first language of French-Canadian writing for some four hundred years.

Whether or not the writings of travellers and other expatriate Frenchmen should be regarded as the origins of French-Canadian literature is uncertain. Leaders of expeditions, missionaries (the great contribution by missionaries is the *Relations Jésuites* (the most scholarly bilingual edition is by Reuben Gold Thwaites, in seventy-three volumes: *Jesuit Relations and Allied Documents: Travels and Explorations of the Jesuit Missionaries in New France* (1610–1791) (Cleveland 1896–1901)), and ghost-writers exploited a variety of genres—chronicle, history, treatise, Utopia, satire, autobiography, official report—often to uphold and defend a particular interest in New France. Jacques Cartier's second voyage is described in the *Bref récit et succincte narration de la navigation fait en MDXXXV et MDXXXVI par le Capitaine Jacques Cartier aux îles de Canada, Hochelaga, Saguenay et autres* (Paris, 1545). A posthumous account of the first voyage appeared in 1534. The French original no longer exists, but Italian and English translations survive and a French version has been reconstructed from various sources. The descriptions of the first sightings of Stadaconé (Quebec), for example, have become part of the legend of Canada's discovery and one of the major intertextual itineraries at the centre of the Quebec tradition (visible in works as diverse as those of Savard, Perrault, Vigneault, and Gatien Lapointe and Paul-Marie Lapointe).

Marc Lescarbot, a Parisian lawyer, left France disgusted with corrupt European society and intent on discovering a lost Edenic paradise. He wrote poems, commemorations (réceptions, in French), and an *Histoire de la Nouvelle France* (three editions, 1609, 1611–12, 1617–18), bringing together all the available material on

Canada's discovery, including writings by Cartier, Champlain, and Biencourt. Lescarbot combines a scientific approach (ethnographical methods, carefully documented) with a personal perspective informed by moral comment and classical allusion. These combine to present a myth of the *bon sauvage* (while compiling the history he also wrote *La Conversion des sauvages*, 1610), and a passionate account of the potential for a New Civilization far from the corruption of Europe.

A number of mysteries surround the life and work of Samuel de Champlain (*c*.1570–1635), generally regarded as the most significant of Canada's explorers and navigators. The three volumes of *Voyages* (1613, the most interesting; 1619; 1632), were almost certainly not written exclusively by Champlain. The moralizing of the third volume is in contrast to the more matter-of-fact style of the preceding two. The Franciscan Gabriel Sagard is surprisingly unmoralizing. *La Grand voyage au pays des hurons* (1632) is an account of his voyage. His *Histoire du Canada* (four volumes) was controversial in part because of the favourable impressions of the Hurons and its corollary: criticism of the treatment of them by the authorities.

Very different is the material written by Louis-Armand de Lom d'Arce, baron de Lahontan. More literary or 'factional', Lahontan's most influential work, his *Supplément aux mémoires de l'Amérique septentrionale où l'on trouve des dialogues curieux* . . . (1703) is a dialogue between Adario, the 'bon sauvage', and an unconvincing interlocutor who attempts to defend French civilization. The authenticity and naturalness of the 'savage' is also described by Joseph-François Lafitau's account of Amerindian culture in *Mœurs des sauvages américains comparées aux mœurs des premiers temps* (1724).

Pierre-François Xavier's contribution is important for a number of reasons. A Jesuit historian, his *Histoire et description générale de la Nouvelle France avec le Journal d'un voyage* (1744) was a long-standing authority. A subtle but important change was the use of the term *canadien* to designate, not the indigenous Indian population, but a new people.

Annals, sermons, and letters are also important genres in the early decades of New France.[12] Although many literary historians have argued that these texts belong more properly within French travel literature or literature of exploration (some have designated it 'colo-

[12] These are described in detail in the 5-vol. *Dictionnaire des œuvres littéraires du Québec* (see 'Guide to Further Reading' below).

nial literature', 'exotic literature', or 'regional literature'), modern
Quebec writers, in exploring their history and origins, have drawn
on and reacted to much of this early writing. A literary tradition is
not constituted by the sum of those texts which meet the definition
of a theoretically construed concept, but rather a web of threads, of
echoes, quotations, influences, and references which are present
within literary texts and which themselves define, to a large extent,
the itinerary of a literary tradition.

In terms of the different genres, poetry dominates literary production in the nineteenth century. Essays and histories are also
important; the novel and drama gradually gain ground. Four types
of poetic production can be usefully identified: poetry drawing on
folklore, patriotic poetry, Romantic poetry (much of it associated
with the Mouvement littéraire du Québec), and the poetry of the
École littéraire de Montréal, sometimes referred to as a Canadian
Parnassus.

The first literary work in French to be published in Quebec (under the French régime printing was forbidden), Michel Bibaud's
Epîtres, satires, chansons, épigrammes et autres pièces de vers (1830) had
previously been published in the editor's papers (Bibaud, a Montreal
newspaper publisher founded a successful French-language newspaper) and in the main represents the first type mentioned above, as
much of it is concerned with folklore. So too is the work of Pierre
Falcon whose songs recount local events in lively satirical or parodic
style, including the confrontation at Seven Oaks (1816).

The Patriotic Movement of the 1830s inspired a number of poets
to celebrate political reform and those who had died for it. Joseph-
Guillaume Barthe is the best known of the patriotic poets. He was
amongst those responsible for the resumption of relations with
France in the middle of the century. Much more important are the
romantic poets whose patriotism (and concern with history) is also
clear but less exclusive.

The most influential literary figure of the nineteenth century was
Abbé Henri-Raymond Casgrain (1831–1904), one of the founders of
the Mouvement littéraire du Québec, who favoured art which offered clear moral lessons. Poets writing under his influence, William
Chapman and Léon-Pamphile Lemay, most notably, celebrate the
cult of the soil and the heroism and moral rectitude of the pioneer.
Chapman visited France where his work met with some success.
Not dissimilar is the work of Nérée Beauchemin, generally regarded
as the finest of the 'poètes du terroir'. His poetry is concerned with

religious themes, the local landscape and its flora and fauna, but it distinguishes itself from the work of his contemporaries (similarly influenced by Romanticism) as these concerns are frequently not at the centre of the poem. Instead familiar domestic objects become the focus for explorations of the mysterious: the passing of time or the beauty of craftmanship, for example. Frequently anthologized, 'Cloche de Louisbourg' is typical. François-Xavier Garneau's poetry is patriotic and rallying, reminiscent of Hugo. He responded to the Durham Report by writing his history of Canada which he described as 'un juste sujet d'orgueil et un motif de généreuse émulation'. His poetry is patriotic and rallying.

Hugo was one of the poets read at gatherings at the Crémazie brothers' bookshop (the hub of the Romantic revival), where members of the Mouvement littéraire du Québec regularly met. Louis Fréchette's *La Légende d'un peuple* (1887) was clearly inspired by Hugo's *Légende des siècles* and the former was decorated by the Académie française. Chateaubriand, Lamartine and Musset were also important sources of inspiration for these writers. Octave Crémazie's poems made him a national hero, in particular 'Le vieux soldat canadien'(1855), which celebrates the arrival of *La Capricieuse* in 1855, the first French naval ship to visit Quebec for almost a century, and 'Le Drapeau de Carillon' (1858), which celebrates the centenary of Montcalm's victory at Fort Carillon (Fort Ticonderoga). Crémazie's verses are concerned with the land (in the French senses of both *terroir*, territory, and *terre*, soil), the language, and the traditions of Quebec.

The École littéraire de Montréal was a group of friends who shared a common commitment to a philosophy of 'art for art's sake', and who despised the reactionary patriotism of their predecessors. Important members of the group included Jean Charbonneau who was both a poet and philosopher, but above all the tragic figure of Émile Nelligan who spent more than forty years confined in asylums and hospitals. Greatly influenced by Verlaine and the Belgian symbolists and adhering to the École's principle of refusing to attend to political and religious questions, his poems are concerned with mood and musicality. His poems do, of course, have political and religious corollaries. They represent a refusal of the doctrinaire, of narrow prescriptions, and are concerned instead with inner experience, with spirituality, with the importance of the individual, and with the power of language not only to describe but also to explore and create the individual's world. His childhood poems, for example, are both descriptive of childhood (and very probably his own), but they also, like so much literature concerned with childhood, exploit it as a metaphor for all kinds of freedom, most importantly perhaps imaginative freedom which allows normal boundaries to be breached. Their spirituality is not orthodox, but many of his poems are not unreligious. His 'posthumous' poems (published while he was alive but deemed insane), display surrealistic elements: a celebration of the anti-rational and anti-logical, the negation of realism, free rein to the instinctual and the subconscious; the revelation of hidden worlds. These features of the later poetry further emphasize Nelligan's status as a revolutionary and subversive poet.

Just as much of the poetry of the nineteenth century was didactic and polemical and closely concerned with patriotism, so the first French-Canadian novel, *L'Influence d'un livre* (1837), was written, according to its author, Philippe-Ignace-François Aubert de Gaspé (hereafter Gaspé, jun.) in an attempt to initiate a French-Canadian literature, a phenomenon which would encourage a threatened country. The veracity of the extraordinary adventure story in which local superstitions and witchcraft play an important part, was attested by its author, and literary historians have subsequently ascertained that at least some of the novel's bizarre happenings did indeed take place. It is ironic, given the novel's title, that the book should have survived only in a heavily edited form and re-entitled *Le Chercheur de trésors*. References to unedifying European novelists and much of the love interest was removed under the direction of Abbé Casgrain. André G. Bourassa, in his important study, *Surrealism and Quebec Literature* (1977 in French, 1984 in translation), affords *L'Influence d'un livre* an important status as the first proto-surrealistic Quebec text (particularly because of its cabalistic romanticism). Drawing parallels between the works of Edgar Allan Poe and Achim von Arnim, Bourassa argues that these aspects of *L'Influence d'un livre* represent a denial of the established order (and parallel the disputes in which the author was involved which led to his exile).

The title, *L'Influence d'un livre*, is also curiously appropriate in terms of the suspicion in which the novel as a genre was held during the nineteenth century. In *Les Infortunes du roman dans le Québec du XIXe siècle* (1977), Yves Dostaler has examined attitudes to the novel during the period. As early as 1817, Ludger Duvernay was warning against the potential for immorality offered by the novel. It was for this reason that many novelists wrote *apologia* which prefaced their work.[13] These texts generally argue for the patriotism, didacticism, and morally edifying nature of their novels. This context of antipathy for the genre explains, to some extent, the relative success of just three types of novel: the *roman fantastique*, the *roman historique*, and the *roman du terroir*. The first was essentially a highly improbable adventure story which, if necessary, could make the appropriate moral gestures. The second was made popular by Philippe Aubert de Gaspé (father of Philippe-Ignace-François Aubert de Gaspé), whose novel, *Les Anciens Canadiens* was an immediate popular success, partly thanks to the support of Abbé Casgrain. In 1866 Aubert de Gaspé published his *Mémoires* which brought together anecdotes and reminiscences that form a detailed and compelling social history of Quebec at the end of the nineteenth and beginning of the twentieth centuries.

The titles of some of the adventure stories which followed *L'Influence d'un livre* underline the genre in which they are written: *Les Fiancés de 1812* (a 500-page adventure story in the manner of Eugène Sue or Alexandre Dumas—both widely read in Quebec— published in 1844 by Joseph Deutre), and most notably works by Henri-Émile Chevalier: *La Huronne de Lorette* (1854), *L'Héroïne de Chateauguay* (1858), *Le Pirate du Saint-Laurent* (1859), and *L'Île de sable* (1862).

More significant in terms of the French-Canadian tradition are the more obviously polemical *romans du terroir*. The first, *La Terre paternelle* (1846) describes rural life in considerable detail. The lesson of the narrative is that a price has to be paid by those who fail to remain loyal to the land. Pierre-Joseph-Olivier Chauveau's *Charles Guérin: roman des mœurs canadiens* (1853) as its title suggests, is equally detailed in its descriptions of the society of the day but is most famous for its use, in dialogue, of popular speech (included for the first time in French-Canadian fiction). This was a decision which he was keen to justify. Similarly, the storyteller Honoré Beaugrand, at the end of the century, claimed that his transcriptions of ordinary speech were those of 'des hommes au langage aussi rude que leur difficile métier'.[14]

Jean Rivard, économiste, by Antoine Gérin-Lajoie, is a didactic

[13] See in this connection Guido Rousseau, *Préfaces des romans québécois du XIXe siècle* (Montreal, 1970).

[14] Honoré Beaugrand, *La Chasse-galerie* (Montreal, 1973), 15.

novel about colonization. Equally political is Jules-Paul Tardivel's novel, *Pour la patrie*, the first novel to advocate a separatist ideology.

Women novelists contributed to the genre of the historical novel, but *Angéline de Montbrun* (1884) represents the first psychological novel. Written by Laure Conan (whose real name was Félicité Angers), it is one of the few nineteenth-century novels to have stimulated considerable contemporary critical debate as opposed to historical or sociological discussion. It is in part the form of the novel which accounts for its critical interest. The first part is epistolary: a father, his daughter Angéline, and a young man (Maurice) and his sister correspond. Angéline and Maurice fall in love. This is followed by a short section of text in the third person. Angéline's father has died in an accident and Angéline has been disfigured and therefore assumes that Maurice can no longer be in love with her. The engagement ring is returned. The final section is .nade up of Angéline's diary in which descriptions of her solitude and religious commitment (manifested in her devotion to the poor) constitute the text. By combining the epistolary, third-person narrative, and diary forms, much remains only suggested. The confessional dimension of the diary has led critics to explore biographical details. Angéline's masochism (there is no clear evidence of Maurice's change of heart), and incestuous elements (in Angéline's relationship with her father) are two obvious strands which psycho-analytical critics have explored. *Angéline de Montbrun* has also been read, predictably but no less convincingly, as a frightening testimony of women's entrapment in nineteenth-century Quebec society.

The text's literary-critical importance lies in the invitation which it extends to a multiplicity of interpretative modes. By abandoning an authoritative narrator who remains stable and consistent throughout the narrative (as is the case with most other nineteenth-century works), *Angéline* allows for ambiguity and in the manner of a *récit*, leaves the reader to judge. Like Nelligan's poetry, Anger's novel (and others by her which followed) is concerned with the inner self, with emotional states, and with the potential offered by language and literary form to suggest mental and psychological states.

If the novel as a genre had to contend with the suspicions of the Catholic Church, theatre throughout the eighteenth century and until the last quarter of the nineteenth, was almost totally supressed. The influence of French touring companies finally stimulated playwrights to produce drama. Up until this point the 'tradition' is no more than a few disparate texts. The first plays are réceptions, written to celebrate the return or visit of a distinguished person. *Théâtre de Neptune en la Nouvelle-France* (1606) was written to welcome the return of the colony's leaders from an expedition. It is interesting in its attempt to create a New World setting, in including in the cast four 'Indian' roles, and in its occasional use of words from indigenous languages. Although plays by French writers were performed from time to time—a great controversy surrounded attempts to show Molière's *Tartuffe* in 1694—it was not until the Treaty of Paris (1763) that any number were staged. The first operetta composed in the New World was written by French-born Joseph Quesnel and entitled *Colas et Colinette: ou le bal dupé* (performed in 1790). Most of the plays written during the nineteenth century, however, are strongly patriotic and historical. Most famous are L. H. Fréchette's plays, *Félix Poutré* (1871), and *Papineau* (1880). A number of plays based on successful novels were also produced, for example, *Les Anciens Canadiens*, performed in 1865. As the influence of foreign troupes increased, so the clergy compensated by writing their own moralizing plays, very different from the increasingly popular and light-hearted comedy tradition which was beginning to establish itself. Amid the essays whose didacticism and moralizing is still more overt than in much of the poetry, novels, and plays of the nineteenth century, are those of Arthur Buies (1840–1901). He attempted to found an anticlerical journal, *La Lanterne* (1868–9), and wrote essays which attacked the obscurantism, narrowness, and censorship of Quebec. He participated in the Institut canadien, a liberal institution which was the target of the ultramontanists. He spent time in Paris and fought with Garibaldi.

It was, of course, the narrowness of Quebec society which militated against creativity. Prescriptions for literature were repeatedly written in prefaces, manifestos, essays, and letters, warning against foreign literatures (particularly the immoral and frivolous literature of France) and laying down narrow guidelines for a national literature. Casgrain's are the most famous and were among the most influential: 'notre littérature a compris sa mission: favoriser les saines doctrines . . . faire aimer le bien, admirer le beau et connaître le vrai'.[15] Less well-known but equally important are James Huston's pronouncements made in the preface to his *Répertoire national* (4 vols., 1848–50). The texts he is introducing are: 'utile[s]

---

[15] Quoted by May, *Breaking the Silence*, 36.

aux jeunes gens studieux, aux écrivains du Canada, à toutes les personnes qui aiment la littérature nationale et qui voudraient en étudier l'enfance, le progrès et l'avenir'.[16] It is the practical utility required of nineteenth-century writing which discouraged experimentation and, with the exception of various writers described above (most particularly and notoriously, Aubert de Gaspé jun. and Émile Nelligan), encouraged orthodoxy in every aspect of the literary text. Both were exiled from Quebec society (one abroad and the other in a mental institution).

Censorship dogged the development of a French-Canadian literary tradition throughout the nineteenth century, despite attempts by writers and critics to establish the existence of a French-Canadian literature and to define its relationship with French literature. Its development was viewed as a subversive activity by the English-speaking conquerors for whom writing in French was tangible evidence of a resilient French-speaking community, and also by the powerful Catholic clergy who regarded literature as both pernicious and seditious in terms of their authority. Nevertheless a literature emerged, but it remained, in Crémazie's famous words, a 'littérature de colonie' despite the appearance in 1848–50 of a *Repertoire national*, in three volumes.

Most of the writers who participated in the École littéraire de Montréal were born during the 1870s and most were writing at the end of the nineteenth and beginning of this century. Albert Laberge is best known for his novel *La Scouine* (1918), often cited as the first realistic novel in Canada, which was originally published in an edition of sixty because it was considered too offensive for its time.

Among those members of the École littéraire de Montréal not mentioned at any length is Charles Gill who was a central figure. His *Le Cap éternité* (1919) is an ambitious (unfinished) attempt to write narrative verse. Set on the Saruenay River the verses (reminiscent of Laforgue) describe the vastness and grandeur of the Canadian landscape and its mysteriousness. Unlike the landscape of Europe (made significant in art for millenniums), this landscape still had to be given meaning. The meaning attributed to it by indigenous peoples was largely disregarded. Gill studied painting both in Montreal and in Paris, and the landscape is of supreme importance in his writing.

Many of the debates initiated in the nineteenth century continued in the twentieth. Regionalists and exoticists opposed one another,

---

[16] Quoted by May, *Breaking the Silence*, 39.

and central to their argument were questions about the language (in the sense of both tongue and system) of literature and its function. The regionalists sought to preserve tradition and to root the literature in the place. The exoticists argued for aesthetic and formal considerations. Societies and organizations sprang up, including the Société du parler français du Canada (1902). Camille Roy's *Manuel d'histoire de la littérature canadienne de langue française* (1918) provided the basis for the study of French-Canadian writing as an autonomous literature.

Just as the nineteenth-century writers who are today regarded as influential were rarely the prominent writers of their day, so, during the first half of this century, the most important poet, Hector de Saint-Denys Garneau, was little known in his time. However, Paul Morin, a well-known exoticist, cofounder of *Le Nigog* (1918), won considerable critical acclaim both for his poems (*Le Paon d'émail*, 1911, for example), and for his translations. His evocations of extraordinary sensations and his handling of the alexandrine explain his popularity. *Le Nigog*, the first arts magazine in Quebec, grew out of meetings held by the architect Fernand Préfontaine in his Montreal home. Articles published were on music, literature, and the plastic arts. It was influential in its call to abandon the official utilitarian themes favoured by the regionalists. Instead it called for a modern approach.

Founder of the Société des écrivains de l'est which flourished in the 1920s and 1930s, Alfred DesRochers was also well-known during his lifetime although his critical writings (*Paragraphes. Interviews littéraires*, 1931) were only 'discovered' in the 1960s. His first collection of poetry, *L'Offrande aux vierges folles* (1928) is, like Morin's and Arthur Bussières's poetry (Bussière is regarded by many as the most important Canadian *parnassien*) is Parnassian in inspiration. *A l'ombre de l'Orford* (1929) is made up of poems and sonnets inspired by rural life, the appeal of the North, freedom, and adventure.

The most important poet of the first half of the century is, however, Hector de Saint-Denys Garneau who continues to attract considerable critical attention. His collection, *Regards et jeux dans l'espace* was published in 1937, but it was the appearance of his *Œuvres complètes* in 1949 which ensured that his poetry would be more widely read. Garneau had trained at the École des beaux arts in Montreal and knew the work of the Impressionists. His early poetry is often concerned with *effets de lumière*. In *Regards et jeux dans l'espace*, however, the object of the poetic quest lies beyond the visible, illuminated world. In an autobiographical and self-reflexive poem, Garneau describes a move towards something outside this world:

> Autrefois j'ai fait des poèmes
> Qui contenaient tout le rayon
> Du centre à la périphérie et au-delà
> Comme s'il n'y avait pas de périphérie
> mais le centre seul.[17]

Interested in metaphysics, spirituality, and surrealism, of which he knew through his reading of the *Nouvelle revue française*, Garneau sought to find the 'joint entre le physique et le métaphysique, entre la matière et l'esprit [. . .] entre le rationnel et l'irrationnel, entre l'être enfin [. . .] qui se noue dans le *moi* et le non-être [. . .], entre la nature, la sur-nature, et l'anti-nature'.[18] Describing *Regards et jeux dans l'espace*, Claude Gavreau wrote: 'L'univers subsiste en Saint-Denys Garneau, libéré des étaux inférieurs, l'univers vit de sa vitalité imminente, défiguré par le vice d'aucun stigmate préceptoral.'[19] The image of the eye travelling at great speed through space and time suggests both the cosmic and metaphysical, and a liberation from 'real' space and time:

> Et maintenant
> Les yeux ouverts les yeux de chair
> trop grands ouverts
> Envahis regardant passer
> Les yeux les bouches les cheveux
> Cette lumière trop vibrante
> Qui déchire à coups de rayons
> La pâleur du ciel de l'automne
> Et mon regard part en chasse effrénément
> De cette splendeur qui s'en va
> De la clarté qui s'échappe.[20]

If failure of various kinds becomes important in much of Garneau's later poetry, so too do the associated figures of night and death. Often described as the poet who liberated Quebec poetry, allowing for the total adventure of the poetic self, Garneau has also been described as the 'poète-martyr' whose violence was directed to-

---

[17] Quoted by André-G. Bourrassa, *Surréalisme et Littérature québécoise* (Montreal, 1977), 41.
[18] Quoted ibid.   [19] Quoted ibid.   [20] Quoted ibid.

wards himself rather than towards the repression and injustice around him (he abandoned poetry and withdrew to the family house at Sainte Catherine-de-Fossambault where he died in 1943, aged 31).

A major novel of the first half of the twentieth century was by the Frenchman, Louis Hémon: *Maria Chapdelaine: récit du Canada français*. Published first in France in serial form in 1914 and in book form in Montreal two years later, it is a *roman du terroir* in which the heroine has to choose between marrying a man who will take her to an easier life in the United States, and marrying a man who can offer her nothing more than a continuation of the hard life she has so far led. Her choice symbolizes a commitment to a rural, Catholic, traditional (French) way of life threatened by a modern, urban (English) way of life.

The literary merits of the novel, its language and form, have often been ignored in arguments which seek to demonstrate, on the one hand that the novel faithfully portrays the merits of a particular way of life and one which should be perpetuated and on the other, that the novel is peopled by submissive characters who are consequently enslaved in a harsh, if not brutal, way of life By allowing for different interpretations, *Maria Chapdelaine* has continued to provoke debate and to act as a catalyst for other novels which foreground their relationship with the earlier text.

Félix-Antoine Savard's *Menaud, maître draveur* (1937) is explicit in establishing a relationship with Hémon's novel. The eponymous hero, a veteran of the log-drive, attempts to reverse the process of foreign (Anglo-Canadian) exploitation of the lumbering region of north-eastern Quebec.

The vision proposed by *Menaud, maître draveur*, reminiscent of Giono's rural novels of the same period, is very different from that which had been proposed by Claude-Henri Grignon, *Un Homme et son péché* (1932). The sadomasochistic relationship between the miser and his wife is the sordid human corollary of the economic crisis of the 1930s. In *Précisions sur 'Un homme et son péché'* (1936), Grignon defended his text against those who accused him of great exaggeration. Equally denunciatory of the rural idyll (and its textual lyricism), Philippe Panneton (better known under his pseudonym, Ringuet) in *Trente arpents de neige* (1938), subverts the romantic idealization of rural life and opposes urban and rural, young and old, progress and tradition, life and death, in a pessimistic narrative which questions, above all, submissiveness to the land. The title refs, of course, to Voltaire's dismissal of French Canada as nothing more than 'trente arpents de neige'.

What had been romantic and mythical moves towards realism and historical writing. *Les Engagés du grand portage* (1937) by Léo-Paul Desrosiers is a fascinating account (in the present tense) of the life of Nicolas Montour, an unscrupulous *voyageur* who climbs to the top of the North West Company, dealing in the fur trade in the early 1800s. The bitterness of personal rivalries is set against a backdrop of the harshness of the environment.

During the 1930s, *La Relève* was founded. It lasted from 1934 until 1941 and was supported by Robert Charbonneau, Paul Beaulieu, Saint-Denys Garneau, and Robert Élie. Its concerns were for the spiritual, the universal, and the transcendent. In the first issue, a brief manifesto, 'Positions', described the journal's intentions: '*La Relève* se propose de refléter la mentalité et les tendances des jeunes catholiques canadiens, et par ressor des jeunes catholiques du monde entier.'[21] *Amérique française* pursued these themes from 1941 to 1964, but placed them within the context of a culture which is both North American and French. This question of French Canada's allegiances was central to debates during the 1940s stimulated particularly by the six-year period during which Canada was cut off from France. It provoked both a revival of interest in French culture and an awareness that this was different from French-Canadian culture. The founding in 1944 of the Académie canadienne-française is symptomatic of this realization of cultural distinctiveness. Editors and publishing houses also responded to this climate, recognizing their importance for modern French-Canadian cultural production.

During the 1940s a number of poets testified to the modernity of French-Canadian poetry. Alain Grandbois published *Les Îles de la nuit* (1944), followed by *Rivages de l'homme* (1948). Saint-Denys Garneau's *Poésies complètes* appeared in 1949 and both Alphonse Piché and Éloi de Grandmont published significant early collections. A considerable legacy had freed Grandbois to travel extensively throughout his life and he thus belongs within a group of globe-trotters of the inter-war period. He met Cendrars, Supervielle, and Hemingway, for example, in Paris. Love, death, and the potential of and for art are the dominant concerns of his poetry. Grandbois's poetic self is alone, protesting in an inhospitable universe. His modernity can in part be explained by the importance of the image in

---

[21] 'Positions', *La Relève*, 1/1 (1934), 1–3 (p. 1).

his poetry. Here the influence of the Surrealists (for a while he was in touch with the Port Cros group of French writers) is visible. Michel van Schendel, himself a poet, has accounted for Grandbois's influence: 'On trouve chez Alain Grandbois ceci qui est précieux pour l'avenir de la poésie canadienne: une expérience de l'espace, un plein air qui cogne, toute la rose des vents, même quand il rentre au plus profond de lui.'[22]

The novel of the 1940s reflected the urbanization and industrialization of the period and experienced sudden popularity. While a degree of homogeneity is visible in the common locus for many novels (an urban setting among the poorer community), many novels, while equally contemporary, take place elsewhere. Gabrielle Roy's *Bonheur d'occasion* (1945), in which a Montreal slum family's fortunes ironically rise, Roger Lemelin's *Au pied de la pente douce* (1944) and its sequel *Les Plouffe* (1948) belong clearly within the first group. Roy's *Bonheur d'occasion* was the first Canadian work to win a major French literary prize (the Prix Fémina). It is both poetic and powerful and is often cited as the text which acted as the major catalyst for the explosion of protest literature in the 1960s. It is also notable—and this should not be regarded as separate but as part of the complex matrix of the text's poetics—for the inclusion of Joual. It is a much more successful attempt than, for example, Ringuet's in *Trente arpents de neige*.

Lemelin's *Les Plouffe* describes the city of Quebec and the hopes and battles of a group of adolescents whose rebellion does not translate into ideas or action. Roger Viau's *Au milieu, la montagne* (1951) is also important. The Quebec urban novel constitutes a significant genre both because it reflects the growing contemporary industrialization of Quebec and because it represents a rejection of the *roman du terroir* and everything about it.

André Giroux's *Au delà des visages* (1948) is essentially a psychological novel; Germaine Guèvremont's *Le Survenant* belongs within the tradition of the *roman du terroir* but also subverts it, just as the novel's protagonist disturbs the order of the rural setting into which he arrives. The most subversive moment of the 1940s, however, was the publication of *Refus global*. Rejecting certain dominant features of contemporary Quebec (and their historical origins), the painter Paul-Émile Borduas and his colleagues published a manifesto, *Refus global* (1948): 'Fini l'assassinat massif du présent et du

---

[22] Joubert *et al.* (eds.), *Les Littératures francophones*, 324.

futur à coup redoublé du passé.' Published privately in 400 copies, the appearance of *Refus global* is generally regarded as marking the beginning of modern Quebec. The title-essay was signed by Borduas, the main text by fifteen others also. Variously described as surrealist, anarchist, nationalist, Marxist, and Freudian, *Refus global* is above all a document descriptive of, and a catalyst for, French-Canadian revolt.

Four relatively distinct narratives can be separated out: first, a brief history of the colony of French Canada living in fear, psychologically incapable of free thought and expression (and also subject to censorship). The second points to the possibility for change by appealing to war in Europe, travel, and the liberating texts of writers such as Lautréamont, Sade, and André Breton. The third strand is a polemical attack on the Catholic Church and capitalist powers for maintaining Quebec's submissiveness, and stifling originality. Finally *Refus global* proposes the means of personal and collective liberation above all through spontaneous artistic creativity. The text was crucial in its forceful proposition that art and action, and artistic, social, and political revolution were all intimately bound up with one another.

From 1950 on, criticism of the conservative and reactionary power groups became more forceful. For example, intellectuals associated with *Cité libre*—principally academics and writers—called for modernization, liberalization, and more progressive institutions. Maurice Duplessis, the authoritarian and anachronistic Provincial Premier of the time, came under increasing and ever more overt criticism. The war (which has been the subject of a number of novels including Gabrielle Roy's *Bonheur d'occasion*, 1945; Roch Carrier's *La Guerre, yes sir!*, 1968; Antonine Maillet's *La Sagouine*, 1971), had brought a number of French writers to Quebec which, combined with the publication of various works by French classical writers on the index, was a significant stimulus to new writing. Jean-Paul Sartre's plays had been performed for the first time during the early 1940s (*Huis clos* in 1946).

During the 1940s, and particularly towards the end of the decade, the range of types of novel increased: urban social realism, the political novel, the psychological novel, the subverted traditional novel, emerged as relatively distinct types. Gabrielle Roy published a second novel set in Montreal, *Alexandre Chenevert* (1954). In the same vein as the novels of Roger Martin du Gard, through the life and death of a city bank clerk, the novel raises questions about economics, culture, religion, and metaphysics. Place and climate play important roles. Other urban novels include Ringuet's *Le Poids du jour* (1949) which is concerned not with the poor but with the making of an industrialist in the period between the wars.

Among the psychological novels of the 1950s are those described by Pierre Baillargeon as 'romans de conscience'. In *La Fin des songes* (1954), two school friends, meeting in their 30s, question the significance of their lives and the authenticity of their emotions and feelings. One commits suicide and the other struggles to commit himself all the more fully to life. Suicide is a recurrent event in André Langevin's novels. In *Evadé de la nuit* (1953), *Poussière sur la ville* (1955), and *Le Temps des hommes* (1956), the meaninglessness of life and human isolation are the themes often explored by means of the orphan figure. Other novelists are concerned with moral and metaphysical questions; Langevin rejects traditional religion in favour of existentialism, in a manner reminiscent of Camus's *Le Mythe de Sisyphe*.

The novels of a number of satirical writers can also be broadly described as psychological and moral. Jean Simard, who published *Félix* in 1947 and *Hôtel de la reine* in 1949, continued to criticize bourgeois conformity and provincialism, the clergy, and the educational system (in *Mon fils pourtant heureux*, 1956). Bertrand Vac's *Saint-Pépin, P.Q.*, like Yves Thériault's equally compelling *Les Vendeurs du temple* (1951), is a satirical tale of electoral antics in a small Quebec town. A prefatory note testifies to the veracity of the account.

It was not until the 1950s that industrial conflict became common and widespread. It was at this point that a more properly political novel appeared in Quebec. In the 1940s industrial disputes had been written about in the novel (a printers' strike occurs in Lemelin's *Les Plouffe*, for example), but it is not central to the narrative. During the 1950s the quest for meaning which had been the concern of the individual (within socialist-realist, psychological, religious, or existentialist novels) is transformed into a collective quest for greater social justice within the political novel. Jean-Jules Richard's *Le Feu dans l'amiante* (1956), Pierre Gélinas's *Les Vivants, les morts et les autres* (1959), and Gérard Bessette's first novel, *La Bagarre* (1958), are amongst the most important. Central to Richard's novel is the 1949 Asbestos strike. In *Les Vivants* conflicts in Dominion Textile and the Dupuis Frères Department Store, occupy central positions in the narrative, as do sweepers at the Metropolitan Transport Company in Bessette's *La Bagarre*. Bessette's novel is also about the writing of a novel, however, and inaugurates a self-reflexive tradition within the Quebec novel. *Les Vivants* is also notable for its transcriptions of Joual, and concern for the significance of different registers of language.

While the terms 'urban realist', 'psychological', 'moral', and so on indicate a certain range, they are, of course, of limited applicability. Many important novels of the 1950s challenge these categories.

Yves Thériault's work falls into numerous categories. One of Quebec's most prolific and adventurous writers, his first book, *Contes pour un homme seul* was published in 1944. Three of his best-known early novels, *Aaron* (1954), *Agaguk* (1958), and *Ashini* (1960), are concerned with ethnicity and its significance in the modern world whether urban or rural. The eponymous heroes, Aaron, Agaguk, and Ashini are an orthodox Jew, an Inuit, and a Montagnais respectively. Each struggles to discover the degree to which he should live within or outside the ethnic and religious group into which he has been born. Some critics have seen in the ethnographic richness of Thériault's novels what might be described as an 'ethno-exoticism', which is also an escape from the contemporary francophone reality of Quebec. Others regard Thériault's protagonists as the 'little people' of modern Quebec, battling against conformity whether moral, religious, or social.

During the 1950s French touring theatre companies achieved considerable success and the first works of contemporary Quebec drama appeared including Gratient Gélinas's *Tit-Coq* (1950). Paul Toupin, principally an essayist, published *Brutus* in 1952. The Théâtre du rideau vert opened in 1948 and three years later the Théâtre du nouveau monde was founded. *Tit-Coq* was staged in Montreal in 1948. The French-Canadian 'little rooster' of the title is the hero who searches hopelessly for love and a family. Written in the popular spoken French-Canadian of the day, it demonstrated the possibilities of properly French-Canadian drama. Marcel Dubé's *Zone* (1953) and *Un Simple Soldat* (1958), Jacques Ferron's *Les Grands Soleils* (1958), and Jacques Languirand's *Les Grands Départs* (1958), further demonstrated the possibilities for French-Canadian theatre. The poor in the east end of Montreal take to the stage in Dubé's early plays. During the 1960s his work was to dominate not just the theatre but television also.

During the 1950s a number of poets established themselves as the older generation, Anne Hébert and Rina Lasnier in particular.

Hébert's *Le Tombeau des rois* (1953; reprinted in *Poèmes*, 1960, with *Mystère de la parole*) is intimate, anxious, and introspective. Images of confinement signal one of the important themes of her later prose writing (from *Les Chambres de bois*, 1958, to *Les Fous de Bassan*, 1982). Lasnier's poetry is profoundly religious. Her major works are *Présence de l'absence* (1956), *Mémoire sans jours* (1960), *Miroirs: prose* (1960), *Les Gisants* (1961), and *L'Arbre blanc* (1966), whose title points to one of the images which binds inseparably the devotional and the *québécois*, in Lasnier's writing. The tree is, it might be added, one of the most important symbols in Quebec literature.

Numerous publishing houses and groups appeared in the 1950s: Erta, Orphée, l'Hexagone. Among the most interesting (and representative) of the collections published during this period were Gilles Hénault's *Totems* (1953), which is a quest for and a celebration of origins, and Roland Giguère's *Les Armes blanches* (1954), which explores the origins of society's repressiveness in a poetry which invites psychoanalytical readings.

The literary-critical tradition which had become more important during the late 1940s (for example the contribution of journals such as *La Relève* (1934–41; *La Nouvelle Relève* (1941–8)), is marked, in the 1950s, by texts such as *La Poésie et nous* (1958), the proceedings of the first Rencontres des poètes, and Fernande Saint-Martin's *La Littérature et le non-verbal* (1958). In 1959 the journal *Liberté* was launched, providing a forum for both English and French writers to discuss questions such as the responsibilities of the writer, cultural difference, French unilingualism, and nationalism. Le Moyne's essays, *Convergences* (1961), written between 1941 and 1961, are underpinned by an unorthodox but unshakeable faith, and range over every aspect of contemporary French-Canadian life with peculiarly penetrating insights into the effects of the Church and the role of women. The writings of Le Moyne, Ernest Gagnon, Pierre Trottier, and Pierre Vadeboncœur (particularly his essay on independence of mind, *La Ligne du risque*, 1963), show a steady throwing off of orthodoxy and the birth of what has been described as 'la pensée québécoise'.[23]

In 1960 the phenomenon of the *Révolution tranquille* accelerated with the advent of the Lesage government. Figures such as René Levesque brought in major reforms and many structures in Quebec

---

[23] For a discussion of this see e.g. Robert Vigneault in *Études littéraires*, 5/1 (1972).

changed, from government to local pressure groups, from trade unions to press organizations, from school boards to feminist groups. Significant new organizations came into being: in 1961 the Ministère des affaires culturelles and the Office de la langue française. Some French-Canadians responded to these institutions by proclaiming their 'colonized' status (colonized from within, as much as from outside their society). 1961 was also the year in which the RIN (Rassemblement pour l'indépendance nationale) was founded and the Mouvement laïque de langue française. The FLQ (Front de libération du Québec), founded in 1963, announced its brief to use clandestine violent action in its cause. It was also during the 1960s that uncertainties about identity and allegiance, visible in the myriad terms *canadien, canadien-français, canadien d'expression française, canadien de langue française*, were displaced by the certainty of a Quebec reality. As Gaston Miron, receiving the Prix Athanase-David in 1983 declared:

le fait majeur intervenu dans la littérature de ces trente dernières années, c'est celui du passage de la littérature canadienne-française en littérature québécoise [. . .] Il revient donc à trois générations d'écrivains, par leurs œuvres, d'avoir forgé le concept de littérature nationale québécoise, hissant celle-ci au rang des littératures nationales de par le monde.[24]

The cultural and literary corollories of this growing confidence were increased production and diversification. The essay was renewed as an important and distinct genre. Jean Le Moyne's *Les Insolences d'un frère Untel* (1960) initiated debates about the education system and about language, in terms of both its state and status. Throughout the decade important individual essays and collections appeared including (the titles are frank): Pierre Vadeboncœur's *La Ligne du risque* (1963), Fernand Dumont's *Le Lieu de l'homme* (1968), Gilles Marcotte's *Une Littérature qui se fait* (1968), Pierre Vallière's *Nègres blancs d'Amérique* (1969), Marcel Rioux's *La Question du Québec* (1969), Jean Bouthillette's *Le Canadien français et son double* (1971).

Many of the ideological and literary debates of the 1960s were discussed in *Parti pris*, a journal and publishing house of the same name founded in 1963. Although a heterogeneous group, they were agreed about their radical political aim: an independent (projected as 'post-colonial'), socialist Quebec. The experience of colonialism and the post-colonial condition were much discussed particularly in

---

[24] Joubert *et al.* (eds.), *Les Littératures francophones*, 323.

terms of psychological fall-out. The relationship between literature and politics was also an important subject of debate. Literature as an institution was investigated, particularly the role of writing in upholding or overturning the status quo. Works published by members of the group drew attention to the relationship between the oral and the written (*oralité* and *textualité*) and the 'problématique de l'écrit'. Jacques Renaud's *Le Cassé* (1964), for example, both describes and enacts a slow process of degeneration and dispossession associated with the adoption of Joual by the novel's unemployed (although textually employed) hero.

Already established writers, Gabrielle Roy, Yves Thériault, Andrée Maillet, and Claire Martin for example, continued to publish during the 1960s, joined by numerous younger authors. Every level and group in society, and every register and type of language became a source in the quest for personal or collective liberation. Values and roles were questioned and relations between the individual and society (the family, the church) were contested. The formal, textual, technical, and linguistic formulations of these concerns in the novel were often the abandonment of linear narrative in favour of experimentation with new patterns and new treatments of time. The French narratologist Gérard Genette, exploring the dynamics of narrative progression (in 'Vraisemblance et motivation') demonstrates the extent to which narrative *significance* can only be reconstructed retrospectively. The teleological structure of plot can be subverted, however, if endings are open, suggestive of circular narratives, or multiple. Rather like the French *nouveaux romanciers*, Quebec novelists of the 1960s sought to subvert the rules of narrative in forms which become exploratory and playful. Réjean Ducharme's *L'Avalée des avalés* (1966) foregrounds language as its subject in a narrative in which the novel's half-Jewish, half-Catholic heroine invents (in a ludicrous gesture of refusal) a new anti-social and incomprehensible language in order to escape the absurdity of her entrapment within traditional structures. Later novels include *Le Nez qui voque* (1967), *L'Océantume*, the least cynical of Ducharme's novels (1968), *La fille de Christophe Colomb*, a mock epic (1969), *L'hiver de force* (1973), and *Les enfantômes* (1976). Ducharme's novels are described by Gilles Marcotte as both the apotheosis and the negation of the novel.

Gérard Bessette's *L'Incubation* (1965) is a *récit* or fictionalized autobiography (Bessette later explained the novel in these terms albeit 'with a great many distortions and changes') which, in a single paragraph, recounts both the events of a life (what is outwardly visible) and the strategic moves of a consciousness, brought into symbiotic and symbolic relationship in the labyrinthine basement of the library where the hero works. Many of the text's strategies are those of the *nouveau roman* as practised by, for example, Robbe-Grillet. The extreme repression of the novel's male characters is thrown into relief by Néa, the only passionate character, who commits suicide.

Jean Basile's *La Jument des mongols* (1964) is the first of a trilogy (*Le Grand Khan*, 1967; *Les Voyages d'Irkoutsk*, 1970). Each is a first person narrative (there are three distinct voices), made up of fantasy, humour, and reflective passages. As Basile began to experiment with drugs his writing became dense and fantastic, representative of the turbulence of the 1960s and now regarded by criticism as of 'documentary' as well as literary interest. In *La Jument*, place, action, and conversation merge and the disorientation experienced by the reader mimics the disorientation which is one of the defining characteristics of the underground culture in which Basile's texts deal. It is not so much that taboos have been consciously exorcised, rather they have been ignored.

Une Saison dans la vie d'Emmanuel (1965) by Marie-Claire Blais, on the other hand, is immediately recognizable as belonging within a long tradition: that of the reactionary, rural, *roman du terroir*. Amid a bleak and brutish existence, in which all hopes are frustrated or end in waste (the talented son, one of sixteen children, who wants to become a writer, dies of TB, which is seen as a welcome release), presides one warm figure, the grandmother, whose large feet (seen close up and from a low angle) dominate the youngest child's view. Her words at the end of the novel, that you get used to everything, articulate not hope but stubborn endurance.

Roch Carrier's *La Guerre, Yes Sir!* (1968) is an ironic treatment of traditional village mores. Equally emblematic of the novels of the 1960s are Jacques Godbout's *Salut Galarneau* (1967) and Jean-Jules Richard's *Journal d'un hobo* (1965). The former celebrates the freedom of writing ('vécrire') or the necessity of writing (as an urgent form of action) in a society from which the hero (who writes a novel while tending his hot-dog stand) is alienated. Richard's *Journal* rejoices in the choice of nomadism which takes the novel's homosexual hero from Acadia to British Columbia.

The Quebec historical and mythological novel is continued and transformed in Jacques Ferron's *La Nuit* (1965) and *Papa Boss* (1966) which combine, in post-modern fashion, contemporary current events, history, and fiction. More obviously related to contemporary events, Claude Jasmin's *Ethel et le terroriste* (1964) is based on the first fatal FLQ attack of 1963. *Prochaine épisode* (1965), by Hubert Aquin, is generally regarded as the great novel of the revolutionary period by one of Quebec's most colourful and uncompromising writers. His mythical status was finally reinforced, after an eventful and public life, by his suicide in 1977, aged 48. Where revolution dominates, the narrative is lyrical, where Quebec's present is described, the language is prosaic. The hero, a Quebec separatist in Switzerland, hesitates, not able to act but only to write. The man it is his mission to kill, a banker, historian, and lonely aristocrat, represents the hero's antitype, the English-Canadian who is the corresponding half of the French-Canadian. A narrative about a moment in Quebec's history, *Prochain épisode* is also about the constant desire for revolutionary change and its attendant problems.[25]

In the same way that novels of the 1960s challenged a narrow definition of the genre, so poetry was no longer to be contained on the page. Poetry readings and demonstrations became historical events, blurring the distinction between poetry and action. The emotions vented at these happenings included anger, despair, mockery, compassion, love, and hope; influenced by Marx and Frantz Fanon, Paul Chamberland's work is illustrative of this period. In *L'Afficheur hurle* (1964) and *L'Inavouable* (1968), the poem becomes an angry cry, a moment of violent rupture. Poetry is subversive, Chamberland declared in *Parti pris*, or it is not poetry.

Michèle Lalonde's early poetry (beginning with *Songe de la fiancée détruite*, 1958) reveals the influence of Saint-Denys Garneau and Anne Hébert. From the mid-1960s on, however, she became increasingly 'committed', that is to say more overtly concerned with the socio-political reality of Quebec. 'Speak white' is her most famous poem, performed at the Nuit de la poésie in 1970. *Terre des hommes*, an epic poem set to music by André Prévost, inaugurated Expo 67 in Montreal.

Influenced by Roland Barthes, Maurice Blanchot, and Gilles Deleuze's later writings, Gatien Lapointe's *L'Ode au Saint-Laurent, précédée de j'appartiens à la terre* (1963) is one of a number of collec-

---

[25] The complexities of the modern Quebec novel and the corresponding complexities of the literary-critical approaches which it has inspired, are analysed in *Le Roman québécois depuis 1960: méthodes et analyses*, ed. Louise Milot and Jaap Lintvelt (Laval, 1992).

tions in which the naming of the Quebec landscape creates the poem. The territory can only be claimed, this poetry implies, if the trees, rivers, and faces of the place exist both linguistically and textually. *Mémoire* (1965) by Jacques Brault is, as its title suggests, about memory, particularly as the supreme act of introspection. Brault's poetry also explores the landscape and Quebec's 'shameful' history. Gérald Godin, in *Les Cantouques* (1967) employs Joual in an act which he describes as a 'poetic sit-in'.

The denouncing of the 'élitism' of poetry is also an important moment in the history of Quebec poetry of the 1960s and *poésie-spectacles*, combining aural and visual elements, are one of the tangible corollaries. It is during this period that sex and, later, drugs are proposed as the liberating cornerstones of the counter-culture. Linguistic and formal limits are transgressed in the writings of Claude Péloquin and his group Le Zirmate which, in multi-media productions at the Musée de l'art contemporain, attempted to synthesize different modes of artistic expression. His *Manifeste infra suivi des emissions parallèles* (1967) was dedicated to the NASA scientists. Louis Geoffroy's pornographic or erotic work (in, for example, *Les Nymphes cabrées*, 1968), and Denis Vanier's mixture of the erotic, the sacred, and the violent, in *Pornographic Delicatessen* (1968), are still more radical in their rejection of the taboos of society and the conventions of art.

Songs are transformed from folklore into vehicles for the expression and exploration of group aspirations. Instrumental in promoting songs as a significant genre was Félix Leclerc and his group the Bozos. Typical of their activity was the rewriting of the famous song 'Alouette' as 'Alouette en colère'. By the end of the 1960s Quebec songs had become known abroad, particularly those of Robert Charlebois. Poetry and songs were performed during the Nuit de la poésie (1970) which brought together some 5,000 people and marked the end of a decade in which poetry and action had been closely associated.

Theatre also flourished in the 1960s, exaggerating and accelerating the trends of the 1950s. New companies were established, the École nationale de théâtre (1960) added to the opportunities for young actors and dramatists alongside the already existing Conservatoires d'art dramatique of Montreal and Quebec. The Centre d'essai des auteurs dramatiques, a more experimental enterprise, as its name suggests, was founded in 1965. New dramatists and plays emerged, most displaying a preoccupation with the language of theatre. Marcel Dubé's *Les Beaux Dimanches* (1965) and *Au Retour des oies blanches* (1966), are concerned above all with family relations as a focal social microcosm. Dominating the theatre of the 1960s were the plays and personage of Michel Tremblay. *Les Belles-Sœurs* (1968), which provoked enormous controversy, made legitimate 'le français parlé québécois' or Joual as spoken in the east end of Montreal.

That same year, 1968, the Parti Québécois, committed to independence, came into being focusing the hopes of a people. The four huge volumes which make up the *Histoire de la littérature française du Québec*, published in 1968, testified to the existence of a Quebec literature, a significant independent institution in a modern Quebec.

No longer intimately and overtly bound up with political and social action, the Quebec literature of the 1970s is often self-reflexively and theoretically preoccupied. Often self-conscious, playful, and open-ended, the problems and significance of writing and the problematic of women's writing, become important themes. The impact of structuralism on literature and literary criticism (*La Barre du jour* was founded in 1965, and *La Nouvelle Barre du jour* in 1977), encouraged these tendencies and are witnesses to them. In the first issue of the former, a 'Présentation' declared:

La Barre du jour ne défendra aucune idéologie politique, mais elle ne pourra qu'acquiescer à tous les textes de valeur littéraire qui lui seront soumis, bien qu'ils fussent empreints de caractère politique. Car s'il n'y a pas de poésie engagée, il y a une poésie essentielle qui veut tirer l'image de l'homme vers la lumière et assurer à tous une place dans cette conscience culturelle qui s'éveille rapidement aux nécessités et par là se définit comme nécessité.[26]

Hugues Corriveau, in the later incarnation of the journal, refers to a 'nouvelle écriture' which he describes as 'l'ephémère de la recherche, c'est le plaisir du passager, de l'incertain, de l'indécidable'. Equally influential and central to literary activities in the 1970s was the journal *Herbes rouges* (1968). Interest in what constitutes the 'literariness' of the text widened the field of literature to include advertisements, comic strips, and 'contemporary myths' as material. *Mainmise* (1970–5) and *Hobo-Québec* (1972–80) are two other significant journals of the period. *Estuaire* published in Quebec, was the first of a number of journals published all over the province (Rimouski, Trois-Rivières, Sherbrooke) which allowed for diversity and individuality. Lyricism was no longer associated with *mauvaise conscience* as it might have been in the 1960s.

[26] *La Barre du jour*, 1/1, (c.1965), 2.

In 1976 the Parti Québécois came to power and in 1977 the Union des écrivains was founded, signalling, in a sense, that writing had become a profession. As literature moved still further away from direct social and political involvement, so interpretative models were proposed which challenged the easy distinctions between public and private, collective and individual, political and psychological. Marxist structures were explored in *Stratégies* (1972–7) and *Chroniques* (1975–8). Feminist 'strategies' were also proposed, often departing from the contention that 'le privé est politique'. *Les Têtes de pioche* (1976–9) and *La Vie en prose* (1980–1) were the forums for discussions about patriarchal power and women's specificity.

One of the most interesting readings of Quebec women's writing which remains to be explored would take as its guiding principle the idea that this corpus of texts mimics, or can be read as, a microcosm or meta-Quebec literature. The 'colonized', relative powerlessness of women, the desire to write a language of difference, questions of influence and allegiance, are exaggerations of many of the problems of Quebec literature as a whole.

In the theatre, women playwrights have been supported by women's theatre groups based in Montreal, such as Le Théâtre des cuisines, formed in 1974, Le Théâtre expérimental des femmes, founded in 1979, and by women's publishing companies such as Les Éditions du Remue-Ménage (meaning 'stirring' in the colloquial sense of 'creating trouble') and Les Éditions de la Pleine Lune. A number of plays produced in the 1970s were collective productions (an important current in Quebec theatre since the mid-1960s). *La Nef des sorcières* (1976) was both drama and manifesto. Published by a collective, six monologues are superimposed. In the Preface they declared:

Pièce de théâtre ou spectacle de femmes? Six femmes prennent ici la parole. De personnages aucun. Car aucune de ces femmes que sont l'actrice, la ménopausée, l'ouvrière, la fille, la lesbienne et l'écrivain ne se donne en spectacle. Point de spectateur à l'abri: le drame se joue entre la salle et six femmes. Chacune isolée dans son monologue, comme elle l'est dans sa maison, dans son couple, incapable de communiquer du projet à d'autres femmes, inapte encore à tisser les liens d'une solidarité qui rendrait crédible et évidente l'oppression qu'elles subissent et qui les fissure sur toute la surface de leur corps. Du dedans, du dehors.[27]

---

[27] L. Guilbeault, M. Blackburn, F. Théoret, O. Gagnon, M.-C. Blais, P. Pelletier, N. Brossard, *La Nef des sorcières* (Montreal, 1992), 9.

Denise Boucher's *Les Fées ont soif* (1978) is equally polemical. It became a *succès de scandale* and was picketed by religious groups for what was perceived as its blasphemy and profanity. Nicole Brossard, founder and editor of *La Barre du jour* and for a time a member of the editorial board of *Tête de pioche*, is best known for her novels, influenced by the *nouveau roman* as practised by Sarraute, Robbe-Grillet, and Butor. She participated in *Le Nef des sorcières* (1976) and the title of 'text' (a term she prefers and uses to signify process and production), *L'Amer ou le chapitre effrité* (subtitled 'Theoretical fiction', 1977), demonstrates both her concern with words ('l'amer' conflates, opposes the meaning of 'mer' (sea) 'mère'(mother), and 'amer' (bitter)) and her desire to subvert genre (in the subtitle). The word-play is a linguistic equivalent of the layering of the human consciousness and subconscious. Brossard's concern as a feminist is to liberate women's suppressed desires. The text is about writing and constitutes a lesbian critique of heterosexual feminism. Her poems (*Amantes* and *Le Sens apparent*, both 1980) associate the processes of writing, reading, and sexual (lesbian) pleasure. Anne Hébert is one of Quebec's best-known writers. Her four-novel cycle (*Kamouraska*, 1970; *Les Enfants du sabbat*, 1975; *Héloïse*, 1980; *Les Fous de Bassan*, 1982) is varied, violent, and dramatic. The first and last are concerned with murders, the second is about witchcraft, and the third is about the influence of a dead woman on a young man. Other important women writers include France Théoret, Louky Bersianik, and Marie Laberge (among a large number of impressive writers).

A pessimism permeates much of the theatre of the 1970s: failed love, dreams unrealized, tragedy, and absurdity dominate. That these are on the whole collective rather than individual experiences, is reflected in, for example, the use of the chorus (often used in plays of the period). Some plays escape the bleakness of the majority. At the other end of the emotional spectrum, *spéctacles* such as *T'en pas tamée Jeanne d'Arc* (1970) represents the ludic and joyful, and combines music, puppets, and clowns. The meanings of 'play' are playfully enacted. A theatre of cruelty is inaugurated by the young playwright Normand Chauvette, and theatrical successes such as Jean-Pierre Ronfard's *Vie et mort du roi boiteux* (1981), made up of six interconnected plays, and Robert Lepage's *La Trilogie des dragons* (1987), have encouraged lively discussion about theatricality and the techniques of production.

In the novel of the 1970s and 1980s it is above all use of language (*langue*) which is foregrounded. Whereas the inclusion of Quebec

French had previously been a technique associated with exoticism or regionalism, it now becomes an integral part of the fabric of the text, rarely foregrounded. Permeating or constituting the whole text, Quebec French moves surreptitiously from direct speech into third person narrative. Michel Tremblay's linguistic itinerary is illustrative of this general trend (and one which he was important in trail-blazing, to use an appropriately North American metaphor). While *Les Belles-Sœurs* was revolutionary in its use of Joual, this was theatre, and the choice of language was associated with realism: this is how people in that particular area of Montreal spoke at that time. In his chronicle of life again set in Montreal, *Chronique du Plateau Mont Royal*, different registers are subtly interwoven to create a linguistic complex which transcends realism.

Louis Caron's *L'Emmitouflé* (1976) is about the conscription crisis of 1917. Victor-Lévy Beaulieu's three cycles of novels, the first about the Beauchemin family (*Race du monde*, 1969; *La Nuitte de Malcolm Hudd*, 1970; *Jos Connaissant*, 1970 rev. 1978), belong, crudely speaking, within Quebec's storytelling tradition. The social frescoes of his earlier writing (marred according to many by the persistent recurrence of sexual fantasies), give way, however, to more complex patchwork texts in which visual images and quotations (in the form of epigraphs, for example) create dense and interesting composites constantly preoccupied, according to the author, by the idea of creating something properly and uniquely *québécois*.

Gilbert LaRoque's œuvre is uneven. *Serge d'entre les morts* (1976), however, is widely regarded as a major Quebec novel. It tells, in a poetic and hallucinatory prose, of the incestuous liaison between Serge (an orphan) and his cousin, whose marriage ends their relationship. His novel *Les Masques* (1980) is the object of literary analysis in Bessette's novel *Le Semestre*.

Jean-Yves Soucy's work, particularly *Un Dieu chasseur* (1976) celebrates a primitivism within a lyrically evoked landscape. On a much grander scale, Antonine Maillet's epic fresco (*Les Cordes-des-bois*, 1977, *Pélagie-la-charrette*, 1979) chronicles the return of the Acadians, dispersed (by British troops in the 1750s) and scattered through the British colonies in America and the West Indies. Maillet is one of Acadia's most important writers and her work has drawn the attention of a large public to Acadia's rich oral culture and language. The success of *La Sagouine*, performed by Viola Léger, attracted interest in all her novels. Among a number of important prose writings *On a mangé la dune* (1962), tales about children, and

Par derrière chez mon père (1972), a collection of portraits, exhibit the lightness of her storytelling touch, her humour and folkloric lack of pretension.

The breadth of the trilogy *Histoire de déserteurs* (1974–6) by André Major, is also considerable, and exploits features of the thriller in a depiction of a violent society severed from its roots. The title of Yolande Villemaire's *La Vie en prose* (1980) could equally well belong to most of the novels of the 1970s. *La Vie en prose* is an urban novel *par excellence* and the town functions not as a locus or backdrop but as a character or agent of the narrative. During the 1980s the novel continued to be exploited for its flexibility as a genre. Chronicles similar to Tremblay's have been written by Yves Beauchemin (*Le Matou*, 1980) and Francine Noël (*Maryse*, 1983, and *Myriam première*, 1987). These novels have been enormously popular successes. The impetus for the plot of *Le Matou*, a fast-moving narrative, is delightful. The protagonist, in a gesture which he assumes will be without long-term significance, helps a man who has been hit on the head by a bronze quotation mark which has fallen from a sign! What dominates the novels of the 1980s is, on the one hand, a concern for history and its power and, on the other, a desire to explore minutiae. As in the *nouveau roman* or in the *proèmes* of Francis Ponge, small everyday objects are re-created linguistically. If the Quebec landscape was also a 'landscape of the mind', intellectually, psychologically, and emotionally significant, particularly for writers of an earlier generation, the small objects which dominate life in the city (with all its consumerism and materialism) are equally 'symbols of the mind'. The short story is a genre sympathetic to these ideas. Practitioners include: Gaëtan Brulotte, Monique Proulx, Marie-Josée Thériault, Daniel Gagnon, André Berthiaume, Gilles Péllerin.

More recently, Pauline Harvey's *Encore une partie pour Berry* (1985) is *réalisme magique* where the familiar and the strange are part of the same world. *Petites fins du monde* (1988), by Geneviève Amyot, is a philosophical novel. Science fiction has been accepted as a serious genre (Esther Rochon, Milovan Rajic, Elizabeth Vonaburg). The best-seller has also attracted critical interest, testifying to the broadening of the literary field.

The post-modern scene questions genres, investigates writing, texts, reading, and language(s). Simultaneously, and to an extent paradoxically, a desire to establish a canon of Quebec literature (a cultural system), has also been an important concern in recent years. Literary critics and members of the pedagogical community have set about this in predictable ways, writing histories, bibliographies, literary encyclopedias, syllabuses, essays on language (Jean Marcel, *Le Joual de Troie*), on aesthetics (G.-André Vachon, *Esthétique pour Patricia*), and on the phenomenology of criticism (*Essais critiques*, by André Brochu), critical works (including altogether new types of academic writing, socio-criticism, semiology, mytho-criticism, 'textologie'), and so on. Most emphasize language, both *langue* and *language*, as, for example, the title of *Le Joual de Troie* so cleverly suggests. Literary texts (if a degree of separateness between the critical and literary text can still be supposed), use quotation and citation to establish a network of cross-references. Thus Quebec literature has its own codes and models which constitute, in a textual sense (as opposed to the autonomy of production, for example, guaranteed by Quebec publishing houses) its autonomy. There is no sense, however, that Quebec literature is turning in on itself, forming a closed, incestuous system. Travel writing, construed by some as the origins of Canada's own literature, has become an increasingly important genre in recent years. *Volkswagen Blues*, by Jacques Poulin, takes the novel's hero to America (the most popular destination for travel writing), in search of the American dream. Parodying, in many ways, Kérouac's *On the Road*, Poulin's text is also a satirical rewriting of the classic American dream of the 'road west'. Like all travel writing (and exotic literature), the subject is as much the place against which the exoticism is measured, in other words, home. Demystifying and uncovering the emptiness of the seductive power of the Other has been the focus of recent Quebec travel writing. Confronting the Other also entails introspection. Louis Gauthier's *Le Pont de Londres* and Yvon Rivard's *Les Silences du corbeau* are about interior journeys which accompany the outward journey. The journey, like the Other, is central to many francophone texts, associated with the multilingualism and exile which are often the corollaries of the francophone literary space.

Part of this pattern of outward and inner journeying is made up of writing by groups who have recently arrived in Quebec or who consider themselves a minority community. A corpus of Jewish writing exists in English and is one of the most significant of these 'literatures within a literature'. In French the journal *Dérives*, founded in 1975 by Jean Jonassaint, originally from Haiti, has become an important forum. Fulvio Caccia and Lamberto Tassinari, of Italian origin, founders in 1984 of the journal *Vice-versa*, have sustained an important debate concerning the notion of a 'transculture'. *La Parole métèque*, founded by Ghila Benesty Sroka in 1986, is a feminist journal which, by definition recognizes the solidarity of women, and also recognizes cultural difference and explores the tensions, potentially creative but always problematic, which feminist and cultural allegiances can provoke. Identity, origins, difference, and language are the subjects at the centre of texts by writers such as Anne-Marie Alonzo, Marilu Mallet, Serge Legagneur, Èmile Ollivier (who is also discussed in Chapter 5), and Régine Robin. Quebec's best-known immigrant writer is probably Dany Laferrière however, whose *Comment faire l'amour avec un nègre sans se fatiguer* (1972), *Cette grenade dans la main du leune nègre est-elle une arme ou un fruit* (1979), and *Chronique de la dérive douce* (1982) have all been immensely successful. Texts by these writers challenge the definition of Quebec literature and its limits, and ask of literary critics and historians a question posed throughout Quebec's literary history: what constitutes Quebec literature?

That literature is, first and foremost, a linguistic exercise is a truism on which literary theory has focused. From the Russian formalists onward, attempts to define the literariness of literature have depended largely on defining the nature of literary language. In these debates what is important is language as a system, the 'nationality' of language has rarely been a major concern. The peculiarities of Quebec's linguistic position demanded that, early on, language (in the sense of a 'tongue') and its role in literature, be at the centre of literary debate. It was in 1918 that Camille Roy published his *Manuel d'histoire de la littérature canadienne-française* and here the question as to what constitutes the distinctiveness of French-Canadian literature, its difference from French literature, is clearly articulated:

Notre littérature est distincte de la littérature française, sinon par la langue et les procédés généraux de composition, du moins, en général, par la matière dont elle est faite, par les pensées et les préoccupations qui sur le fond français de notre mentalité et notre conscience, se sont lentement et solidement superimposées.[28]

He also advocated a programme of nationalization, albeit a cautious one: 'nationaliser, dans la mesure où cela peut se faire sans nuire à la formation générale de l'esprit, notre enseignement'.[29] The impor-

---

[28] *Manuel d'histoire de la littérature canadienne-française* (Quebec, 1918), 8.
[29] Ibid. 114.

tance of the process is, however, underlined: 'La nationalisation est une réaction contre une habitude trop fréquente de regarder les choses de chez nous à travers des souvenirs de lectures françaises, et de traiter cette matière en imitant trop directement des livres ou des écrivains de France.'[30]

The problem had been succinctly articulated by Octave Crémazie in a much quoted letter of 1867:

Ce qui manque au Canada, c'est d'avoir une langue à lui. Si nous parlions iroquois ou huron, notre littérature vivrait. Malheureusement, nous parlons et écrivons, d'une assez piteuse façon il est vrai, la langue de Racine et de Bossuet . . . Je le répète, si nous parlions huron ou iroquois, les travaux de nos écrivains attireraient l'attention du vieux monde . . . On se pâmerait devant un roman ou un poème traduit de l'iroquois, tandis que l'on ne prend pas la peine de lire un livre écrit par un colon de Québec ou de Montréal. Nous avons beau dire et beau faire, nous ne serons toujours, du point de vue littéraire, qu'une simple colonie.[31]

At the beginning of the twentieth century the opinion of Camille Roy was held by many writers. Unlike Crémazie he emphasized the importance of writing for a Quebec, rather than French, audience, and suggested that the French language had a degree of flexibility that was anathema to Crémazie's academicism:

N'écrivons pas pour satisfaire d'abord le goût des lecteurs étrangers, ni pour chercher par-dessus tout leurs applaudissements . . . La langue française, maniée par d'habiles artistes canadiens, sera toujours assez souple, assez large, assez belle, pour leur permettre d'imprimer sur cette matière [les thèmes canadiens] le cachet d'une suffisante ou puissante originalité.[32]

As early as 1902 the Société du parler français au Canada was founded whose brief was to promote the French of Canada. It also encouraged authors to write literary works: 'propres à faire du parler français au Canada un langage qui réponde à la fois au progrès naturel de l'idiome et au respect de la tradition, aux exigences des conditions sociales nouvelles et au génie de la langue française'.[33] The degree to which the French language (that of the Académie)

[30] *Manuel d'histoire de la littérature canadienne-française* (Quebec, 1918), 114.

[31] Letter to Canon Henri-Raymond Casgrain, 29 Jan. 1867, *Œuvres complètes* (Montreal, 1882), 40–1.

[32] C. Roy, 'Critique et littérature nationale', *Regards sur les lettres* (Quebec, 1931), 235–6.

[33] 'La Société du parler français au Canada', *Bulletin de la société du parler français au Canada*, 1 / 1 (1902), 3.

should be modified/corrupted/subverted/bastardized became a subject of much polemic at the beginning of the century and remains so today. Marcel Dugas's claim, made in *Le Nigog*, a journal which opposed the use of anything but 'proper' French, represents one extreme: 'Il existe une langue française; il n'y a pas de langue canadienne. L'idiome canadien, ce n'est pas une langue, c'est une corruption.'[34] In the early 1960s the 'corruption' of Joual was not denied. What mattered was that it existed. In highly emotive language, Jacques Renaud declared:

Nous refusons de devenir de beaux eunuques de la peste; les derniers français d'une 'Province of Quebec' composée d'une part de Canadiens-anglais et d'autre part d'ex-Canadiens-français anglicisés. Nous refusons d'être les Français de service; une couronne française sur une tête jouale. Nous refusons de servir à maquiller par notre beau langage le langage pourri de notre peuple.[35]

Although an oversimplification to describe it as such, Gaston Miron's article, 'Décoloniser la langue', published in *Maintenant* in 1973, represents, in many ways, a culmination of the Joual debate:

Il y a beaucoup de confusion autour de ce terme [joual], on ne sait plus très bien ce qu'il recouvre. Pour le moment, le n'est pas là, il n'est pas entre les dialectes québécois. Il se situe entre la langue québécoise et l'anglais . . . L'alternative juste est la suivante: faut-il dire horse ou tous les autres: cheval, joual, ouéoual, etc. Qu'on dise un arbe, un âbe, un arbre, tant qu'on ne dit pas *tree*, on parle québécois. Ceci étant dit, un créateur a toute liberté d'utiliser tous les niveaux de langue séparément ou en même temps, pour créer une œuvre.[36]

The political dimension of Miron's argument was accompanied by a more literary one: he emphasized the playful aspect of the literary project.

Since 1977 French has been the only official language of Quebec and this has coincided with the disappearance from literary debate of the subject of language. As Lise Gauvin put it in an important article on the language(s) of Quebec writing, 'we have passed from exorcism by Joual to the exorcising of Joual and so to the great diversity of writers' languages'.[37]

[34] Marcel Dugas, 'Jeux et vies littéraires', *Le Nigog*, 8 (1918), 254.
[35] 'Le Joual politique', *Parti pris*, 2/7 (Mar. 1965), 57.
[36] Témoignage avec Gaston Miron, 'Décoloniser la langue', *Maintenant*, 125 (Apr. 1973), 12–14 (p. 14).
[37] Lise Gauvin, 'From Octave Crémazie to Victor-Lévy Beaulieu: Language, Literature and Ideology', *Yale French Studies*, 65 (1983), 30–49 (p. 49).

If it is a writer's responsibility to renew language (*langage*), the Quebec writer has been equally responsible for defending the language (*langue*), in order to ensure that it remains the language of the State, culture, and communications. This is a literary dilemma which has excited numerous textual strategies and has guaranteed Quebec literature's self-consciousness, an important aspect of its (post-)modernity

The *français pluriel*, to which Quebec writers have made an important contribution, challenges the ideas of linguistic norms and margins, and the relationship between the centre (Paris remains by far the most economically powerful city in the francophone world) and those other 'centres' on the periphery.

Guide to Further Reading

Belgium

Unless otherwise stated place of publication is Brussels.

Novels

Susanne Lilar is undoubtedly one of Belgium's most important writers. Defying genres, her best-known text is the *Journal de l'analogiste* (1954). Her autobiographical text, *Une Enfance Gantoise* (1976) explores her identity as a Belgian. Conrad Detrez's writing (for example *Ludo*, 1974) is also important. Marguerite Yourcenar, whose sense of nationality is complex (*La Labyrinthe du monde*, i. *Souvenirs pieux*, ii. *Archives du Nord*), and Dominique Rolin (in particular *Le Corps*, 1969) have both met with considerable success internationally. Pierre Mertens (in particular *Nécrologies*, 1975), Jacques Crickillon (most famously the texts of *Supercoronada*, 1980), and Anne-Marie La Fère (*Le Semainier*, 1982) are all major voices.

Poetry

Maurice Maeterlinck is Belgian's most famous writer. Bibliographies, guides to, and criticisms of, his writing are listed below (Secondary Material).

Belgian Surrealism was a major movement. The painter René Magritte and the writers and poets Paul Nougé and Christian Dotremont are three of the many creative artists who were involved. A useful guide to the many works of poetry is provided in Mariën's study (see Secondary Works below). Belgian *avant-garde* poetry is most significantly represented by Jean-Pierre Verheggen (beginning with *La Grande Mitraque*, 1968). Werner Lambersy (*Silenciaire*, 1971), Jacques Izoard (*Terre Ultime*, 1970), Jacques Crickillon (*L'Ombre du prince*, 1971), and William Cliff (e.g. *Homo sum*, 1973), are all key writers.

Theatre

For a long time it was plays by Belgian writers Maeterlinck, Fernand Crommelynck, and Michel de Ghelderode, which, one after another, dominated Parisian theatre. After the war Susan Lilar (*Tous les chemins mènent au ciel*, 1947, is a most accomplished play), and Paul Willems (most famously *L'Autostoppeur*, 1977), make important contributions. René Kalisky's plays are also major Belgian cultural events, from *L'Impossible royaume* (1968) to *Falsch* (1983).

Secondary Material

The major bibliography is Robert Frickx and Raymond Trousson, *Lettres françaises de Belgique, Dictionnaire des œuvres*, i. *Le Roman* (1988) ii. *La Poésie* (1988), iii. *Le Théâtre* (1989), iv. *L'Essai* (1989). Two useful introductions are A. J. Mathews, *La Wallonie* (1947) and R. Burniaux and R. Frickx, *La Littérature belge d'expression française* (1973). V. Mallinson, *Modern Belgian Literature* (1966) is, as its title suggests, narrower in its concerns. More specialized still is Marcel Mariën, *L'Activité surréaliste en Belgique* (1979). The major introduction to Maeterlinck is J. Hanse, *Introduction, Poésies complètes de Maurice Maeterlinck* (1965).

Switzerland

Unless otherwise stated place of publication is Geneva.

Novels

Charles Ferdinand Ramuz (his last two novels *Farinet ou la fausse monnaie*, 1931, and *Derborence*, 1934, are high points) is undoubtedly Switzerland's most famous writer. A substantial body of studies of his work exists (see Secondary Material). Charles-Albert Cingria (*Œuvres complètes*, 1968, made up of *chroniques*) is also a major writer. Jacques Chessex, winner of the Prix Goncourt for *L'Ogre* in 1973, has produced an extremely significant œuvre. A younger but equally major writer is Étienne Barilier, see e.g. *Passion* (1974). Maurice Chappaz is most famous for *Le Testament du Haut-Rhône* (1953). S. Corinna Bille (*La Demoiselle sauvage*, 1974) is important. Georges Haldas (*Boulevard des philosophes*, 1966) and Albert Cohen, beginning with *Après minuit, à Genève* (1925), are major novelists from Geneva.

Poetry

Pierre-Louis Matthey (see e.g. *Muse anniversaire*, 1955) and Gustave Roud (e.g. *Air de la solitude*, 1988) are two of Switzerland's many significant poets. Jacques Chessex (see under Novels) is also a poet (e.g. *Le Calviniste*, 1983); so too are Alexandre Voisard (see e.g. *Louve*, 1972), and Jean Cuttat (*Bravoure du Mirliflore*, 1970, is typical).

Secondary Material

The most useful bibliography is A. Berchtold, *La Suisse romande au cap du XXe siècle* (1986).

The major introduction is C. Guyot, *Écrivains de Suisse française* (1961). Focusing on the modern period, M. Gsteiger, *La Nouvelle Littérature romande* (1978) and J. L. Flood, *Modern Swiss Literature* (1985) are both important. An interesting special issue of *La Revue des Lettres Modernes* devoted to C. F. Ramuz was published in 1983.

Quebec and French Canada

Unless otherwise stated place of publication is Montreal.

Novels

Major canonical texts from the modern period include: F.-A. Savard, *Menaud maître-draveur* (1938), Gabrielle Roy, *Bonheur d'occasion* (1945), Anne Hébert (*Le Torrent*, (1950), followed by a large number of other important texts), Marie-Claire Blais (*La Belle bête* (1959), also the first of a substantial number of publications), Jacques Renaud (*Le Cassé*). Jacques Godbout *Salut Galarneau* (1967) is a seminal novel. Also important from this period are Réjean Ducharme, *L'Avalée des avalés* (1966), Roch Carrier, *La Guerre, Yes Sir!* (1968). Notable are Nicole Brossard (*Suite logique*, 1970, is typical of her later work in the manner of the French *nouveaux romanciers*) and Michel Tremblay (see under Theatre below; *La Grosse Femme d'à côté est enceinte*, 1978). Antonine Maillet, the most famous Acadian writer, won the Prix Goncourt for *Pélagie-la-Charrette* in 1979, one of a large œuvre.

Poetry

Three early major poets are: Octave Crémazie (*Œuvres, i. Poésies*, with an introduction by O. Condemine, 1972), Emile Nelligan (*Poésies complètes*

1896–1899, 1952, compiled by Luc Lacourcière), and Saint-Denys Garneau (*Œuvres*, ed. Benoît Lacrois and Jacques Brault, 1971). During the second half of this century a large number of highly influential poets emerged including Paul-Marie Lapointe (*Choix de poèmes—Arbres*, 1960), Gilles Henault (*Totems*, 1953), Roland Giguère (*La Main au feu, 1949–1968*, 1973), Paul Chamberland (*L'Afficheur hurle*, 1964), Jacques Brault (*Mémoire*, 1965; 1968), and Gaston Miron (*L'Homme rapaillé*, 1970). Of the very large number of poets published since the 1970s Claude Beausoleil (*Il y a des nuits que nous habitons tous*, Saint-Lambert, Quebec, 1986) and Michel Beaulieu (*Kaléidoscope*) are undoubtedly major voices.

Theatre

Major works include Gratien Celinas, *Tit-coq* (1948), Michel Tremblay, *Les Belles-Sœurs* (1968), Réjean Ducharme, *Le Cid Maghané* (1968), a parody in Joual, and Claude Gauvreau, *Les Oranges vertes* (1972).

Essays

Paul-Émile Borduas, *Refus global* (1948) is essential for an understanding of modern writing. It is also reproduced in *Borduas et les Automatistes, Montréal 1942–1955* (1971), 95–151.

Secondary Material

Two bibliographies are indispensable research tools: *Dictionnaire des œuvres littéraires du Québec* (Montreal, 1976; later volumes in press) and *Dictionnaire pratique des auteurs québécois* (1976). The Bibliothèque nationale du Québec also published a *Bibliographie des bibliographies québécoises* (1979, 2 vols.; supplements published annually since).

Major Studies

A relatively short account is given in the 'Que sais-je' (PUF) series by L. Mailhot, *La Littérature québécoise* (Paris, 1975). Gérard Tougas, *La Littérature canadienne-française* (1974) is also an accessible introduction. More polemical is Jeanette Urbas, *From Thirty Acres to Modern Times: the Story of French-Canadian Literature* (Toronto, 1976). G. Miron's *Écrivains contemporains du Québec* (1989) is, as its title suggests, more specialized. W. Toye, *Oxford Companion to Canadian Literature* (Oxford, 1983) is a useful research tool with substantial entries on *québécois* and French-Canadian writing.

Studies of a more theoretical kind and books and articles relevant not only to Quebec and French Canada but to other areas also, are to be found in the Select Bibliography at the end of the book.

PART II   CREOLE ISLANDS

4

ANTILLES AND
FRENCH GUIANA

De la littérature? oui. Littérature de sucre et de vanille. Tourisme littéraire
[. . .] Allons la vraie poésie est ailleurs. Loin des rimes, des complaintes, des
alizés, des perroquets. Bambous nous décrétons la mort de la littérature
doudou. Et zut à l'hibiscus, à la frangipane, aux bougainvilliers. La poésie
martiniquaise sera cannibale ou ne sera pas![1]

Suzanne Césaire's characterization of literary production on
Martinique, in an article in *Tropiques* (1941), 'Misère d'une poésie',
holds for French writing in the other French territories in the
Caribbean. Poetry was the dominant genre and romanticism,
Parnassianism, and symbolism had been the literary movements to
which West Indian writers had contributed. The poets regarded as
models were Baudelaire, Hugo, Verlaine, Leconte de Lisle (born on
La Réunion), Théodore de Banville and José-Maria de Heredia (both
born in Cuba). Classical forms dominated and the themes were
conventional: the description of 'exotic' landscapes, melancholic
meditations in the twilight hours, and so on.

In the French territories of Martinique, Guadeloupe, and Guiana
(*la Guyane*), there was little to encourage the idea of a distinct or
national literature in countries where the administration, and the
policy of cultural assimilation, were very much against such a development. Edouard Glissant describes the general atmosphere as one
which 'déclenche la non-créativité, renforcée en l'occurence par la
consommation passive des produits culturels extérieurs'.[2] The essential problem for West Indian writing in French had been identi-

---

[1] S. Césaire, 'Misère d'une poésie', *Tropiques*, 4 (Jan. 1942); reprinted by J.-M.
Place (2 vols., 1941–2; 1943–5), i. 48.
[2] E. Glissant, *Le Discours antillais* (1981), 166.

fied by Oruno Lara early in the century. In *La Guadeloupe littéraire* he wrote:

Comment nous imposer, nous affirmer notre personnalité, quand il nous faut nous fondre dans l'esprit français? Nous vivons, nous inspirons des œuvres françaises, nous avons la culture française; tout de nous, nos pensées, nos gestes, nos espoirs sont français. Comment dans cette assimilation de notre être dans la civilisation française, conserver notre caractère propre?[3]

Recently, in an important essay-manifesto, *Éloge de la créolité* (1989), three of Martinique's most prominent writers and critics argued very similarly:

La littérature antillaise n'existe pas encore. Nous sommes encore dans un état de prélittérature: celui d'une production écrite sans audience chez elle, méconnaissant l'interaction auteurs/lecteurs où s'élabore une littérature. Cet état n'est pas imputable à la seule domination politique, il s'explique par le fait que notre vérité s'est trouvée mise sous verrous, à l'en-bas du plus profond de nous-mêmes, étrangère à notre conscience et à la lecture librement artistique du monde dans lequel nous vivons. Nous sommes fondamentalement frappés d'extériorité. [. . .] Nous avons vu le monde à travers le filtre des valeurs occidentales, et notre fondement s'est trouvé 'exotisé' par la vision française que nous avons dû adopter. Condition terrible que celle de percevoir son architecture intérieure, son monde, les instants de ses jours, ses valeurs propres, avec le regard de l'Autre.[4]

Guadeloupe, French Guiana, and Martinique remain French. They are overseas departments (*départements français d'outre-mer*) and constitute, along with a number of smaller dependent islands, the French West Indies. Yet many would argue, whether or not the polemic of *Éloge* is accepted as valid, that contemporary French writing from this area is amongst the most exciting in the French-speaking world.

Guadeloupe, like Martinique to the south, is in the Caribbean Sea. French Guiana is on the north-east coast of South America,

---

[3] Oruno Lara, *La Guadeloupe littéraire*, 18 Feb. 1912, n.p.

[4] Jean Bernabé, Patrick Chamoiseau, Raphaël Confiant, *Éloge de la Créolité (In Praise of Creoleness)* (1993; first edn. in French, 1989), 14. The denial of the existence of literatures is common in francophone literary critical discourse. Jacques Mercanton argued, for example: 'une littérature se définit par la langue dans laquelle elle est écrite. Or il n'y a point de langue romande. Ainsi donc le terme *littérature romande* [. . .] n'a aucune signification.' Quoted by Bertil Gallant, *La Littérature de la Suisse Romande expliquée en un quart d'heure* (Geneva, 1986), 11.

between Brazil and Surinam. Columbus arrived in Guadeloupe in 1493 and in Martinique in 1502; the Spanish arrived in Guiana in 1499. Colonized by the French in the seventeenth century, slaves were brought to Martinique after the extermination of the island's native Indians. Sugar, coffee, and indigo were the principal crops of the plantations. The Dutch made an unsuccessful attempt to invade in 1674, and the British occupied the island in the eighteenth century, but the Treaty of Paris in 1763 restored Martinique to the French. Creole planters took power during the French Revolution; the black population revolted. The British then took control from 1794 to 1809. The island became French again in 1814. During the nineteenth century the island's wealth increased due to the success of sugar-cane in particular.

The history of Guadeloupe is similar. 'Discovered' by Columbus on his second great voyage in 1493, Guadeloupe (the name is Spanish), together with the islands of Marie-Galante, la Désirade, Saint-Barthélemy, and the French area of Saint-Martin, has been a DOM (*département français d'outre-mer*) since 1946. The French first occupied the island in the seventeenth century, driving out the Caribs (whose name for the island was Karukera). Sugar-cane, coffee, and cotton were introduced during the seventeenth century and worked by African slaves. From the middle of the eighteenth century until 1816 the British occupied for brief periods, in particular taking advantage of the chaos which followed the abolition of slavery at the end of the eighteenth century. Slavery was, however, re-established on the island until the middle of the nineteenth century when Victor Schoelcher finally brought about its eradication. Since the second decade of the nineteenth century the island has been French. The July Monarchy of 1833 established a Conseil Colonial giving the island limited autonomy. By the end of the nineteenth century, as on Martinique, the economic strength of the island began to weaken rapidly on account of cheaper sugar production in Asia and the introduction of sugar-beet in Europe.

La Guyane, French Guiana, is a territory of some ninety thousand square kilometres on the north-east coast of South America, between Brazil and Surinam, with a population of roughly 100,000. Cayenne is the principal town. Reaching the mouth of the Orinoco, Columbus was the first European to arrive here. The coast was later explored by Vicente Yanez Pinzon, a Spaniard. A number of attempts to colonize the area were made by the French during the seventeenth century, but these failed due to the prevalence of disease and the hostility of the climate. English and Dutch attempts also failed. It was not until 1677 that the French finally established a settlement, but colonization proper, overseen by Choiseul between 1763 and 1765, failed hopelessly resulting in a large number of deaths. Between 1765 and 1775, however, Malouet and Guisan, the latter Swiss, succeeded in establishing plantations worked by African slaves. Although slavery was abolished in France at the time of the 1789 Revolution, it was re-established by the 1804 *Consultat*. In Guiana slaves revolted, fleeing to the forests. The territory was used mainly as a *lieu de déportation*. The Portuguese successfully invaded in 1809 and the French won the area back only in 1814. The definitive abolition of slavery, freeing some 12,000 in Guiana, in 1848, ruined the plantations. Under the Second Empire, Guiana became a penal colony where some 18,000 prisoners were sent. At the end of the nineteenth century other groups of colonizers arrived, from the Caribbean, India, and China. In 1946 Guiana became, like Guadeloupe and Martinique, a DOM (*département d'outre-mer*).

The first texts to emanate from this context were written by priests. They are largely descriptions of how the inhabitants of the territories lived, whether colonials, slaves, or savages, and belong broadly within the genre of travel writing. The best representative of the genre is Père Labat's *Voyage aux îles d'Amérique*, an account of his travels between 1693 and 1705, published in 1705. Eighteenth-century doubts about the institution of slavery, expressed by such writers as Montesquieu, were nourished by texts such as this. Labat's name has entered West Indian folklore as that of the ogre who punishes disobedient children. His *Voyage* describes in extraordinary detail the sadistic brutality of the punishment meted out to those who practised African religions, for example.

Occasionally *marronage* (the same term is used in Martinique and Guadeloupe), or escape by groups of slaves, took place and those who were successful settled in otherwise uninhabited parts of the islands or the Guianese forest. Although small-scale rebellions took place (and were brutally suppressed), it was not until the abolition of slavery in 1848, that society began to change, if slowly. There are only very rare examples of descendants of slaves gaining an education during the nineteenth century.

Well-known nineteenth-century writers include Nicolas-Germain Léonard (1744–93), a Guadeloupean, who attracted the attention of Sainte-Beuve and Poirié de Saint-Aurèle (1795–1856)

who, during the second quarter of the nineteenth century, published three collections in which whites' superiority over blacks was
one of the themes. Slavery was God's will, or so he argued. His
interest in West Indian folklore and legend accounts for the view
expressed by Jack Corzani, author of the most substantial history of
francophone West Indian literature: 'Ce grand Blanc créole, dans
le fond, est moins loin des futurs poètes de la négritude et de
l'antillanité que ne le seront beaucoup de mulâtres et de Noirs
aliénés par la culture française.'[5]

The same could be said of Marbot (1817–66), author of adapta-
tions of La Fontaine's *Fables*, entitled *Les Bambous* and first published
in 1846. Both Poirié and Marbot draw on Creole culture. A more
radical shift is visible in the first poems by a Black West Indian,
Eugène Agricole's *Fleurs des Antilles* (1900). The first Guianese novel,
Atipa (1885) was written by Alfred Parépou, about whom nothing is
known. Here and there, however, among nineteenth-century
French West Indian texts are works which, in retrospect, stand out
as early attempts to assert, however tentatively and inconsistently,
differences: J. Levilloux's *Les Créoles ou la vie aux Antilles* (1835), and
Louis-Xavier Eyma's two works, *Peaux noires* (1857) and *Le Roi des
tropiques* (1860).

Very little distinguishes francophone writing which emanated
from the three French regions during the nineteenth century. Although works such as J. Levilloux's *Les Créoles ou la vie aux Antilles*
and Eyma's *Peaux noires* or *Le Roi des tropiques* are often cited as
works which go beyond the narrowly prescribed limits of nineteenth-century exoticism and are concerned accurately to document cultural difference, their titles indicate the degree to which
differences *between* the French territories were not, at this point,
deemed to be of any significance. The differences which the French
were concerned to propose and on which they insisted at the Exposition universelle in Paris in 1900, for example, were rather those
which distinguished Black Africans ('primitifs et sans culture') from
the West Indian 'évolués'. But the writers so regarded, Victor
Duquesnay (*Les Martiniquaises*, 1903), Drasta Houel (*Vies légères*,
1916), and above all the highly regarded poet Daniel Thaly (*Lucioles
et Cantharides*, 1900), are not today seen as the founders of a modern
Martinican literature but rather as writers so fully assimilated into

---

[5] Quoted in J.-P. de Beaumarchais, D. Conty, A. Rey (eds.), *Dictionnaire des
littératures de langue française* (3 vols.; Bordas, 1984), 364.

French culture that their works display little to distinguish them from those of French exotic writers.

Gilbert Gratiant is generally proposed as the first major writer of modern Martinican literature. *Cris d'un jeune* (1926) is a seminal text in its refusal of exoticism. Gratiant is also important in terms of the history of West Indian literature as an early exponent of writing in Martinican Creole (some of his Creole poems were included in Senghor's famous *Anthologie*), and as founder of *Lucioles*. Published between 1926 and 1928, the object of the journal was to make available 'des œuvres qui tinssent compte de notre qualité de *Martiniquais* d'origine ou adopté'.[6] His early opposition to a simplistic exoticism and his desire to define something specifically West Indian account for his status as 'Père de l'Antillanité'.

A number of Martinican intellectuals made important contributions to a *discours antillais* (to use the title of Édouard Glissant's later essay (1981)) during the first half of the century: the Nardal sisters were important for their contributions to the *Revue du monde noir* during the 1930s, and the political and literary manifesto, *Légitime Défense* (1932), was essentially the initiative of three Martinicans: Jules Monnerot, Étienne Léro, and René Ménil. Léro declared: 'L'Antillais, bourré à craquer de morale blanche, de culture blanche, de préjugés blancs, étale dans ses plaquettes l'image boursouflée de lui-même. D'être un bon décalque d'homme pâle lui tient lieu de raison sociale aussi bien que de raison poétique.'[7] Their revolutionary tone is visible in poetic form in the work of the Guianese writer, Léon-Gontran Damas in *Pigments* (1937), Aimé Césaire, Martinique's most famous poet and dramatist, in his *Cahier d'un retour au pays natal* (1939, and 1947 in book form), and by the Senegalese writer, Léopold Sédar Senghor, in his more lyrical *Chants d'ombre* (1945).[8] These three writers are generally regarded as the founders of Negritude.

A minor and isolated Martinican literary event which took place before the end of the war was the publication of Clément Richer's first work, *Ti Coyo et son requin* (1941). It constitutes the seminal

---

[6] G. Gratiant quoted by Régis Antoine, *Les Écrivains français et les Antilles* (1978), 214–16, my italics.

[7] Étienne Léro, 'Misère d'une poésie', *Légitime Défense* (1932), 10–12 (p. 10).

[8] Raphaël Confiant's recent *Aimé Césaire: Une traversée paradoxale du siècle* (1993) is one of a small number of recent and more critical studies of Césaire. It explores the complex and often problematic relationship between Césaire's politics and poetics.

work in what could be construed as a marginal but not insignificant tradition of West Indian writing: works of fantasy which are also humorous and lighthearted.

A very wide range of different descriptions of Césaire's *Cahier* testifies both to its complexity and its difficulty. It is both interesting and significant that a work which is generally regarded as relatively inaccessible should be as widely read and highly regarded both in the West Indies and Africa (where it is frequently a central text on literature syllabuses). A neologism, the word 'negritude' first appeared in print in the *Cahier* in the famous lines which begin, 'ma négritude n'est pas une pierre . . .' (see Chapter 13 for fuller quotation). That the *Cahier* was written at a critical moment in Césaire's life is undeniable. This has naturally led many commentators to approach the text biographically or more particularly in terms of the psychological need which it satisfied for Césaire. The description in *Les Littératures francophones* is typical in this respect:

Le *Cahier* . . . a été écrit en son principe pour combattre le déracinement de l'étudiant Césaire, transplanté à Paris, élève de l'École normale superieure, passionné de culture classique et grand dévoreur de poésie moderne. Les premiers lecteurs (André Breton, Jean-Paul Sartre) y ont reconnu le cheminement d'une quête orphique: plongée au fond de soi-même pour dépouiller les masques blancs de la mauvaise foi, descente aux enfers de l'oppression raciale pour y conquérir la fierté d'être nègre. Orphée vainqueur, le poète noir ramène au jour son Eurydice: la négritude. (p. 94)

Born in 1913 in Basse-Pointe, the figure of Aimé Césaire is inseparable from both the literary and political history of the French West Indies since the war. Educated at the Lycée Schoelcher, Fort-de-France, he later won a scholarship allowing him to travel to Paris where he attended the Lycée Louis-le-Grand (1931). It was in Paris that he met Senghor, Damas, and the group associated with the *Revue du monde noir*. In 1935 he was admitted to the École normale supérieure and the following year began work on the *Cahier*: 'J'ai pris un titre extrêmement neutre: cahier. Il est devenu en réalité un poème. Autrement dit, j'ai découvert la poésie à partir du moment où j'ai tourné le dos à la poésie formelle.'[9]

In 1939 he failed the *agrégation* and returned to Martinique to

[9] Quoted in Alain Rouch and Gérard Clavreuil (eds.), *Littératures nationales de langue française* (1986), 311.

teach at the Lycée Schoelcher. Frantz Fanon and Edouard Glissant were among his pupils. In 1941 he founded the review *Tropiques*, published until 1945. Concerned with both a relatively narrow regionalism and broader concerns associated with Surrealism and Modernism, Césaire wrote in the 'Présentation' of the first issue: 'Terre muette et stérile. C'est de la nôtre que je parle. Et non ouïe mesure par la Caraïbe l'effrayant silence de l'Homme. Europe. Afrique. Asie.'[10] It was also in 1941 that he met André Breton who was to become an important friend.

In 1945 he was elected both mayor of Fort-de-France and *député* (as a member of the Communist Party). He supported *départementalisation* but urged considerable decentralization and devolution. In 1956 he left the Communist Party and formed the Parti progressiste martiniquais. Politics and poetry have dominated his life, and his plays have been highly influential, particularly in Africa. The *Cahier* has also been read as a record of Césaire's political commitment to Martinique.[11]

In addition to readings which privilege the autobiographical and psychological—the discovery of an authentic black identity and commitment to Martinique—the *Cahier* also represents a radically new intertextuality. In his book *Modernism and Negritude*, A. J. Arnold argued, not unproblematically:

Whereas the European artists introduce bookish reminiscences between self and world, Césaire as a Martinican writing on the identical subjects presents nature as the everyday experience linking self and world. This is not to suggest that Césaire's poetics should be considered a purely natural upsurge of affect [*sic*] and emotion. Such a neoromantic reading of the negritude poets effaces the extraordinary complexity of Césaire's relation to modernism. At the same time it is equally important to recognize [. . .] that Césaire lacks the patent exoticism of the European surrealist. When Césaire practices a poetics of intertextuality, as he has frequently done, his intertexts are functional elements within his poems, not the references to the outside world that we find in Breton's and Masson's work.

More thorough analyses of specific aspects of Césaire's intertextuality may be more theoretically complex and satisfactory but Arnold's study remains important in terms of its overall argument:

[10] A. Césaire, 'Présentation', *Tropiques*, repr. Place, i. 1.

[11] A. Césaire, *Cahier d'un retour au pays natal*, *Aimé Césaire: The Collected Poetry* (bilingual edn.), trans. with an introduction and notes by Clayton Eshleman and Annette Smith (Berkeley, 1983), 34–85.

Césaire's 'references' are not evidence of successful cultural assimilation, but rather subversive strategies.[12]

Les Armes miraculeuses, published by Gallimard in 1946, contained twenty-seven surrealist poems many of which had appeared earlier in *Tropiques*. A long dramatic poem, 'Et les chiens se taisaient', published separately in an adapted form as a dramatic script in 1956, was published with *Les Armes*. Many of the poems of *Soleil cou coupé* (1948) and *Corps perdu* (1950) were republished, with changes, in *Cadastre* (1961). *Ferrements*, published a year earlier and *Moi, laminaire* (1982), although separated by more than twenty years, testify to the permanence of Césaire's poetic vision. This is based on repeated patterns (of death and rebirth), an elemental imagery (often combined with sexual imagery); the juxtaposition of size and scale, foreground and background, violence and revolution are important in most of his poetry (in terms of poetic structure, syntax, and themes); the lexis is frequently one which situates many of his poems in a specifically West Indian landscape.

Césaire's plays have reached large audiences, having been performed regularly in the West Indies, but also in Africa, Europe, and elsewhere. The stage version of 'Et les chiens se taisaient' was published in 1956. The hero of the piece, 'la Rebelle' reappears, although not always so named, in all Césaire's drama. Politics, power, and the physical and linguistic articulation of these are central to his plays. Bertold Brecht's drama and stagecraft have been profound influences. French seventeenth-century heroic drama and dramatic theory (exemplified in the plays of Corneille, for example), have also been a significant influence. His plays include *La Tragédie du roi Christophe* (1963), a play about Haiti's independence, *Une Saison au Congo* (1966), about the (former) Belgian Congo and the events which surrounded its move to independence, and *Une Tempête* (1968), one of a number of versions of Shakespeare's drama written by black writers.

The first appearance of Césaire's *Cahier* went relatively unnoticed. It was after the Second World War that it became better known. It was also at this point that other young Martinican

---

[12] A. J. Arnold, *Modernism and Negritude: The Poetry and Poetics of Aimé Césaire* (Cambridge, Mass., 1981), 92–3. An account that furthers this discussion is given by Mireille Rosello, ' "One More Sea to Cross": Exile and Intertextuality in Aimé Césaire's *Cahier d'un retour au-pays natal*', *Yale French Studies*, 83/2 (1993), *Post-Colonial Conditions: Exiles, Migrations and Nomadisms*, 176–95.

writers brought out their first works. For example, it was in 1946 that Joseph Zobel published *Diab'la* (Zobel is, of course, best known for his novel, *La Rue cases-nègres* (1950), made into an important film).

In 1947 Raphael Tardon published *Bleu-des-îles* and in 1948 Mayotte Capécia published her *récit autobiographique*, *Je suis martiniquaise*, on which Frantz Fanon based much of his analysis of sexual relationships between white men and coloured women (see below).

Léonard Sainville's first novel also belongs to the immediate post-war period (*Dominique*, 1951). He is best known for his important two-volume anthology, published by Présence Africaine in 1963, *Romanciers et conteurs africains*.

It is equally to this period that Frantz Fanon's work belongs. *Peau noire, masques blancs* was published in 1952. Fanon was born in Fort-de-France in 1925 and left to fight with the Free French during the war. In 1945 he began his studies in medicine and philosophy. In 1953 he went to Algeria to work as a psychiatric doctor but was expelled from the country in 1956. A member of the National Liberation Front, he spent time in Tunisia, Ghana, and Mali. He became terminally ill and sought medical attention first in Moscow, then in the States where he died in 1961. *Peau noire, masques blancs* is a seminal work: a socio-psychiatric study of the effects of colonization. Its impact has been immense. *Les Damnés de la terre* (1961) was written during the last months of his life. It is a theory of violence and its necessity at certain points in human history. *Les Damnés* also denies Europe a monopoly of power which she has long assumed:

Quittons cette Europe, qui n'en finit pas de parler de l'homme tout en le massacrant partout où elle le rencontre. [. . .] L'Europe a pris la direction du monde avec ardeur, cynisme et violence. Et voyez combien l'ombre de ses monuments s'étend et se multiplie. Chaque mouvement de l'Europe a fait craquer les limites de l'espace et celles de la pensée [. . .][13]

Together with Césaire and Fanon, Édouard Glissant should be cited as one of Martinique's most influential writers, although his work has aroused more controversy on the island than that of Césaire and Fanon. His writing belongs principally to two genres: poetry and the novel. He was born in 1928 and having completed his

---

[13] Quoted in Beaumarchais, *et al.* (eds.), *Dictionnaire*, 787–8.

secondary school education, left the island for Paris with a scholarship. He enrolled at the Sorbonne but quickly abandoned his studies to concentrate on writing. In 1951 he resumed his studies however, and successfully completed his *licence* in philosophy. From this point on he committed all his energies to writing, working for both *Présence Africaine* and *Les Lettres modernes*. In 1959 he was actively involved in the founding of the Front Antillo-Guyanais, a small group concerned to promote the independence of the *départements français d'outre-mer*. This militant activity led to his expulsion from the island; he was forced to live in France until 1965 when he was allowed to return. He founded the Institut martiniquais d'études, an educational centre, and the review *Acoma*, published between 1971 and 1973. For many years (from 1983), he edited the *Courier de l'UNESCO*, a weekly publication which appears in twenty-six languages and is distributed in 158 countries.

All Glissant's writings could be subtitled *Le Discours antillais*, the title of a collection of his essays, written during a ten-year period, and published in 1981. At the centre of each text is a concern to find a language, a discourse, appropriate to the West Indian condition in all its imaginative, sociological, psychological, historical, linguistic, political, and economic complexities. But Glissant's *antillanité* does not aim for coherence, but rather to explore and allow for plurality, diversity, and difference whilst at the same time avoiding the chaos, at a social level, and madness, at a personal level, which such openness and inclusiveness threaten to bring in their wake:

Chaos ne veut pas dire désordre, néant, introduction au néant, chaos veut dire affrontement, harmonie, conciliation, opposition, rupture, jointure entre toutes ces dimensions, toutes ces conceptions du temps, du mythe, de l'être comme étant, des cultures qui se joignent, et c'est la poétique même de ce chaos-monde qui, à mon avis, contient les réserves d'avenir des humanités d'aujourd'hui.[14]

He is probably best-known for his novel, *La Lézarde*, published in 1958, which won the prestigious Prix Renaudot, but this work had been preceded by three collections of poetry: *Un Champ d'îles* (1953), *La Terre inquiète* (1954), and *Les Indes* (1956). These were followed by further collections of poetry including *Pays rêvé, pays réel* (1985) and *Fastes* (1991), and novels including *Le Quatrième Siècle* (1964), *Malemort* (1975), *La Case du commandeur* (1981), *Mahogany* (1987),

---

[14] E. Glissant, 'Le Chaos-monde, l'oral et l'écrit', in Ralph Ludwig (ed.), *Écrire la 'Parole de nuit': La nouvelle littérature antillaise* (1994), 111–29 (p. 124).

Tout-Monde (1993), and a play *Monsieur Toussaint* (1961; reprinted 1986).

Glissant's poetic quest for *antillanité* begins with what is at times a questioning, a refusal, a refinement, or a reiteration of the West Indies already linguistically articulated. Among the poets with whom his work establishes the most complex relationships is that of Saint-John Perse. Glissant is explicit, in *L'Intention poétique* (1969) about the way in which his poetry engages with Perse's. Whilst the latter's writing posits a 'fragile antillanité' his vision is also one which universalizes. Glissant, on the other hand, seeks to inscribe the humble particularities of the West Indies. The sea is at the centre of Perse's collection *Amers*, and becomes the central symbol of man's desire to transcend, to go beyond the known and familiar, to travel beyond known limits. Glissant's collection *Les Indes*, suggests the sea's status as witness to the terrible deeds of history, as a record of 'ce qu'on n'effacera jamais de la face de la mer': the slave trade. Thus Glissant writes: 'On a cloué un peuple aux bateaux de haut bord, on a vendu, loué, troqué la chair [. . .] Il n'est plus de mystère ni d'audace: les Indes sont marché de mort; le vent le clame maintenant, droit sur la proue!'[15]

In *Vents* and *Anabase*, Perse describes the heroism and grandeur of human exploration and settlement, while Glissant, in *Les Indes*, treats the weak and oppressed: those who were massacred, deported, enslaved, sold. The nature of Perse's 'antillanité' is fundamentally questioned and contested by Glissant's texts. His later work testifies to his desire to move beyond his dialogic relationship with Perse's texts (and other writers' representations) in order to discover an indigenous imagery, that is, one dependent on elements of the 'réalité martiniquaise' as opposed to an earlier 'discours antillais'. The influence of Martinican Creole is visible not in a specific vocabulary—which inevitably runs the risk of introducing an unwelcome exoticism for the non-Creole reader—but in a certain eclecticism in terms of imagery, and rhythmic discontinuities. Formal elements, the turns of phrase associated with the riddle, for example, further suggest indigenous genres. Thus the emphasis, in the poems of *Boises*, is on ways in which an appropriate process of naming can take place, in order to take possession of a landscape

---

[15] J.-L. Joubert *et al.* (eds.), *Les Littératures francophones depuis 1945* (1986), 108. Interesting parallels exist with the Congolese poet J.-B. Tati-Loutard. See my article 'Death and Identity in the Writings of Jean-Baptiste Tati-Loutard', in Abdulrazak Gurnah (ed.), *Essays on African Writing: A Re-evaluation* (1993), 126–41.

which is 'sans arrière-pays'. The metaphorical association between history and hinterland, and the present and immediate surroundings is important:

Il n'est pas d'arrière-pays. Tu ne saurais te retirer derrière ta face. C'est pourquoi dérouler se tarir et descendre dans tant d'absences, pour sinuer jusqu'à renaître, noir dans le roc.[16]

Pays rêvé, pays réel is equally self-reflexive. The process of naming, of poeticizing, is often emphasized. The paradox is that the tangible world is a chaos which language makes concrete. Language gives significance to a place whose history has not bestowed the *sense* which the history of other places might have bestowed:

Je t'ai nommée Terre blessée, dont la fêlure n'est gouvernable, et t'ai vêtue de mélopées dessouchées des recoins d'hier
Pilant poussière et dévalant mes mots jusqu'aux enclos et poussant aux lisières les gris taureaux muets
Je t'ai voué peuple de vent où tu chavires par silence afin que terre tu me crées
Quand tu lèves dans ta couleur, où c'est cratère à jamais enfeuillé, visible dans l'avenir.[17]

Time past and future time, the invisible and the visible, landscape and the numinous: these are the essential aspects of Glissant's poetics and it is from the relationships established between these that the strength of his poetic vision emerges.

The absence of continuity which is a function of the peculiarities and brutalities of West Indian history is palliated, poetically, by an emphasis on landscape, not as a permanent and unchanging *locus*—the changing activity (and threat of eruption) of the volcano on the island is also a source of poetic meaning—but as a place of belonging. Within his novelistic œuvre, a certain coherence, a sense of belonging, the idea of a 'people', is conferred by the reappearance of characters in a range of novels. Whatever the ruptures and discontinuities brought by history, genealogies cannot be denied. A knowledge of generations and blood relationships may be lost and circumstance may deny them their social significance, but—they cannot cease to be. Slavery and slave society—and *marron* society too—may have disrupted genealogies, but there is always a possibility of reconstructing them. Hence the inclusion of the genealogical tables in *La Case du commandeur*, subtitled 'essai de classification, sur

---

[16] Ibid. 109.   [17] Ibid.

les relations entre les familles Beluse, Targin, Longoué, Celat'.[18] The relationship between his texts, similarly, is made clear at the beginning of *Tout-Monde* in a three-page section entitled 'Rappel des péripéties qui ont précédé'.

Glissant's remarkable novel, *Le Quatrième Siècle* is essentially a historical novel, but also a parody of the genre at least in its nineteenth-century French form. Treating the four centuries of Martinican history which have elapsed since the island was first populated, the novel's structure neither presents history chronologically nor, however broadly defined, within the conventions of realism; a mythological dimension is important too, and there is an underlying ambiguity inherent in the notion of *l'histoire*: history/ story. Whilst the *békés* (white plantation owners) are important in the novel, it is principally the descendants of two *frères ennemis* (rival brothers) who people the novel. Two ways of life are contrasted: that of the slaves and that of the *marrons* (a small minority of slaves who escaped to live, always on the run, in the hills). The relationship between the two groups has never been straightforward, but the novel is not without a certain optimism. The linguistic success of *Malemort*, which is written in a powerful, vivid language poised between French and Martinican Creole, is in ironic contrast to its thematic pessimism which suggests the slow and painful effacement, decay, and death of the West Indies. The success of the linguistic synthesis suggests the continuing possibility of creating cultural and political solutions.

The language of *La Case du commandeur* is very similar, but here the novel's temporal framework is more complex. The novel at once projects into the future and reflects back upon the past. What is sought—and the sense of quest is strong—is an origin which will confer significance on all that followed, and on a future yet to be lived. The death of Marie Celat (who also appears in *La Lézarde* and *Tout-Monde*) and her descent into madness, is *one* corollary of the impasse in which the West Indies finds itself.

Madness is an important feature of Glissant's poetics and in other West Indian literature. Like the fool in classical mythology, the utterances of the mad can be meaningless—or original and visionary. Glissant's understanding of the writer and the significance of writing is analogous: poised between sense and nonsense, between pure fiction (which may bear no great significance for contemporary

---

[18] Glissant, *La Case du commandeur* (1981), 249.

society) and writing which confers meaning and significance. The latter proposes an understanding of the past which is both true and constructive, and a vision of the future which is at once realistic and honest. Finding appropriate forms and an appropriate language are the means to the end identified by Glissant and it could be argued that the relative inaccessibility of his writing—which explains his ambiguous status as a West Indian writer—is a function of the inaccessibility of easy solutions for the West Indian and his island(s). As early as 1956, in *Soleil de la conscience*, he wrote:

J'ai dit chaos de l'écriture dans l'élan du poème. Je le dirai maintenant dans le brouillon des proses. De même que je sus qu'il ne suffit pas qu'un poème soit emporté par un vent de démesure pour qu'il s'accomplisse de manière durable l'été d'un être, fût-il démesuré; de même j'entrevis enfin que la prose ordonne ce qui ailleurs est donné.[19]

Glissant's militancy should not be underestimated, but it is a less overt and more complex militancy than that of many of his compatriots. Auguste Macouba's poems, *Le Cri antillais* (1964) were confiscated on his arrival on the island. His play, *Eia! Man-maille là!* (1968) is based on the popular uprising which took place in Fort-de-France in 1959. Joseph Polius' poems, *Bonheur de poche* (1968) also belong within the protest tradition.

Vincent Placoly's novels, *La Vie et la mort de Marcel Gonstran* (1971), *L'Eau-de-mort guildive* (1973), and *Frères volcans* (1984), are written in a French which incorporates creolisms. The resultant linguistic pastiche suggests a lack of homogeneity appropriate to the cultural context he describes. Like Glissant he is suspicious of an easy and coherent *antillanité* while at the same time believing in the urgency of the country's need to find a sure foundation on which to build. In *Frères volcans*, which is subtitled 'chronique de l'abolition de l'esclavage', he writes:

Il est certain que l'héritage n'est pas facile à assumer, le gigantesque de la mission qui nous échoie n'échappe pas, seulement qu'est-ce qui bâtit le monde sinon la grandeur? Il ne faudrait pas que nous bâtissions aux générations futures cette vie couresse [Creole, 'wandering'] qui ne s'enracine nulle part.[20]

Very different is the writing of Xavier Orville, whose first novel *Délice et le fromager* (1977) won the Prix des Caraïbes in 1977.

---

[19] Glissant, *Soleil de la conscience*, 52.
[20] Rouch and Clavreuil (eds.), *Littératures nationales*, 329.

Orville's novels and short prose texts are fantastical in terms of narrative mode, and lyrical in their tone. His surrealism is reminiscent of South American writing. The titles of his works are consonant with the mysteriousness of much of his writing: *L'Homme aux sept noms et des poussières* (1981), *Le Marchand de larmes* (1985). After teaching for many years in France, Orville later became cultural adviser to Senghor.

One of Martinique's most influential playwrights, Daniel Boukman, describes his work as 'réalisme merveilleux'. His political and cultural convictions emerge most obviously in his criticisms of those who take up positions for the wrong reasons. In *Orphée nègre*, a parody of Sartre's 'Orphée noir', the Preface to Senghor's *Anthologie*, a character asks, 'Monsieur Orphée dont il ne faut pas ignorer les ambitions politiques se sert de la poésie pour escalader les murs du Pouvoir. Sa Négritude une vulgaire échelle!'[21] *Les Négriers* (1971) contrasts the dislocation of the slave trade with the dislocation experienced by immigrants to France. This 'slave trade in reverse' keeps wages in the metropole low while at the same time emptying the West Indies of the young and fit. *Ventres pleins, ventres creux* (1971) is about money, power, hierarchy, and racism.

Since the beginning of the 1970s a number of younger writers have begun to publish: the poets Arlet Jouankaéra, Soucougnan, Alfred Melon-Degras, and the novelists, Xavier Orville (*Délice et le fromager*, 1977), Honoré-Alfred Seitu (*Agodome-Dachime*, 1978), Louis-Charles William (*Le Foliloque en ou dièze mineur*, 1978). During the 1980s, José Alpha published *1902, La catastrophe de Saint-Pierre* (1981) and in 1982 four notable new works appeared: Alain Rapon's *La Présence de l'absent*, Roland Tell's *Le Réprouvé* and Marie-Thérèse Rouil's story for young people, *Le Secret de Monsieur Clodomir* and the poems of Monchoachi's *Nostrom*. The last, a 'bilingual text' does not provide translations of Creole poems into French or vice versa. Rather it juxtaposes poems which have 'versions' in the other language. Inherent in the book's conception is the conviction that translation is an impossibility: real access to a culture is only possible through the language of that culture. There are, however, parallels and equivalents to which appeals can be made. Such a project also suggests the need to allow the coexistence of cultures rather than the creation of what can only be a spuriously homogeneous culture.

A similar polemic is both implicit and explicit in an important

---

[21] Rouch and Clavreuil (eds.), *Littératures nationales*, 306.

recent collection of texts, *Écrire la 'parole de nuit': la nouvelle littérature antillaise* (1994), with contributions by Martinican, Guadeloupean, Haitian, and Guianese writers (there is also an important contribution by the German critic, Ralph Ludwig). The collection bears witness to a new literary and critical vitality in the region and is evidence that aspects of a shared culture are increasingly attracting attention, rather than the literary and cultural production of each island constituting separate fields. Before considering this text however, the literary histories of both Guadeloupe and French Guiana need to be considered independently.

Nicolas-Germain Léonard (1744–93), one of Guadeloupe's first writers, attracted the attention of Sainte-Beuve. Poirié de Saint-Aurèle, during the 1820s, 1830s, and 1840s published numerous poems celebrating the superiority of Whites over Blacks. Léonard and Poirié were both White colonials. Oruno Lara was the son of a slave and his poems and novels which belong to the opening years of this century, assert the dignity of the Black man while exploring differences. Throughout the first half of this century Gilbert de Chambertrand wrote prolifically and not without a degree of originality. Suzanne Lacascade's *Claire Solange, âme africaine* (1924) sets out to emphasize the Africanness of West Indian culture. Jean-Louis Baghio'o's *Issandre le mulâtre* marks a more trenchant break with the tradition of assimilationist writing. A prose translation of an epic 'conte poétique', his later work is equally difficult to describe in terms of European genres. *Le Flamboyant à fleurs bleues* (1973) is closer to the *conte* than novel; *Colibri blanc* (1980), subtitled 'Mémoires à deux voix' is made up of two *récits*.

A further shift away from the exotic tradition is represented by the poetry of Paul Niger. Like a number of West Indian writers of his generation (René Maran most famously), he completed his secondary education on his native island, at Pointe-à-Pitre, and then went to Paris to the École de la France d'outre-mer to prepare for a career in the French colonial service. While in Paris he met other Black writers, in particular Senghor, and was thus made familiar with contemporary debates about Black writing and culture, including those aspects of the debate associated with Negritude. He was posted first to Dahomey and then Niger. This direct experience of Africa no doubt explains in part his rejection of a folkloric, romantic, all-embracing, and uncritical *retour aux sources*. His poem 'Je n'aime pas l'Afrique' is the most obvious and best-known illustration:

Moi, je n'aime pas cette Afrique-là. [. . .]
L'Afrique des yesmen et des béni-oui-oui.
L'Afrique des hommes couchés attendant comme une grâce le
  réveil de la botte. [. . .]
L'Afrique des négresses servant l'alcool d'oubli sur le
  plateau de leurs lèvres.
[. . .] L'Afrique des Paul Morand et des André Demaison.
Je n'aime pas cette Afrique-là.[22]

His collection *Initiation* can be crudely described as belonging within the protest tradition and announces the liberation of Africa and her people: 'L'Afrique va parler | J'entends chanter la sève au coeur du flamboyant.'[23] His novels, *Les Puissants* (1956), and *Les Grenouilles du Mont-Kimbo* (1964), published posthumously, also look to future liberations. Niger's biting satire is accompanied by overt polemic.

The status of Saint-John Perse as a Guadeloupean writer is ambiguous. Born on the island, he left when young. Educated at Pau and Bordeaux, he entered the Ministère des affaires etrangères in 1914 where he worked until 1940. Unwilling to have anything to do with the Vichy régime during the war, he took refuge in America, working as an advisor to the Library of Congress in Washington.

In Perse's early work the profound influence of the island and its people on his imagination, his emotions and sensibility, is evident. 'Pour fêter une enfance' is in part a celebration of the child's intimacy with nature—a near-universal experience—and in part a celebration of the *particular* security and stability experienced by a White child in a colonially structured society, growing up with rare privileges and comforts. But Perse's poetry is above all aesthetically preoccupied; its relationship with the social and political reality of Guadeloupe can only be proposed relatively tentatively. The following quotation is commonly cited in such discussions:

La place couverte du Marché
où debout
et vivant
et vêtu d'un vieux sac qui fleure bon le riz
un nègre dont le poil est de la laine de mouton
noir grandit comme un prophète.[24]

---

[22] Joubert *et al.* (eds.), *Littératures francophones*, 105.
[23] Beaumarchais *et al.* (eds.), *Dictionnaire*, 1641.
[24] Rouch and Clavreuil (eds.), *Littératures nationales*, 176.

The texts of Glissant and Césaire establish interesting relationships with those of Perse.

Sonny Rupaire's writing belongs to the protest tradition. He first disseminated copies of his poems simply by handing them out at union meetings, for example. He published his collection of protest poems . . . *Cette igname brisée qu'est ma terre natale* in 1970. A number of significant Guadeloupean writers emerged during the 1960s: Florette Morand, Gérard Delisle, Michèle Lacrosil, Guy Tirolien. Like Maran and Niger, Tirolien worked in Africa as a colonial administrator and later for the Organization for African Unity, in Mali, Cameroon, and Gabon. Although he has written relatively little (*Balles d'or*, 1961, a collection of poems, and *Feuilles vivantes au matin*, 1977, a collection of short stories and poems), his work is easily accessible and widely known. 'Prière d'un petit enfant nègre' is one of the most anthologized poems in French about Black experience:

> Seigneur, je ne veux plus aller à leur école
> [. . .]
> Et puis elle est vraiment trop triste leur école
> Triste comme
> Ces messieurs de la ville,
> Ces messieurs comme il faut
> Qui ne savent plus danser le soir au clair de lune
> Qui ne savent plus marcher sur la chair de leurs pieds
> Qui ne savent plus conter les contes aux veillées.
> Seigneur, je ne veux plus aller à leur école.[25]

Lacrosil's writing has aroused considerable debate. Her work belongs within a tradition of largely autobiographical writing by women in which the nature of relationships between Black women and White men is explored. Such a relationship is at the centre of Lacrosil's most controversial novel, *Sapotille et le Serin d'argile* (1960). Jacqueline Manicom's *Mon examen de blanc*, published in 1972, also belongs within this tradition, one which goes back to Capécia's *Je suis martiniquaise* (1948; see above). But it is not only the difficulties of exploring interracial relationships which has attracted criticism of Lacrosil's work. The narrative of *Demain Jab Herma* (1967) suggests that the eponymous hero, a Black chauffeur will, if he possibly can, assume the position of his White masters if they no longer dominate.

Guadeloupe's most outstanding (woman) writer, and publicist of

---

[25] Joubert *et al.* (eds.), *Littératures francophones*, 105.

Guadeloupean and West Indian writing, is Maryse Condé. Born in Pointe-à-Pitre in 1937, Maryse Bocoulon (her maiden name), left the island in 1953. She attended the Lycée Fénelon and then the Sorbonne (graduating as a *licencié ès lettres*). In 1958 she met Condé, an artist whom she followed to Guinea, his homeland. When the reality of Sekou Touré's regime became apparent she left and went to Ghana where she taught at the Winneba Ideological Institute. After Nkrumah's downfall she was expelled from the country and came to London where she worked on French programmes for the BBC. She taught for two years (1968–70) in Saint-Louis and Kaolack, Senegal, before returning to Guadeloupe, making frequent trips to Paris while preparing her doctorate. Since completing her doctorate she has taught in various Parisian universities. She has also collaborated on numerous periodicals (*Africa, Demain l'Afrique, Présence Africaine*) and, in recent years has spent more time on Guadeloupe, campaigning for the cultural life of the island.

Condé's œuvre comprises works of literary criticism, essays (including comparative analyses of anglophone and francophone Caribbean writing—for example, 'Anglophones et francophones: les frontières littéraires existent-elles?'), plays, novels, short stories, and stories for children.[26] She has also produced an *Anthologie de la littérature d'expression française*, published by the Institute of Languages, Accra (1966). Among her critical writings are studies of both the West Indian novel, *Le Roman antillais*, and poetry, *La Poésie antillaise* (both Paris, 1977), a study of Césaire's *Cahier d'un retour au pays natal* (Paris, 1978), and essays, most importantly *La Civilisation de bossale* (1978) and *La Parole des femmes* (1979). Her plays include *Dieu nous l'a donné* (1972) and *Mort d'Oluwémi d'Ajumako* (1973). It is, however, for her novels that she is best known; these include: Hérémakhonon (1976; reprinted as *En attendant le bonheur (Hérémakhonon)*, 1988), *Une Saison à Rihata* (1981), and *Ségou*, a two-volume historical novel, published in 1984 (i. *Les Murailles de terre*) and 1985 (ii. *La Terre en miettes*). The first two are set in Africa and the heroines of both are *Guadeloupéennes*. Their encounter with Africa, with politics and African men, is a largely disillusioning one, and the narrative technique of both is a stream of consciousness which creates an immediacy and a degree of ambiguity which encourage the reader to make sense of a narrative which is rarely explicit in its judgements.

---

[26] A useful recent bibliography is provided at the end of Françoise Pfaff's *Entretiens avec Maryse Condé* (1993).

Ségou is a vast historical chronicle of the Bambara Kingdom. The novel begins at the end of the eighteenth century and ends at the middle of the nineteenth. The manner of narration is dramatic and often rhetorical, suggesting transcription of an oral delivery. The society that is chronicled is one in constant change, initially because of the pressure of Islamic forces and later owing to the arrival of Europeans. But there is a certain stability too and Condé conveys a strong sense of the dignity of the Bambara people and the richness of Peul civilization.

Comparisons are often made between Condé and her compatriot, Simone Schwarz-Bart. She was educated in her home town and later in Paris and Dakar. Her first novel, *Un Plat de porc aux bananes vertes* (1967) was written in collaboration with her husband, André, whose novel, *Le Dernier des justes* had been awarded the Prix Goncourt in 1959, shortly before they met. *Pluie et vent sur Telumée Miracle* (1972) was Simone's first novel written independently. Comparable in many ways to Condé's *Ségou*, *Pluie et vent* is a historical novel which chronicles *la vie guadeloupéenne* over nearly a century. It is the generations of women that provide continuity and stability, in particular the women of the Lougandor family. The novel begins at the point when slavery is abolished; Telumée is the principal character. It is she who narrates and it is her language which accounts, to a large extent, for the power of the novel. Although little Creole is incorporated in the French, Creole idioms are directly translated, conveying a sense of a Creole vision, a Creole worldview. Maryse Condé's description of *Pluie et vent*, 'gigantesque fourre-tout où sont jetés pêle-mêle tous les traits de la vie du peuple antillais' is widely quoted and has sometimes been construed as an adverse criticism of the novel. This is not, however, what emerges from the context in which it was made. Rather it suggests the extent to which the form of the novel reflects the eclecticism and diversity of Creole culture.

Condé's other novels include *Hérémakhonon* (1976), *Une Saison à Rihata* (1981), *Moi, Tituba, sorcière . . . Noire de Salem* (1986), *La Vie scélérate* (1987), *Traversée de la mangrove* (1989), *Les Derniers rois mages* (1992), *La Colonie du nouveau monde* (1993). She has also written short stories and plays. Françoise Pfaff's recent *Entretiens avec Maryse Condé* (1993) provide a fascinating insight into her life and writing.

Three important Guadeloupean writers emerged during the 1980s: Max Jeanne, Daniel Maximin, and Myriam Warner-Vieyra. Jeanne, a schoolteacher in Pointe-à-Pitre, published *Western*, a 'ciné-poème', in 1978 (l'Harmattan) and *Chasse au racoon* in 1980. The latter is based on events that took place in Pointe-à-Pitre in 1967 which culminated in the arrest of eighteen young people and their appearance before the Cours de Sûreté de l'État (February–March, 1968). Jeanne's purpose, however, was not simply to record his own interpretation of these happenings but to suggest possibilities for Guadeloupe's future—and the future of an independent West Indies. Irony is the most powerful technique of the novel, combined with a linguistic register which mixes, unexpectedly, a classical French with a spoken register, interspersed with occasional words from a Creole lexis.

Daniel Maximin's first novel, *L'Isolé Soleil* (1981) is a more formally complex and less overtly polemical work. A composite of genres which include the epistolary novel, poetry, and poetic prose, it reconstructs Guadeloupean history from the time of Delgrès, the last defender of Blacks when Bonaparte's soldiers came to re-establish slavery. The author's intention was to write 'd'une manière impure, parodique, mythique et documentaire à la fois'.[27] *L'Isolé Soleil* is one of a number of formally daring texts published during the 1970s and 1980s. They represent a refusal to homogenize or to be assimilated into a dominant mode, but rather to display and extend the textual possibilities of diversity, plurality, polyphony, and difference.

Born in Pointe-à-Pitre, Myriam Warner-Vieyra completed most of her secondary education in France and qualified as a librarian and archivist. She lives and works in Dakar and her perspective on Guadeloupe is thus that of the writer in exile. Her novels, *Le Puimboiseur l'avait dit . . .* (1980) and *Juletane* (1982) have a number of points in common. Both are principally concerned with women's experience and the ways in which these are largely controlled by social contexts. In *Juletane*, the eponymous heroine discovers after her marriage to Mahmadou, a Senegalese, that she is his second wife. Both novels stage returns or remembrances of Guadeloupe from a present point of exile. More significantly, both are concerned with the processes of psychiatric treatment and the role played by memory in human psychic life. The formal corollary of this in *Juletane* is the inclusion of the heroine's diary which she keeps in moments of lucidity. Madness and death are important topoi.

A number of other important contemporary Guadeloupean writers are best considered in the context of a wider francophone Carib-

---

[27] Joubert *et al.* (eds.), *Littératures francophones*, p. 118.

bean cultural and political community. First, however, a brief account of French Guiana's literary production should be given.

Guiana's most celebrated writers are René Maran and Léon-Gontran Damas. The latter is generally regarded as one of the three writers most closely associated with the genesis of Negritude. Maran's *Batouala*, which won the Prix Goncourt in 1921 amid considerable controversy, drew the attention of a new audience to 'Negro-African' writing in French (it was thus that it was coming to be defined). Previously it had been the colonial institutions which encouraged and controlled writing by Africans, in particular, and Maran's novel was about Africa (see Chapter 13). *Batouala*, subtitled *véritable roman nègre* was clearly not a 'colonial novel' and the subtitle prompted exploration of what the suggested new genre (*roman nègre*) might be. But the novel is no out-and-out indictment of the colonial system, rather a criticism of the behaviour of certain colonial officials.[28] Maran's œuvre is a large one although this is often overlooked because of the notoriety of his first novel. He has written a number of collections of poems and stories, biographies *Livingstone et l'exploration de l'Afrique* (1938), *Savorgnan de Brazza et la fondation de l'A.E.F.* (1940), and a three-volume 'chronique coloniale', *Les Pionniers de l'Empire* (1943, 1946, 1955).

It is important to emphasize that Damas's first collection of poetry, *Pigments*, was published very early in terms of the history of Negritude, in 1937 (he had also published influential poems in *Esprit*—versions of the later *Pigments*—as early as 1934). The title was provocative and unambiguous, both attributes of much of Damas's writing, and although Robert Desnos, who contributed a Preface to the first edition, did not mention Negritude by name, he did recognize features of Damas's text which would, retrospectively be seen as intimately related to Negritude. Desnos wrote, for example: 'Damas est nègre et tient à sa qualité et à son état de nègre.'[29]

Damas was born in Cayenne in 1912. His family was part Indian, part European, and part African. In *Névralgies* he writes: 'debout

---

[28] Two relatively recent articles which provide a sense of the diversity and complexity of opinion surrounding *Batouala* were published in *Semper Aliquid Novi: Littératures comparée et littératures d'Afrique: Mélanges offerts à Albert Gérard* (Tübingen, 1990): Michel Fabre, 'De *Batouala* à *Doguicimi*: René Maran et les premiers romans Africains' (239–49); Hans-Jürgen Lusebrink, 'Batouala, véritable roman nègre: La place de René Maran dans la littérature mondiale des années vingt' (145–55).

[29] Joubert *et al.* (eds.), *Littératures francophones*, 101.

dans ma triple fiérte de sang-mêlé . . .'[30] He was sent to the Lycée Schoelcher (Fort-de-France, Martinique) for his secondary schooling and from there to Paris to study law. In Paris he became interested in Oriental languages, literature, and ethnology and it was lectures on these subjects that he attended at the Sorbonne. He also came into contact with the French Surrealists who were to become a significant influence. Even more importantly, it was at this point that he met Senghor and Césaire. The three collaborated to produce L'Étudiant noir in 1934.

In 1937 Guy-Levis Mano published Damas's Pigments which was to attract considerable attention despite the small size of the edition (500 copies). The collection is preoccupied by two experiences: the unease of assimilation and a nostalgia for Africa. His later collections, in particular Black Label (1956), Graffiti (1952), Névralgies (1966) are written in the same simple language. Rhythm, typology, and jeux de mots are the predominant stylistic features of a poetry which, because of its accessibility, directness, and power has been very widely read.

Gilles Sirder's writing was quickly identified by his compatriot, the writer and critic Serge Patient, as pioneering in its language. In an article in Présence Africaine, Patient wrote: 'Sirder, tout en feignant de créoliser, invente cette langue neuve dont les audaces syntaxiques ne laissent pas d'être familières.'[31]

Bertène Juminer (born in 1927) and Élie Stephenson (born in 1944) are both concerned with the continuation of a Guianese literary tradition. From the poorest of the three Caribbean departements français d'outre-mer, and the most isolated, Juminer has always supported a politics of independence for the French territories. As was the case with his close friend Frantz Fanon, his medical training took him to North Africa to teach, and he also went to Iran and Sénégal. He has written five novels: Les Bâtards (1961), Au Seuil d'un nouveau cri (1963), La Revanche de Bozambo (1968), Les Héritiers de la presqu'île (1979; winner of the Prix des Caraïbes), La Fraction de seconde (1990). As for many West Indian writers, Africa is prominent in his œuvre. Les Héritiers, for example, describes the process of decolonization in Africa with a bitter irony. Each of his novels is essentially concerned with questions of individual identity and its relationship to the social group and culture, and the powers invested in these. The mores of

---

[30] Damas, 'Si depuis peu', Névralgies (1966), 46.
[31] Présence Africaine, 20 (June–July 1958), 44–51 (p. 50).

the group (for example the absurdities of society's *phallocrates*) are also humourously exposed. In *Les Héritiers* a private detective, Bob Yves Bacon, who has been fully assimilated into American culture, finally reveals his true identity. This is expressed both in terms of nationality and name: 'Je suis sénégalais. Je m'appelle Mamadou Lamine N'Diaye!'[32]

Élie Stephenson is often described as Damas's successor. His poems, which also display complex and interesting intertextual relationships with Paul Éluard's, are written in a direct lanquage and are easily accessible. Stephenson's collections include: *Une flèche pour le pays de l'encan* (1975), *Poèmes négro-indiens aux enfants de Guyane* (1978), *Catacombes de soleil* (1979), and *Terres mêlées* (1984). He has also written plays.

Other writers who have contributed to the francophone Guianese tradition include: Christian Rollé (*Le Negoce*, 1975), Raoul-Philippe Danaho whose most recent novels include *Soudain l'aurore* (1983) and *Le Temps d'un amour* (1984), and Eugénie Rézaire (*Pirogue pour des temps à venir*, 1987), and editor of *La Torche*, produced by the Friends of Damas.

Early literary periodicals in the French West Indies were concerned with the literatures of each island; the title of the pioneering *La Guadeloupe littéraire* (founded in 1908) illustrates this, and Suzanne Césaire, in her article in *Tropiques*, cited at the beginning of the chapter, was concerned to prescribe for a 'littérature martiniquaise'. When West Indian writers met in Paris, however, their perspective shifted. Parallels between Black writing in French (and indeed English) from diverse areas were identified; francophone West Indian writing was one such area.

Since the beginning of the 1980s a number of publications have testified to a growing concern to identify French West Indian culture (and French Creole cultures including those of the Indian Ocean) as a homogenous field. A number of titles are sufficient to indicate this new perspective: Edouard Glissant's *Le Discours antillais* (1981), Jean Bernabé, Patrick Chamoiseau, and Raphaël Confiant's *Éloge de la créolité* (1989), Raphaël Confiant and Patrick Chamoiseau's *Lettres créoles: Tracées antillaises et continentales de la littérature, 1635–1976* (1991), Ralph Ludwig and Sylviane Telchid's *Corpus créole: Textes oraux dominicains, guadeloupéens, haïtiens, mauricines et seychellois* (1994), and *Écrire la 'parole de nuit': La nouvelle*

---

[32] Rouch and Clavreuil (eds.), *Littératures nationales*, 225.

littérature antillaise (1994). This last is a collection of texts edited by a German academic, Ralph Ludwig. Four contributors are essentially Guadeloupean: Ernest Pépin, Gisèle Pineau, Hector Poullet, and Sylviane Telchid, three are Martinican: Patrick Chamoiseau, Raphaël Confiant, Edouard Glissant; René Depestre is Haitian and Bertène Juminer, Guianese. The texts that make up the volume: 'témoignent d'une prise de conscience du caractère original de la littérature antillaise, née à un carrefour culturel, lieu de rencontre entre Amérindiens, colons européens, esclaves africains et ouvriers indiens'.[33] Yet as Depestre points out in his text, 'Les Aventures de la créolité':

> Les états de créolité propres aux différentes sociétés de la Caraïbe, quoique historiquement apparentés, quoique issus, à la même époque, du même maelström colonial, dans aucune de leurs expressions—langues, religions, mentalités, arts et littératures—ne se recoupent toutefois entre eux, purement et simplement, comme des échelles de valeurs qui seraient uniformément interchangeables.[34]

However, Bernabé, Chamoiseau, and Confiant, in their *Éloge de la créolité*, are concerned not to describe a present reality but to prescribe for the future: 'Ni Européens, ni Africains, ni Asiatiques, nous nous proclamons Créoles. Cela sera pour nous une attitude intérieure, mieux: une vigilance, ou mieux encore, une sorte d'enveloppe mentale au mitan de laquelle se bâtira notre monde en pleine conscience du monde.'[35] One of the epigraphs for *Éloge* suggests their concern to celebrate difference and diversity, not to delimit and reduce for the sake of tidy definitions: 'C'est par la différence et dans le divers que s'exalte l'Existence. Le Divers décroît. C'est là le grand danger.' (V. Segalen)[36]

The diversity and richness of Creole cultures in the Caribbean are threatened as Juminer argues:

> De nos jours [. . .] le bain culturel créole est en voie de tarissement, et notre langue (qui peut prétendre la maîtriser encore?) tend vers un sabir sans âme ni portée. L'exode rural bat son plein. A l'instar d'un passe-muraille, l'audiovisuel s'introduit partout sans nous renvoyer notre image.[37]

In response to this recognition, the authors of *Éloge de la créolité* propose an *attitude* which will encourage creativity:

---

[33] Ludwig (ed.), *Écrire la 'Parole de nuit'*, 15.   [34] Ibid. 160.
[35] Bernabé, Chamoiseau, and Confiant, *Éloge de la créolité*, 13.
[36] Ibid. 11.   [37] Ludwig (ed.), *Écrire la 'Parole de nuit'*, 148.

Ces paroles que nous vous transmettons ne relèvent pas de la théorie [. . .] Elles branchent au témoignage. Elles procèdent d'une expérience stérile que nous avons connue avant de nous attacher à réenclencher notre potentiel créatif, et de mettre en branle l'expression de ce que nous sommes.[38]

Since the publication of *Éloge* Raphaël Confiant's *Eau de café* (1991) was awarded the Prix Novembre, and Patrick Chamoiseau's *Texaco*, the Prix Goncourt. Both authors started to publish in the mid-1980s and both have already produced significant œuvres. Confiant's texts include: *Bitako-a* (1985), *Kòd Yanm* (1986), *Marisosé* (1987), in Creole, and *Le Nègre et l'amiral* (1988), a historical novel about Martinique under Vichy, *Eau de café* (1991) and *Ravines du devant-jour* (1993), in French. In addition to the texts cited above, Chamoiseau has written: *Chronique des sept misères* (1986), *Solibo Magnifique* (1988), *Antan d'enfance* (1990), *L'Écolier* (1994). Like Glissant's most recent and massive novel *Tout-Monde*, texts by Confiant and Chamoiseau stand in part in place of a continuing oral tradition (though they are not transcriptions from the oral tradition but modern literary texts), inscribing Creole experience in a form which will be preserved and to which, therefore, even if there are years of hiatus, later generations can reconnect.

---

[38] Bernabé, Chamoiseau, and Confiant, *Éloge de la créolité*, 13.

5

HAITI

Wɪᴛʜɪɴ the francophone world, particularly the Caribbean and
Black francophone world, Haiti has an emblematic status:
'Pays où l'homme noir s'est mis debout pour affirmer, pour la
première fois, sa volonté de former un nouveau monde, un monde
libre'[1]. In terms of the literary representation of Haiti's history in
other black literatures, Bernard Mouralis writes:

On comprend l'intérêt que pouvait susciter chez les écrivains négro-
africains l'histoire de l'indépendance haïtienne. Alors que partout ailleurs la
résistance avait succombé [. . .] Haïti offrait au contraire l'exemple d'une
révolte armée qui avait libéré définitivement les Noirs de l'esclavage et
avait abouti à la création [. . .] du premier état noir. Le thème était riche et
devait donner naissance à une abondante littérature historique, théâtrale,
poétique et, plus rarement, romanesque.[2]

Haiti's history is fundamentally different from that of other
francophone Caribbean territories. But as René Depestre argues in a
recent essay, despite the important differences which separate the
Creole societies of the Caribbean, they are differences which issue
from a particular common experience:

Nos identités, à de nombreux égards, ont été déterminés par les mêmes
'contextes médians'. Milan Kundera appelle, très intelligemment, *contexte
médian* 'la marche intermédiare entre une nation et le monde'. Aux
Caraïbes, en effet, nous cohabitons à l'intersection d'une multiplicité de
contextes médians: précolombien, latino-américain, africain, français, voire
nord-américain et canadien. Sur les plans anthropologique et culturel, ils

[1] Aimé Césaire quoted by René Depestre, *Bonjour et adieu à la négritude* (1980),
77.
[2] Bernard Mouralis, 'L'Image de l'indépendance haïtienne dans la littérature
négro-africaine', *Revue de littérature comparée*, 48 (1974), 504–535 (p. 504).

n'arrêtent pas de se croiser, s'interpénétrer, s'interféconder, se contrarier, avant de s'aventurer, avec une sensuelle baroque exubérance, dans le processus de créolisation qui les métisse (ou sur le métier à métisser qui les créolise).[3]

He describes the specificities of francophone Haitian literature thus:

L'oralité africaine, la tradition indienne, l'écriture à la française furent portées sur les mêmes fonts baptismaux, le même *métier à créoliser* qui font aujourd'hui le *mode d'être* qui permet de distinguer d'abord entre elles chacune de nos littératures; ensuite par rapport à la littérature francophone de l'hexagone, aux littératures également francophones de l'Afrique noire, du Québec, du Maghreb, et à celles de la Belgique, de la Suisse; et les pays (créolophones) de l'océan Indien.[4]

Thus Depestre proposes a dynamic field within which Haitian literature can be approached, as one of a group of Caribbean Creole literatures (each with a specific *métier à créoliser*), and one which displays interesting relationships with other literatures, those of France, and francophone black Africa, Quebec, the Maghreb, Belgium, Switzerland, and the Indian Ocean islands.

The Republic of Haiti occupies the western part of one of the islands in the Greater Antilles in the West Indies. The population, of which the majority is black, is estimated at some five million. 'Discovered' by Christopher Columbus in 1492, the Spanish named the island Hispaniola, and, from 1502, began to populate it with African slaves. In the seventeenth century the French took possession of the western part, founded the capital, Port-au-Prince, and established large plantations.

In the wake of the French Revolution of 1789, the black population revolted under the leadership of Toussaint Louverture, whose heroic status is celebrated and explored in numerous modern black francophone texts (Aimé Césaire's essay *Toussaint Louverture*, 1962, is one of the most important). He yielded to the French in 1794 after the temporary suppression of slavery; the British, who had occupied various parts of the island, were expelled. Although the island was placed under the authority of Bonaparte in 1795, in practice Toussaint Louverture remained very powerful. In 1802 however, when slavery was re-established, further revolts took place on the

[3] René Depestre, 'Les Aventures de la créolité: Lettre à Ralph Ludwig', in Ralph Ludwig (ed.), *Écrire la 'parole de nuit': La nouvelle littérature antillaise* (Paris, 1994), 159–70 (pp. 160–1).

[4] Depestre, 'Les Aventures de la créolité', 170.

island and Toussaint Louverture was exiled to France where he died in 1803, a few months before the Battle of Vertières.

It was this last confrontation which resulted in the expulsion of the French and, on 1 January 1804, General Dessalines became Emperor and proclaimed the island's independence. He was assassinated in 1806 and the Spanish took this opportunity to reconquer the eastern part of the island. Their possession of the territory was recognized in the 1814 Treaty of Paris. In the west, the unrest continued. The north and south were divided. In the south the mulatto Alexandre Pétion established a Republic which was to continue for eleven years until 1818. President Boyer then united the north and south in 1820 and in 1822 extended his power east, conquering the newly proclaimed Dominican Republic. The independence of Haiti was formally recognized by the former colonial power in 1838. Boyer's death was followed by the successful revolt of the Dominicans in 1844; two distinct republics came into being once again: Haiti in the west and the Dominican Republic in the east.

F. E. Soulouque, formerly a slave, was crowned Emperor under the name of Faustin I and was in power from 1847 to 1859. His reign was followed during the second half of the nineteenth century by an endless series of revolts and a succession of leaders, some more constructive than others. Amongst the most revered of the later nineteenth-century leaders was Saloman (1879–88).

At the beginning of this century the United States made the first of a long series of interventions. President V. G. Sam had been assassinated in 1915 and the Americans occupied the island, finally withdrawing almost twenty years later in 1934. During the American occupation attempts were made to reconstitute Haitian society, instituting American-style political, administrative, and educational structures. From 1934 increasingly democratic constitutions were drawn up. These changes did not, however, bring an end to the violence which dominated Haitian life.

In 1946 President Lescot was overthrown during a period of unrest. This was the culmination of a series of events largely animated by students and in which literary involvement had been seen as dangerously subversive. Following a lecture by André Breton, the journal *La Ruche* had published a special number devoted to Breton and Surrealism.[5] The issue was seized by the authorities, and mem-

---

[5] See Jacqueline Leiner's essay 'René Depestre ou du surréalisme comme moyen d'accès à l'identité haïtienne', in her *Imaginaire Langage: Identité culturelle Négritude* (Tübingen, 1980), 75–93.

bers of the editorial team, including René Depestre and Jacques-Stephen Alexis, were imprisoned. In response students staged a demonstration and a general strike followed. The unrest was brought under control by further violence.

In 1949 demonstrations were suppressed by military intervention and the election of Colonel Magloire as leader. In 1957 François Duvalier took power, rapidly transforming the political structures of the island into what amounted to a ruthless family dictatorship, supported by the notorious Tontons Macoutes, the Duvalier militia. In 1964 François assumed the role of President. When he died in 1971 he was succeeded by his son, Jean-Claude ('Baby Doc'), who was overthrown by a force made up of both civil and military contingents, assisted by the United States in 1986. A period of considerable instability followed, not helped by a two-year period in which the States withheld aid (1987–9). In December the first multiparty elections were finally held and the radical Catholic priest Jean-Bertrand Aristide became President. The Tontons Macoutes remained powerful, however, and again took control, in 1991, after only seven months. Aristide was forced to leave the country. Tens of thousands of Haitians fled the country in terror. Most were returned by the United States' forces to Port-au-Prince. A trading embargo has been in place since 1991, lifted or softened periodically but it has led, none the less, to further hardship for the people of Haiti. American military intervention has restored Aristide in recent months.

The political instabilities of Haiti's history have not, however, denied the country a rich and influential literary tradition. Independence in the nineteenth century did not bring to an end the playing out of the confrontation of French, Spanish, and American interests on the island so generative in literary terms. These interests are still influential as recent events have demonstrated. The racial, linguistic, religious, and cultural differences which result from these encounters militate against any cultural homogeneity. Questions concerning the nature of Haitian identity, further complicated by large-scale emigration, are thus complex and often central to literary production.

It is the diverse and dynamic nature of Caribbean society that is important in the notion of *créolité* (a development of *Antillanité*, itself a development, and many would argue at least in part a rejection of Haitian Negritude). But as Depestre again points out:

Les états de créolité propres aux différentes sociétés de la Caraïbe, quoique historiquement apparentés, quoique issus, à la même époque, du même maelström colonial, dans aucune de leurs expressions—langues, religions, mentalités, arts et littératures—ne se recoupent toutefois entre eux, purement et simplement, comme des échelles de valeurs qui seraient uniformément interchangeables.[6]

In terms of the country's unique literary history, questions concerning the nature of Haitian nationalism were explored earlier than in the other francophone Caribbean territories, and these debates were to be influential in other regions of the Caribbean. In 1804, for example, the year of the island's independence, Fligneau's play *L'Haytien expatrié* was performed, and in 1817 the island's first literary review, *L'Abeille haytienne*, founded by Solyme Milscent, began publication. As the titles testify, concern to explore identity in terms of the national informed both publications. In the 1830s a number of writers grouped around Coriolan Ardouin and the Nau brothers proposed the idea of a distinctively Haitian literature in French, 'un peu brunie sous les tropiques'. Comparable concerns motivated the historians Madiou and Beaubrun Ardouin to investigate and (re)construct Haiti's history. Implicit in Oswald Durand's poems (as in the Parnassian and symbolist poetry of Massillon Coicou, Edgar Laforest, and Etzer Vilaire) is the notion that specifically Haitian aspects of the landscape (as opposed to an abstract and exotic 'tropical' landscape) offered an appropriate iconography for poetry. The enumeration and celebration of these referents is synonymous with praising the nation:

> J'ai chanté nos oiseaux, nos fertiles campagnes,
> Et les grappes de fruits courbant nos bananiers,
> Et le campêche en fleurs parfumant nos montagnes
> Et les grands éventails de nos verts lataniers.[7]

Not only does the text celebrate features of a particular landscape, it also makes explicit the degree to which literary enunciation raises the referents to emblematic (national) status. Durand also celebrated in verse peasant folklore and local practices such as voodoo rituals. In his poem, 'Le Fils d'un noir' he introduced the theme of the ambiguity of mulatto identity. His poem 'Choucoune' is one of the earliest poems in Haitian Creole.

---

[6] Despestre, 'Les Aventures de la créolité', 160.

[7] Oswald Durant, *Rires et Pleurs: I*, extracts repr. in Louis Morpeau, *Anthologie d'un siècle de poésie haïtienne 1817–1925* (1925); Kraus repr. (Nendeln, 1970), 111.

Also central to much of his poetry are contemporary political problems. Patriotism and national consciousness are aroused in poems reminiscent of Victor Hugo's political verse. 'La Mort de nos cocotiers', for example, draws a parallel between the death of the symbolic indigenous coconut tree, and loss of freedom and idealism:

> Non, tu ne mourras pas, o liberté—quand même,
> Sous le souffle d'un vent mortel,
> Nous verrions se flétrir ce palmier, ton emblème,
> Nos cœurs resteraient ton autel! . . .
> O mes frères, les noirs, rappelons-nous nos pères
> Héros—martyrs des premiers jours,
> Qui prirent corps à corps les gros colons prospères
> Et les chassèrent pour toujours![8]

Verse of this kind was typical of the École patriotique as the contemporary literary movement was known. It was also at this time that essayists such as Anténor Firmin, for example, argued for the equality of the races.

At the turn of the century and grouped around the literary review *La Ronde* (1898–1902), novelists such as Frédéric Marcelin (*Thémistocle-Epaminondas Labasterre*, 1901) and Justin Lhérisson, and the poet Georges Sylvain, were concerned not only with the particularities of Haiti's *état dans le monde*, but also with aesthetic universals. Adapting certain tenets associated with French symbolism, in a manner similar to francophone writing elsewhere, most obviously that of the Belgian symbolists and the École de Montréal, the poetry of the *La Ronde* group has often be described as derivative, a typical manifestation of nineteenth-century assimilationist (and thus 'alienated' writing). To some extent this was clearly the case. But their commitment to a symbolist aesthetic was not a commitment to the abstract rather than the local and particular, but rather bound up with a rejection of 'local colour' as artificial, in the same way that dogmatic commitment to political concerns was obtrusive. Rather they emphasized the need to release creative energies in a way which would necessarily lead to a more authentic discovery of, and later expression of, a specifically Haitian consciousness. What they sought to avoid was poetic conformity and uniformity. As Jean Jonassaint has recently argued, these novels or *récits* from *Thémnistocle-Epaminanondas Labasterre* on (unlike *Stella*, 1859, generally proposed as the first Haitian novel, and others which followed):

[8] Morpeau, *Anthologie*, 107.

'inaugure[nt] une tradition de récits réalistes des problèmes socio-politiques, des us et coutumes d'Haïti ou de ses habitants, dans un français qui intègre des tournures et un lexique haïtiens'.⁹ These features mark out the 'first generation' of Haitian prose writings.

One of the most obvious responses to the American occupation (1915–34), arguably the major catalyst for a new phase of literary production, was the desire to discover an authentic Haitian identity, bound up, in particuiar, with Haiti's 'ancestral' African roots. Thus interest was stimulated in Haitian Creole, in indigenous religions and practices, and certain antitheses which had formerly been accepted were questioned, for example, the opposition between the 'folkloric' and 'superstitious', on the one hand, and the 'cultured' and 'educated' (and, of course, French), on the other. One of the important forums for discussion was the *Revue Indigène*, founded in 1927 by Émile Roumer and associated with the École indigèniste. The École des Griots, whose concerns were similar, was founded in 1938. Jean Price-Mars and Jacques Roumain were the most influential *indigénistes*. Price-Mars's essay, *Ainsi parla l'oncle* (1928) profoundly altered the outlook of a whole generation of Haitians and also West Indians and Africans, in particular the three writers associated with the genesis of Negritude: Aimé Césaire, Léopold Sédar Senghor, and Léon Damas.¹⁰ Price-Mars's name is synonymous with the idea of *Haïtianisme*. He argued for the complete acceptance of the Haitian cultural legacy which embodied universal humane values in microcosm.

Price-Mars's exhortations were translated into a rejection of French models, a recognition of Haiti's rich African heritage and a new excitement about the Creole language and Creole culture. But difficulties were everywhere to be encountered. Sometimes they became the generative source of the literary text as in Léon Laleau's famous poem 'Trahison' from his collection, *Musique nègre* (1930):

> Ce cœur obsédant, qui ne correspond
> Pas avec mon langage et mes costumes,
> Et sur lequel mordent, comme un crampon,
> Des sentiments d'emprunt et des coutumes
> D'Europe, sentez-vous cette souffrance
> Et ce désespoir a nul autre égal,

---

⁹ Jean Jonassaint, 'Des conflits langagiers dans quelques romans haïtiens', *Études françaises*, 28/2–3, *L'Amérique entre les langues* (1992–3), 39–48 (p. 39).

¹⁰ Jean Price-Mars, *Ainsi parla l'oncle* (1928).

D'apprivoiser, avec des mots de France,
Ce cœur qui m'est venu du Sénégal?[11]

His later poetry, influenced by surrealism, does not describe the
confrontation between cultures as in 'Trahison', but in a language
saturated with African referents, and in a syntactically ruptured
French, articulates the complexity and even incoherence of Haitian
cultural identity.

Two other poets of the period, among a large number, who were
concerned with comparable ideas were Carl Brouard and Émile
Roumer. Brouard, one of the founders of Le Griot (1938–40), describes Haitian peasants in a simple French. For Brouard 'le français
n'est pas une langue d'emprunt, c'est notre propre langue. Le créole
ne sera jamais qu'un patois.' Roumer, on the other hand, wrote in
both French and Creole, and language is often a theme as in 'Le
Fiancé a' pantalon unique': 'Dadoune, si je vous aime c'est parce
que vous êtes femme nature, | sans fanfreluche, hypocrisie, parler
français.'

Jacques Roumain's poetry is more overtly political than that of
Brouard or Roumer. J.-F. Brierre's Black Soul (1947), R. Bernard's
Nègre (1945), René Depestre's Étincelles (1945), Un arc-en-ciel pour
l'occident chrétien (1967) and Poète à Cuba (1976) represent a similar
move towards a poetry which is more radically politically preoccupied. Brierre's first collection, Le Drapeau de demain was published in
1931 and his writings, poetry, and novels (he has also published
'sketches'), number some twenty-five texts. Jean Métellus contributed a preface to his collection, Un Noël pour Gorée (1980) in which
he wrote that for Brierre, 'ce qui caractérise le monde noir, c'est
qu'il est encore colonisé [. . .] et qu'on lui refuse toute originalité
sauf d'avoir faim'.[12] Brierre's political activity (he founded the
oppositional paper La Bataille) led to a number of imprisonments
and final exile to Senegal. This clearly accounts in part for his continuing concerns for black solidarity. He is clear that the same forms
of post-colonialism oppression affect 'les Haïtiens, les Africains, les
Noirs américains'.[13] This has sometimes been misconstrued as a
simplistic (post-)Negritude position.

[11] Léon Laleau, 'Trahison', Musique nègre, in Lilyan Kesteloot, Anthologie négro-
africaine (Verviers, 1967), 43.
[12] Quoted in A. Rouch and G. Clavreuil, Littératures nationales d'écriture française
(1986), 238.
[13] Quoted ibid. 238.

Also eventually settling in Senegal (an important country of exile for Haitians), Gérard Chenet's political activities led to the unusual position of being denied entry to both the Soviet Union and the United States. At the age of 19 he founded, with René Depestre and Jacques-Stephen Alexis, the journal *La Ruche* (1946). His most settled employment has been with UNESCO in Dakar. In addition to his collection *Poèmes du village de Toubab Dyalaw* (1974), he has written for the theatre (*Les Fiançailles tragiques* and *Zombis nègres*) and ballet (*Sortilèges* and *Quand les morts vivants goûtent au sel de la terre*. He is concerned to maximize the dramatic effect of different forms of understatement.

Also settling in Dakar, Roger Dorsinville has worked as literary editor for Les Nouvelles Éditions Africaines. Writing in a wide range of genres (beginning with his play *Barrières*, 1947), he has become increasingly preoccupied with Africa (and prose genres) and is often mistaken for a Senegalese writer (using a pseudonym). His writings are often concerned with the specificities, particularities, and detail of African peasant life.

In the poetry of Roussan Camille, René Bélance, and Morisseau-Leroy (*Plénitudes*, 1940; *Natif-natal: conte en vers*, 1948; *Ravinodiab*, 1981), the focus shifts between a wide range of themes which have more or less direct political corollaries: racism and oppression and the need to celebrate Haiti. The revolution that is often called for must be not only political and economic but also psychological or spiritual. Often there is self-reflexive irony in the text's questioning of its own power to bring about actual change (an implicit criticism of the confidence of Senghor's Negritude position in this regard). Morisseau-Leroy's 'Ode au pétrole', written while be was living in exile in Dakar, denounces exploitation and begs questions about the relationship between literature and action: 'Ceci s'appelle ode | et ce veut pourtant prose claire.'[14] He is also the author of an early and influential essay, *Le Destin des Caraïbes* (1941).

There is an anxiety, in the work of Anthony Phelps, bound up with a desire to distance his writing from what Jacques Rancourt describes as 'la négritude duvaliériste'. In attempting to avoid this, he continues:

le 'noirisme', qui, par l'exaltation du racisme, a conduit en Haïti à l'instauration d'un régime protégé par les tontons-macoutes: Anthony Phelps écrit une poésie de combat appelant à la libération effective de

---

[14] *Littératures nationales*, 254.

l'homme noir, comme à celle de tous les peuples opprimés. Mais en même temps qu'il répugne à laisser absorber sa poésie par les seules luttes politiques; aussi parallèlement à ses incursions dans la vie passée et présente du peuple haïtien, poursuit-il une recherche plus personnelle, plus intime, à réaliser dans une certaine autonomie de la démarche poétique: recherche dirigée vers la conquête de la parole et du geste et, par-delà, du silence.[15]

Spiralisme (which succeeded the less influential movements Samba and Haïti-Littéraire, both forms of Haitian Negritude), is a movement which draws eclectically on the *nouveau roman*, structuralism and German modernism, for example, is often highly personal and psychologically charged. But the consciousness at the centre of the poem is always Haitian. Gérard Étienne, Dieudonné Fardin, and René Philoctète are the movement's most obvious practitioners. Étienne's *Le Nègre crucifié* (1974) is a self-questioning dialogue between a self and its double. Interpolations, apostrophic utterances and recollections make up the 'action' of the narrative, as the narrator awaits his own death: 'Je n'ai pas le droit de crier ma souffrance, de dire que ma croix est lourde, qu'elle est le signe de ma Révolution et de ma haine? Je n'ai pas le droit de grincer les dents. Après tout, que me reste-t-il?'[16] The text dramatizes the life of a zombie-figure who, in responding to various challenges serves to demythologize much of contemporary francophone Haitian culture, including the confident certainties voiced by the intellectuals of Port-au-Prince and the idea of 'independence' which is also proposed as largely mythical.

It is within the genre of the novel, however, that contemporary ideas found their most developed expression, in the works of J.-B. Cinéas, Maurice Casséus, Pierre et Philippe Thoby-Marcelin, Milo Rigaud, Jacques-Stéphen Alexis, and above all, Jacques Roumain (*La Montagne ensorcelée*, 1931, and *Gouverneurs de la rosée*, 1944, which was to attract international attention). During the 1930s, 1940s, and 1950s, three types of novel can, rather crudely, be distinguished: novels located in the countryside where rural culture, poverty, and· the oppression suffered by peasants dominate; novels situated in the city which focus on a similar range of urban concerns but which tend to be more politically explicit; and a third type emerging rather later, the novel of exile.

In Roumain's *Gouverneurs de la rosée*, Manuel, like the author, has

---

[15] Ibid. 258.   [16] Ibid. 250.

travelled widely. On his return to his native island from Cuba, where he has seen how unions function, he is concerned to introduce new ideas. He sets out to do something about the drought which threatens to make barren large areas of the countryside. The problem is not, however, caused simply by climatic factors, but also by archaic working practices. Manuel's language is the language of his people, that is the language of the peasants he is hoping to win over to new practices. The figurative language which he uses to persuade is a language with which they are familiar. Looking to a politically-reformed future, for example, he says:

> Nous ne savons pas encore que nous sommes une force, une seule force: tous les habitants, tous les nègres des plaines et des mornes réunis. Un jour, quand nous avons compris cette vérité, nous nous lèverons d'un point à l'autre du pays et nous ferons l'assemblée générale des gouverneurs de la rosée, le grand coumbite [Creole for a kind of co-operative] des travailleurs de la terre pour défricher la misère et planter la vie nouvelle.[17]

Roumain's text is a complex one. It is both a specifically Haitian novel and one which is accessible and interesting (and not simply because of a certain inevitable exoticism) to a wider audience. Different readings are possible and this is not only a function of the text's allegorical levels. Depending on the reader's familiarity with the Haitian reality, the text refers to a more or less specifically Haitian context. Rather than including a significant amount of Creole, for example, which would be necessarily exotic for the non-Haitian, the text is often constructed from a vocabulary whose meaning will be understood differently by different readers. This practice is exemplified by the novel's title which would be understood by the reader to be a poetic, and not a precise, description. The Haitian reader, on the other hand, would recognize the title of 'Gouvénè rouze' which is given, in country districts, to the peasant responsible for irrigation, and the general control and distribution of water.

Manuel seeks water, source of life and renewal, but for those removed from the lives of the people with whom Manuel is involved, his quest is symbolic: in seeking water he is attempting to bring about a revolution by altering established power structures. For those familiar with the novel's context there is no need intellectually to recognize symbolism and allegory, or multiple readings. Manuel's quest is quite literally radical, that is, concerned with the

---

[17] Roumain, *Les Gouverneurs de la rosée* (1946), 80.

'roots' of rural society, and the possibility of supplying those roots with water, source of new life.

From the mid-1950s onwards, the novel becomes more overtly critical of a society in which injustice and corruption affect the lives of the vast majority of Haiti's people. Most influential among the novelists whose work is thus described, is Jacques-Stéphen Alexis, and in particular his famous *Compère général Soleil* (1955), a historical novel which takes place between 1934 and 1938. The hero, Pierre Roumel, like Jacques Roumain (to whom he bears close similarities), discovers politics, which he believes will bring justice and equality to his country, and is killed by his political adversaries. *Les Arbres musiciens* (1957), which is concerned more with individual as opposed to group consciousness, proposes voodoo as a means of resisting a Catholic campaign against 'Haitian superstition'. Alexis's later work, and in particular *Romancero aux étoiles (contes poétiques)* (1960), adapts Haitian forms to create a 'réalisme merveilleux'. Myth and the fantastic dominate these shorter prose pieces (fables and *contes*). Here the fragmentary elements of the texts (which draw on African, Indian, and French traditions) are integrated into a linguistic matrix rich in imagery and colour which represent rather than state what is specific to Haitian culture.

Alexis's move away from the overtly political does not represent a declining concern for the political, but a more complex vision of what *constitutes* the political. As he declared in 1956 at the Premier Congrès des Artistes et Écrivains Noirs in Paris: 'Le réalisme merveilleux est donc partie intégrante du réalisme social [. . .] Qu'est-ce donc le merveilleux sinon l'imaginaire dans lequel un peuple enveloppe son expérience, reflète sa conception du monde et de la vie?' Alexis called on Haitian writers to draw on:

le trésor de contes, de légendes, toute la symbolique musicale, chorégraphique, plastique, toutes les formes de l'art populaire haïtien [. . .] Les genres et organons occidentaux légués à nous doivent être résolument transformés dans un sens national et tout dans l'œuvre d'art doit ébranler la sensibilité particulière des Haïtiens, fils de trois races et de combien de cultures.[18]

A 'réalisme magique' is important in novels of the 1960s. Texts by Pierre Clitandre and Gérard Étienne convey a sense of the dislocated, fragmented experience of city life in texts which dislocate and disorientate the reader in analogous ways. In the former, narrative

---

[18] Repr. in *Présence Africaine* (June–Nov. 1956), 245–71 (p. 268).

technique involves shifting perspectives and the use of Creole, which for non-Creole speakers challenges comprehension and alienates them from the text in a reversal which mimics the Creolespeaker's alienation in a French context.

Whilst a number of writers have moved, during the course of their writing careers, from an overtly political realism in their early writings to texts which are more difficult both linguistically and in terms of the complex vision which they propose, other writers, Émile Ollivier, for example, continue to write overtly political novels. *Mère-Solitude* (1983) also belongs to Haiti's 'writings in exile'. Like many contemporary Haitian writers, Ollivier lives in Montreal. Tourism and its effects is a central concern in *Mère-Solitude*: 'Armés de caméras et de zooms les touristes ne rataient pas une occasion de mitrailler les péquenots [Creole term for peasant] accompagnés de leurs péquenotes, venus en ville, comme ils disent, pour "bousquer" la vie.'[19]

The range of writings by Jean Métellus poses various questions about the *limits* of what is read as Haitian writing. Much of his work, his novel, *Jacmel au crépuscule* (1981), for example, is deeply rooted in a Haitian landscape. *Une eau forte* (1983), however, is set in Switzerland and offers little to a reader in search of Haitian referents. *Anacaona*, staged in Paris in 1985, on the other hand, a play which focuses on a legendary Indian princess, is concerned above all to explore the nature of Haitian identity. Métellus, who lives in exile, in Paris, has also written poems (*Au pititre chantant*, 1978; *Hommes de plein vent*, 1981; *Voyance*, 1985). The range of his writing testifies to his desire to assert his freedom as a writer and not to be constrained by the prescriptions of any ideology.

Theatre has been a significant genre in Haiti since the nineteenth century. The question of audience is a less complex one in Haiti than on other Caribbean islands, and most plays are written in Creole and for a local audience. The first theatrical troupe was founded by André Dupré in 1813. The Haitian theatrical tradition is, however, almost exclusively a Creole one.

What the language or languages of Haitian literature will be in the future is not altogether clear. Numerous poets have chosen to write in Creole, often in addition to publishing in French (for example, Morisseau-Leroy, Roumer)—and in 1977 Rodolph Miller was the first to publish a bilingual collection of poems, *Parole empile/*

---

[19] Quoted in Rouch and Clavreuil, *Littératures nationales d'écriture française*, 257.

parolapil. It would seem likely that in a country where the language of education and the language of the majority is Creole, that Haitian literature will become increasingly monolingual in that language. However, the problems of exile to disparate regions and the desire to reach an international audience may mean that Haitian texts continue to be written in French (sometimes with Creole versions). As Jean Métellus writes: 'Le créole haïtien reste un des fondements essentiels de notre identité. Mais nous vivons à une époque où la rapidité de circulation et de diffusion des idées nous impose d'utiliser une langue d'audience internationale pour faire entendre notre voix.' Nor is the use of Creole within Haiti an entirely unproblematic one: 'Actuellement, l'utilisation systématique du créole en Haïti risque d'être un nouveau facteur d'enfermement et donc d'obscurantisme'. More parallels emerge most obviously with North African writers who view Arabic similarly. Métellus's perspective is at least in part a resolutely historical one: French was Toussaint Louverture's medium of expression and thus the medium of expression associated with Haiti's moment of independence:

Toussaint Louverture, encore lui, l'a bien compris en s'appropriant la langue du dominateur et en s'y installant avec tout son pouvoir de subversion. Il n'a pas commis l'erreur d'identifier Napoléon et langue française et colons blancs. Il en a fait l'instrument de libération de tout un peuple, en face d'un monde hostile et stupéfait.[20]

---

[20] Jean Métellus, 'La Langue de Toussaint Louverture', La *Quinzaine Littéraire*, 436 (16–31 Mar. 1985), 'Écrire les langues françaises', 34.

6

MAURITIUS

Je prophétise le sang mêlé comme une langue de feu
(E. Maunick)

The Mascareignes are a group of islands in the Indian Ocean, most importantly Mauritius (formerly the Île de France) and La Réunion (formerly the Île Bourbon), but also the tiny island of Rodrigues. The two larger islands are less than a hundred nautical miles apart. The journey takes less than twelve hours by sea and roughly three-quarters of an hour by air. Rodrigues is 320 miles from Mauritius and 420 from Réunion.

When Europeans first landed on the islands in the sixteenth century, they found them uninhabited. It was not until the seventeenth century that the Dutch attempted to colonize, first bringing slaves from Indonesia and Madagascar in 1638. Their efforts lasted only twenty years. In 1664 they tried again, this time sending a fresh expedition from the Cape which they had occupied in 1652. This attempt and subsequent efforts failed and, disappointed with the lack of progress, the Dutch abandoned the island in 1710 when the French took possession and renamed it Île de France. The only permanent trace of the Dutch sojourn on the island were sugar cane and the sambhur deer, both of which had been introduced from Java. The Île de France became the administrative centre of the Compagnie française des Indes, charged with the responsibility for the exploitation of the Mascareignes. This privilege was abolished in 1767 when the island came under royal control. An infrastructure was then planned and developed: plantations, the building of a transport system (the port and dockyards were expanded and developed), roads, hospitals, and barracks. The abolition of slavery at the time of the French Revolution was ignored. Bonaparte rescinded the decree. In 1815 the French were defeated by the invading British who renamed the island Mauritius, and brought it under the laws of the Treaty of Venice. The French colonizers resisted, however, and continued to practise slavery until it finally disappeared after 1825. It was during the course of the nineteenth century that groups of indentured labour were brought from India and they, by the beginning of this century, constituted one of the largest landowning groups, controlling a third of the island. Independence was granted in 1968 when Sir Seewoosageur Ramgoolam became Prime Minister.

The diversity of the island's population is most obviously manifest in the diversity of spoken languages: seventeen are used on the island. Four of these play a major role: Hindi (in its Bodjpuri variant), is spoken by 40 per cent of the population. This is the day-to-day language of the biggest community on the island. Creole is spoken by 32 per cent of the population, French by 4.5 per cent, and English by 0.3 per cent. French is the language of the media and culturally the most prestigious. English is the language of administration, a British colonial legacy. Chinese and a number of Indian languages also constitute a significant linguistic presence. Within this diverse group French has held a privileged position since the nineteenth century as far as the country's literary production is concerned. Since 1960 various works in English testify to the beginning of an anglophone literary tradition. A Hindi literature has equally asserted its presence. Abhimanyu Unnuth is the best-known Hindi writer. As on Réunion and in the West Indies, Creole has also been increasingly used as a literary language. Dev Virahsawmy's theatre, *Disik Salé* (1976) and *Bef dâ disab*, and the first novel in Mauritian Creole, *Quand montagne prend dife* (1977), are not experimental texts or linguistic curiosities but amongst the island's most important contemporary written literature. The first literary work to be published in Creole, however, was François Chrestien Desnoyer's *Les Essais d'un bobre africain* (1822).

Before the exploitation of Creole as a literary language however, French was the only important one. Jean-Georges Prosper, author of the seminal *Histoire de la littérature mauricienne de langue française* (1978), describes Bernardin de Saint Pierre's *Paul et Virginie* (1789) as 'le roman de l'île Maurice' and Baudelaire's contact with the Mascareignes finds its way into *Les Fleurs du mal*. Whether or not literary history will continue to cite these texts as constituting the origins of francophone Mauritian literature, it was the exotic tradition which was perpetuated by the first francophone Mauritian writers. This has created what might be described as a 'literary historical oxymoron'. The etymology of the term 'exotic' is, of course, from the Greek *exotikos*, foreign. For French writers who visited the island, whether imaginatively or in reality, the place was exotic. For Mauritian writers, however, it was home, familiar and unremarkable. It could not, by definition, be exotic. They therefore assumed the perspective of the French writer and celebrated those features of the island strange and attractive to someone from outside. This 'francotropisme', as Prosper has termed it, dominated francophone literary production, and is exemplified by Léoville l'Homme's writings which proclaim their loyalty to, and admiration for, France. A moment of transition is represented by Clément Charoux and Savinien Meredac. In their work, 'scènes de la vie mauricienne', devoid of romantic lyricism, testify to a desire for mimeticism, for a realism concerned with aspects of Mauritian life which do not find their way into the work of writers coming from an exotic perspective. In Meredac's tales, *Pauvres Bougres* (1880–1939), for example, the focus is on the poor of the island.

The most important writer of the first half of the century however, and one whose literary itinerary is exemplary, is Robert-Edward Hart (1891–1954). Productive within a number of genres, the works which make up his œuvre draw on, and are representative of, different aspects of what constitutes 'the Mauritian' and more particularly the 'francophone Mauritian'. His early work is Parnassian in inspiration. A Gidean phase in which sensory, carnal experience is paramount gives way to a poetic phase where musicality and mystery dominate. The poetry is less obviously accessible to the French reader than his earlier work because of the influence of Indian philosophy, as the titles of some of the collections indicate: *Bhagavad-Gita* (1936) and *Poèmes védiques* (1941), for example.

His most significant work, however, is the novel-cycle *Pierre Flandre* (1928–36). Again Indian philosophy (as understood within Mauritian culture) is important. Comparable to numerous other francophone texts, the novels constitute a quest for origins, in this case represented by a lost childhood. The novels are a rite of passage which enables the hero (and reader) to be put in touch with a mysterious but defining past. The landscape of the island is important not because of its exoticism but because of the relationship between place and cultural and religious identity.

This move to create a symbolism in which the constituents of the landscape are significant in a new way (that is, different from the significance afforded it within the exotic tradition) is based in part on a refusal of that tradition. The new significance emerges from a denial, a rejection of an earlier attribution of meaning.

A preoccupation with origins (one of the important strands of francophone Mauritian literature), is also central to Marcel Cabon's literary project. His novel *Namasté* (1965) is a *roman paysan* which recounts the tale of a young man's attempts to modernize his village. The protagonist is an Indo-Mauritian and the novel celebrates Indo-Mauritian culture and a nostalgia for the country of origin. This desire to discover and celebrate roots characterizes the first phase of a modern francophone Mauritian literature and is then gradually replaced by a literature focused less on the past and where Mauritians came *from*, and more on contemporary problems of identity and in particular what constitutes the 'Mauritian'. Belonging to the first phase is the poetry of Hart and Cabon who celebrate Madagascar and India. China is important to the poetry of Joseph Tsang Mang Kin. Africa is celebrated in the poetry of Jean Erenne in a way similar to Negritude's celebration and desire for a *retour aux sources*. The recognition of Mauritius's Africanness also resulted in the resurgence of the *sega*, a rhythmic song and dance, performed at night on the seashore beside a woodfire. The large, flat *ravane* (drum) is stretched by the heat from the fire in preparation for the performance. An improvised phrase (linguistic and musical) is repeated, supported by the *ravane*, and the dancing begins. It is erotic in its movements, but partners must not touch. One of the most tangible cultural events linking Mauritius with its African past, the *sega* has become a symbol of the island's past rooted in slavery.

Origins are of central importance in the theory and writings of Malcolm de Chazal, one of the island's most remarkable figures. 'Discovered' by André Breton and Jean Paulhan, Chazal was regarded by the latter as an 'occultiste sans tradition', very much as Breton had proclaimed the West Indian writer, Aimé Césaire, a 'natural surrealist'. Part of Chazal's *Pensées*, first published on the island in 1940, was republished by Gallimard as *Sens-plastiques* in 1948. These aphoristic statements, apparently arranged arbitrarily, allude to theosophy and cabbalism, understanding that certain analogies and correspondences order the world and that it is structured by particular intentions. His texts, including the earlier *La Vie filtrée* (1949), *Sens magique* (1956), and *Poèmes* (1959), are above all preoccupied by the relationship between humans and the environment, and especially the Mauritian landscape. In *L'Homme et la connaissance* (1974) what is sought is an original harmony. The *locus* for this quest was the Mauritian landscape and in *Sens unique* (1974), Chazal describes its origin, an experience he had in the Jardin Botanique de Curépipe on the island: 'Un jour, par une après-midi très pure, je marchais quand, face à un bosquet d'azalées, je vis pour la première fois une fleur d'azalée me regarder. C'était la fée. 'Sens plastique' était né. La plume à la main, en marchant, j'ai écrit tout 'Sens plastique' aisément. Car tout m'était dicté.'[1] Then, in 1951, the stars spoke and Chazal had only to record their cosmic discourse. These were burned because his transcription failed to do them justice. Finally, and most interestingly, Chazal's realization that the Mauritian mountains also had a language. The landscape, its geography and geology could be decoded to reveal 'la Geographie Universelle de l'esprit'.

In 1951 Chazal published *Petrusmok* in which he recounts his experience of visions and revelations. The mountains of Mauritius, for example, revealed to him that the island was all that remained of the continent and brilliant civilization of Lemurie. Chazal's mythopoesis (most extravagantly that the island 'renfermerait tout le mystère du monde') has created a rich tradition on which later writers draw. Nor was Chazal 'sans tradition' as Paulhan thought. An important intertextuality exists with Hart and, more importantly, the Réunionnais writer Jules Hermann and the Mauritian writers Loys Masson and Bernardin de Saint-Pierre. The idea of the 'fairy island' is Hart's, as is the notion of a return to an ideal childhood. *Les Révélations du grand océan* (1927) by Hermann, then Président du Conseil Général de la Réunion, describes the discovery of sculpted mountains, all that remains of the fomer Lemurie. This bizarre text clearly suggested ideas to Chazal. Similarly, Chazal's theory of universal analogies and cosmic unity are to be found in Hart's novels and more importantly Bernardin de Saint-Pierre's *Études de la nature* (1784), where the islands are a microcosm, a text which if decoded will reveal the mystery of the world.

Rather than the work of an *inspiré*, Chazal's writings represent a synthesis of traditions, a drawing into relationship of myth, the geology of the island, its nature, and, of course, man and his desire to make sense of the world. His texts subvert traditional genres (essay, autobiography, *récit*, *Pensées*—the difference between these is

---

[1] Malcolm de Chazal, *Sens unique* (Toulouse, 1985), 6–7.

blurred), and his style is often described not simply as 'unliterary', but 'awkward', 'abrupt', even 'incorrect'. In one sense his texts deny the true history of the island (slavery and the cultural incoherence that many describe as its consequence), and suggest a romantic myth closely bound up with its beauty. In another sense, his often violent texts with their subversion of genre and 'literary' language are a textual/linguistic analogue of Mauritius.

Chazal's cosmic perspective is also visible in J.-G. Prosper's *Apocalypse mauricienne* (1964) and in the work of Raymond Chasle (*Le Corailleur des limbes*, 1970; *Vigiles irradiés*, 1973; *L'Alternance des solstices*, 1975). Uncertain voice and syntactic and linguistic rupture and a typographical explosion mimics the apocalyptic origin of the island. The text becomes a linguistic, literary, and typographical enactment of a historical and mythical tradition.

Discontinuity of imagery, rupture, ellipsis, a syntax which is less French and more Creole, Edouard Maunick's writing displays similarities, beginning with the poetry of *Ces oiseaux du sang* (1954), and reaching a high point in the poetry of *Les Manèges de la mer* (1964), *Jusqu'en terre yoruba* (1969), and *Mascaret ou le livre de la mer et de la mort* (1966). In *Les Manèges* Maunick celebrates multiple origins:

> Moi est enfant de mille races
> pétri d'Europe et des Indes
> taillé plus profondément
> dans le cri du Mozambique.[2]

Myth and apocalypse, important in the early poetry are displaced more and more by a central idea: that of the *métis*. Rather than celebrating a distant place of origin, or creating a mythical origin on the island, Maunick celebrates his status as *métis*: 'métis est mon état civil' even if there is a desire for a less ambiguous identity: 'je suis nègre de préférence'. The idea of plurality is important at a number of levels: racial and linguistic, but also in terms of the 'significance' of his texts. Ambiguity allows for a multiplicity of meaning. Exile also takes on new significance in Maunick's writing. Rather than signifying the abandonment of 'home', exile represents accession to a state of pluralism.

Exile is a dominant theme of modern Mauritian writing. For Jean Fanchette the distance between here and there has somehow to be

---

[2] Edouard Maunick, *Les Manèges de la mer*, cited in J.-P. de Beaumarchais, D. Conty, A. Rey (eds.), *Dictionnaire des littératures de langue française* (Bordas, 1984), 1439.

reconciled—but cannot be. *Alpha du Centaure* (1975) dramatizes the differences between Paris and Mauritius. Associated with this is the central notion of identity. The title of his 1965 collection, *Identité provisoire*, points both to this and to the instability of identity. This ties in with uncertainty about the past. The temporal framework of much of his poetry allows for a merging of past and future:

> L'île en jaillit avec la véhémence de la race
> De nouveau le sang gagne sur les marées basses
> Souvenir redis-moi le nom de ce voyage
> A rebours au pays de trop-d'enfance
> Je n'ai rien renié de ma part de lumière.[3]

Although most of his work has been regarded as 'French literature', Loys Masson, who lives in exile in France, has also set much of his work in the landscape (or more often seascape) of his childhood. Certain recurrent scenes in which sexual interaction between people (often including a child) of different races are involved, and a confessional tone (which suggest a guilt experienced by the writer), can also be read as metaphors for the violent history of Mauritius, and the multiple transgressions of the island's past.

Loys's brother, André, less tempted by exile, has also written a number of important texts including *Le Chemin de pierre ponce* (1963). Violent images also dominate his hallucinatory and psychological realism.

Other Mauritian writers living in exile, Marie-Thérèse Humbert in *A l'autre bout de moi* (1979), for example, have created a place and psychology that is Mauritian. In that novel the central characters are twins. The claustrophobia which is the dominant atmosphere of the novel finds its psychological analogue in their common heredity. For Chazal the mountains of Mauritius had a language, one to which he was to listen in order to transcribe it for others. This is analogous to the process of semiotics: the study of signs and symbols, in particular the relationship between written or spoken signs and their referents in the physical world or the world of ideas. The semiotics of the Mauritian landscape was made infinitely more complex than it had been by 'exotic' writers who reduced it to a relatively straightforward 'reality' with a relatively straightforward meaning: that of a lost Eden. Chazal's mythopoeia invented a geological archaeology which revealed a lost civilization, thereby ex-

---

[3] Fanchette, *Identité provisoire*, cited in J.-L. Joubert *et al.* (eds.), *Les Littératures francophones depuis 1945* (1986), 165.

plaining Mauritius's present autochthonously. A crucial relationship between the landscape, history, and identity was suggested. This coherence is further foregrounded by stylistic and linguistic fragmentation which is analogous to the superficial reality of the island. Beneath the superficiality, however, order, intention, and significant meaning can be discovered.

Contemporary Mauritian literature, unlike contemporary writing on Réunion, explores and celebrates diversity and hybridity. The island's independence, and wise political decisions taken since, have encouraged tolerance and understanding of difference. On Réunion, on the other hand, which remains a French *département d'outre-mer*, the language debate focuses a range of political concerns and tends to become polarized between a pro-French and a pro-Creole lobby. Contrasting the linguistic and wider social differences between the two islands, Françoise Lionnet cites Axel Gauvin (whose writing is discussed in the next chapter): 'The only solution to consider is true bilingualism: two official languages (Creole and French), two languages for justice, two languages for radio and television. . . . The promotion of Creole is, even if this appears to be a paradox, the indispensable condition for the widespread use of French.' And Lionnet concludes:

The experience in Mauritius has largely proven that the presence of many linguistic codes serves only to reinforce strongly bi- or trilingualism. In a pluricultural state, it is clear that the only basis for peaceful cohabitation is mutual respect and tolerance. These can only be achieved when each group is allowed to clear a space for itself, and to enjoy the same rights as the majority without being forced into a (post-)colonial form of mimicry.[4]

---

[4] Françoise Lionnet, '*Créolité* in the Indian Ocean: Two Models of Cultural Diversity', *Yale French Studies*, 82/1 (1993), 'Post-Colonial Conditions: Exiles, Migrations, and Nomadisms', 101–12 (p. 112).

7

LA RÉUNION

T<small>HE</small> literary history of La Réunion begins, according to some, with Évariste de Parny and Antoine de Bertin. Both left the island at the age of 9, and for both the island served primarily as a place of beauty inviting lyrical evocations. During the nineteenth century, exoticism triumphed and a number of writers from the island contributed texts which were to become well-known in France: Eugène Dayot, poet and journalist, Auguste Lacaussade (secretary to Sainte-Beuve), Léon Dierx, elected 'Prince des Poètes' on Mallarmé's death. The most significant writer of the period, however, was Charles Marie René Leconte or Leconte de Lisle (1818–94), who was to become one of the fathers of Parnassianism. He was to assume the place of Victor Hugo at the Académie française in 1886. Although there is considerable range in the poetry of these nineteenth-century writers, images of the island as an earthly paradise predominate and the coloured 'natives' are 'primitifs beaux et purs'.

A significant moment in the literary history of the island was the publication of the first anthology of poetry from Réunion edited by Raphaël Barquiseau and Louis Ozoux. The former also wrote history, criticism, essays, and poetry. Other notable nineteenth-century writers include the poet Cazamian who published two collections, *Sous le voile* (1912) and *Les Feuilles de l'arbre* (1920). That year, Auguste Brunet published his first collection, *Exils dorés des îles* and four years later Marius and Ary Leblond (literary historians, ardent propagandists for the 'colonial novel', and novelists who had won the Prix Goncourt in 1910) published *L'Histoire dorée d'un noir*. The titles of these last two testify to the extent to which the island

and its people continued to represent a blissful lost paradise peopled by happy, simple people.

It is not until the appearance of P. C. Jean-François's poetry, which displays a move away from French classical forms, that a desire for mimetic representation begins to emerge and equally a sense of local cultural identity. With the publication of Jean Albany's *Zamal* (1951) a sudden and fundamental reversal takes place: France becomes the place of exile, the 'outre-mer'. Equally the title, a Creole word, asserts a difference from French literature and locates the text in a specific place (as opposed to a universal paradisical, tropical island). Connected with this is an emphasis on the specificity of the island's landscape, flora and fauna, in addition to its history. Slavery as the historical origin of the island is explored and the possibilities of language and form are considered. Albany's use of Creole (some of his later collections are in Creole, and he also produced a *P'tit glossaire: le piment des mots créoles*, 1974, and *Supplement*, 1983) and has explored and exploited local forms, the *sega* and *maloya* (songs and dances), for example. This relationship between language, in the French sense of *langue* ('tongue'), history, and identity is enacted in Boris Gamaleya's *Vali pour une reine morte* (1973). Written in a number of languages, French, Creole, Malagasy, African languages (spoken by slaves), and Indian languages (spoken by indentured labourers), the poem begins in French and the first six stanzas are alexandrines, four to a stanza. The first three are in rhyming pairs. As the text progresses, it is separated into the speeches of a number of voices, interspersed with unattributed verse.

Just as the diversity of languages which makes up the text represents the linguistic diversity of the island's people and works as a metaphor for racial and cultural diversity, so the text is made up of fragments of different genres and forms. This represents the literary history of the island and reads rather as a palimpsest; the 'parchment' on to which Gamaleya writes, still has traces of former texts. The 'narrative' recounts the genesis of the island but it is its present, exemplified by the form and language(s) of the text, which matters most.

Creole is equally important, though not as the language (*langue*) of Alain Lorraine's *Tienbo le rein* (1975), which is relatively accessible poetry and written in French. The title means 'stick together in the fight', or, in another context, 'embrace intimately'. The first meaning associates a political militancy with the Creole language. The collection is dedicated 'aux z'enfants de la misère de ce pays qui vient'. The title poem is long and complex, reminiscent in many ways of Aimé Césaire's *Cahier d'un retour au pays natal*, but the shorter poems which follow it are accessible and largely descriptive of daily life on the island.

Although his work has been largely in French, Gilbert Aubry is generally regarded as the Father (he is Archbishop) of 'la Créolie': 'Ici nous sommes tous fils ou filles de la Créolie. Ici nous vivons de créolie comme ailleurs de Négritude ou d'Occitanie.' Yet both these were concerned (in part) with celebrating a common racial heritage. The 'Créolie' that Aubry (and Jean-François Sam Long) has campaigned for is a notion of integration of all the island's groups and a recognition of the important features which it shares with the neighbouring (however distant) islands. A desire to confront history (and in particular the experience of slavery) and to emerge proudly from the encounter, is perhaps the feature which links 'la Créolie' and Negritude most closely.

Much of the more recent poetry of the island enacts problems: Jean-Henri Azéma's work is about the difficulties of exile, of separation, of severance from one's roots (he settled in Argentina). Agnès Guéneau's text, *Une Île, un silence* (1979) is highly self-reflexive and explores the problems if not impossibilities of an authentic Réunionnaise literature.

Riel Debars, in *Sirène de fin de l'alerte* (1979), writes about the unauthenticity of those literary texts which create an island not remotely like the island he knows. Unauthenticity and *mauvaise conscience* are a direct consequence of choice of language (*langue*) according to the writer and critic, Carpanin Marimoutou. Until French is abandoned in favour of Creole, he has argued, contradictions and failure will continue to dominate literary projects which seek to discover and express (at least in a good many cases) an identity which is foreign to ('exotic' in) French.

Nor is the tension between the two languages only a feature of the genre of poetry. The Réunionnais novel, which is a relatively recent phenomenon (Anne Cheynet's *Les Muselés*, 1977, is generally cited as the first example), has been written in both languages. Daniel Honoré's *Louyuis Redona* (1980) was the first novel written in Creole.

Most of the novels written during the last twenty years have been simple accounts particularly of the lives of the island's poor, and historical novels which conform more or less to a narrower or looser definition. The experience of the Indian indentured labourer in the nineteenth century is recounted by Firmin Lacpatia. Daniel Vaxelaire's novels, *Chasseur d'esclaves* (1982) and *L'Affranchi* (1984), focus on slavery and its consequences in the eighteenth and nineteenth centuries. Linguistically more unusual (and more controversial) is Axel Gauvin's *Quartier Trois-lettres*. While remaining a witness to a social reality, the novel's language is a French often syntactically closer to Creole and broken up by the frequent occurrence of Creole words. Gauvin has also translated his text into standard Creole (*Kartye trwa let*, 1984).

One of the most significant recent publications is *La Littérature réunionnaise d'expression créole 1828–1982*, edited by Alain Armand and Gérard Chopinet and published in 1983 by L'Harmattan in Paris. An anthology supported by biographies and descriptions of various genres ('contes', 'proverbes', 'jeux de mots' (zed-mo)), the collection is divided into four sections ('les premiers textes créoles', 'l'héritage culturel de la colonie', 'le "bazadour" de la litterature réunionnaise', and 'explosion littéraire de la langue créole') and ends with an important 'essai d'analyse'. The apparent irony of the book's French title is mitigated by the perspective of the collection which serves to emphasize not the difference between French and Creole but rather a *linguistic continuum*. The extraordinary range of perspectives on language(s) is also admirably foregrounded. One end of the spectrum is illustrated by Frère Didier's view of Creole as a light-hearted source of entertainment (although there are contradictions in his description): 'Ce patois, (ce n'est pas une langue) est le lait et le miel vert du premier âge, le chant du vent, la plainte de la pluie, mais soyons sérieux, c'est pour rire que nous l'utilisons.'[1] Somewhere in the middle of this sliding scale of attitudes to the value of Creole is the view which forms an integral part of the polemic of 'La Créolie'. Here Creole is seen as a means of *enriching the French language*. J.-F. Sam Long argues: 'il n'y a pas à privilégier la langue française par rapport à la langue créole au niveau de l'expression poétique, du fait qu'elles sont toutes chargées d'un potential d'affectivité inestimable susceptible de permettre le choc de la rencontre'.[2] The hope is that 'la culture française accepte nos rapports multiples et ne refoule pas nos mots et nos images'.[3]

More radical (and necessarily more overtly political, given the

---

[1] Alain Armand and Gérard Chopinet (eds.), *Littérature réunionnaise d'expression créole 1828–1982* (1983), 319.
[2] Ibid. 419.   [3] Ibid.

force of French) is the view that 'la promotion d'une littérature en langue créole est une dimension essentielle du combat pour une construction cohérente de l'identité du peuple créolophone'.[4] Grouped around the review *Bazadour*, writers committed to the use of Creole argue, 'laissez-nous d'abord être nous-mêmes et nous serons alors mieux préparés pour accueillir la culture universelle'. Rather than celebrating and exploiting the instability of Creole (serious discussions about the normalization of Creole were initiated only in the early 1970s), the desire is that literary writings will tend naturally towards a certain Creole and thus literature will form the language rather than the other way round.

Language within Réunionnais literature should not simply be a matter of choices between different languages (and the baggage which goes with them), but a question which greatly enriches the literary and linguistic possibilities of writing which is rarely 'in' a single pure language (were such a thing to exist). More interestingly the range of languages spoken and written on the island, as on Mauritius, and as in so many francophone areas, creates an atmosphere of linguistic sensitivity and awareness which should act as a literary stimulus. The island's status as a *département* greatly reduces linguistic freedom.

Guide to Further Reading

Antilles and French Guiana

Novels

Edouard Glissant is the most important West Indian novelist writing in French (beginning with *La Lézarde*, 1958). He has now produced a substantial œuvre which includes poetry and essays (see below). An early and influential novelist is René Maran (winner of the Prix Goncourt for *Batouala*, 1921). Other major novelists include Joseph Zobel (his first novel *Diab'la*, 1942, was banned under Vichy). The production in 1983 of the film *Rue cases-nègres* based on his 1955 novel brought him to the attention of an international audience. Mayotte Capécia's novels (*Je suis martiniquaise*, 1948, and *La Négresse blanche*, 1950), are controversial. Simone Schwarz-Bart's historical novels are important (most famously *Pluie et vent sur Telumée miracle*, 1972). Daniel Maximin's work is an ambitious pastiche of genres (*L'Isolé soleil*, 1981). Michèle Lacrosil's *Demain Jab Herma* (1967) is

---

[4] *Littérature réunionnaise*, 420.

also formally innovatory. Vincent Placoly and Xavier Orville are equally important. Maryse Condé is both a writer and feminist critic (see for example *La Parole des femmes: Essai sur des romancières des Antilles de langue française*, 1979).

Poetry

Two of the three key poets associated with Negritude are West Indians: Aimé Césaire and Léon-Gontran Damas. The former's *Cahier d'un retour au pays natal* (1937) is a major text, as is the latter's early collection *Pigments*, published the same year. Césaire's poetic œuvre is a substantial one. Other important West Indian poets include Guy Tirolien (*Balles d'or*, 1961) and Georges Desportes (*Cet île qui est la nôtre*, 1973).

Theatre

Aimé Césaire is the French West Indies' most influential dramatist (most famously *La Tragédie du roi Christophe*, 1963, *Une Saison au Congo*, 1966, and *Une Tempête*, 1968).

Essays

Both Césaire and Glissant (see above) have also contributed important essays—*Discours sur le colonialisme* (1955) and *Le Discours antillais* (1981)—respectively and most importantly. A more recent collection of essays, including work by a number of younger writers is important: Ralph Ludwig (ed.), *Écrire la 'parole de nuit': La nouvelle littérature antillaise* (1994).

The major literary history of the area is A. J. Arnold (ed.), *A History of Literature in the Caribbean*, i. 'Hispanic and Francophone Regions' (Amsterdam, 1994), published as no. 10 of the series, A Comparative History of Literatures in European Languages.

Haiti

Novels

Haiti's most important novelist is no doubt Jacques Roumain (beginning with *La Montagne ensorcelée*, 1931). Jacques-Stéphen Alexis (*Compère général soleil*, 1955, is his first novel) and René Depestre (*Le Mât de cocagne*, 1979) are also important, among a large number.

Poetry

Émile Roumer (*Rosaire Couronne Sonnets*, 1964) is less overtly militant than many Haitian poets, for example J.-F. Brierre (*Black Soul*, 1947), René

Depestre (*Poète à Cuba*, 1976). More individual is the poetry of René Philoctète (*Ces îles qui marchent*) and Jean Métellus (*Au pipirite chantant*, 1976).

Studies

The standard literary history is A. Viatte, *Histoire Littéraire de l'Amérique française*. N. Garret, *The Renaissance of Haitian Poetry* (1963) is concerned only with that genre. M. Dash, *Literature and Ideology in Haiti* (1981), and L.-J. Hoffman, *Haiti: lettres et l'être* (Toronto, 1992), are both concerned with the relationship between literature and society.

Mauritius

Novels

Robert-Edward Hart's major work, the novel cycle *Pierre Flandre* (1928–36) is arguably the island's major prose text. Marcel Cabon's *Chroniques*, tableaux of Mauritian life, are also important, as is his novel *Namasté* (1965).

Poetry

Feted by André Breton and Jean Paulhan, Malcolm de Chazal is the island's most celebrated poet (*Sens plastique*, 1948) was published by Gallimard, part of *Pensées* published on the island between 1940 and 1945). Numerous other collections and often cryptic essays followed. *Sens unique* (1974) is his intellectual autobiography. Édouard Maunick is also a major poetic voice (beginning with *Manèges de la mer*, 1964).

Studies

Jean-Georges Prosper, *Histoire de la littérature mauritienne de langue française* (Mauritius, 1978) is the major history. Camille de Rauville, *Chazal des antipodes* (1974) is an interesting study of an extraordinary writer. See also under Studies for La Réunion.

Studies of a more theoretical kind and books and articles relevant not only to the Creole islands but to other areas also, are to be found in the Select Bibliography at the end of the book.

La Réunion

Novels

The novel is a relatively recent genre. Anne Cheynet, *Les Muselés* (1977) is the seminal modern novel. Axel Gauvin, *Quartier Trois-lettres* (1980) is important both as *reportage* and for its integration of Creole idioms into French. He is also author of an important essay on language (see Essays, below).

Poetry

Poetry is the island's most important literary genre. The first major modern poet is Jean Albany. His collection *Zamal* (1951) announces a break from either a colonial or exotic poetry (the two types of poetry which precede it). Alain Lorraine (*Tienbo le rein*, 1975) is also important, as is Boris Gamaleya (*Vali pour une reine morte*, 1973), Agnès Guéneau (*La Réunion: une île, un silence*, 1979), Gilbert Aubry (*Rivages d'alizé*, 1976), and Jean-Henri Azéma (*Olographe*, 1978).

Essays

An insight into the complex debates concerning language, in particular the language of literature, is provided by Axel Gauvin, *Du créole opprimé au créole libéré* (1977).

Studies

A useful account of the island's literature is given in R. Chaudenson (ed.), *Encyclopédie de la Réunion*, vii. 'La Littérature réunionnaise'. See also the author's entry in the *Oxford Companion to Literature in French* (Oxford, 1995). *Notre Librairie*, 72 (1983), is devoted to 'Littératures de l'Océan Indien'. An interesting study of poetry is provided by Daniel-Rolland Roche, *Lire la poésie réunionnaise contemporaine* (St Denis, La Réunion, 1992). Also interesting from a comparative point of view is Alain Armand and Gérard Chopinet, *Anthologie de la littérature réunionnaise d'expression créole* (1984).

PART III NORTH AFRICA AND THE NEAR EAST

THE MAGHREB

THE Maghreb (Arabic for West) is essentially made up of Algeria, Morocco, and Tunisia. Maghrebi literatures are as hybrid, protean, and defiant as any francophone literature. Challenging literary typologies and prognoses, they embrace writing which has 'come out of' the Maghreb, oral texts which circulate in that space, texts which participate in an *imaginaire maghrébin*, texts written, published, and read principally in the Maghreb, and those written by authors born there, but often living elsewhere, in 'exile'. These literatures are written in numerous languages: classical and dialectal Arabic, Berber, and French are the most significant. Nor do these remain distinct in written texts. Translations and transcriptions of material may constitute parts of a text written largely in (an)other language(s).[1]

Francophone Maghrebi writing is a bastard literature, as one of North Africa's most important early writers argued: 'le colonisé a reçu le bienfait de la langue de la civilisation dont il n'est pas l'héritier légitime. Et par conséquent il est une sorte de bâtard.'[2] Francophone North African theorists have explored these early worries (also visible in discourses which focus on otherness, linguistic exile, treachery, etc.) to propose an aesthetics of difference. In *Maghreb pluriel* (1983), for example, Abdelkebir Khatibi proposes deconstruction as a philosophical equivalent of decolonization. Contesting the idea of an absolute legitimizing origin which authenticates meaning and truth, Khatibi deconstructs Frantz Fanon's call

[1] Samia Nehrez, 'Subversive Poetics of Radical Bilingualism: Postcolonial, Francophone North African Literature', in D. LaCapra (ed.), *Bounds of Race: Perspectives on Hegemony and Resistance* (Ithaca, NY, 1991), 255–77.

[2] Cited by Abdelkebir Khatibi, *Le Roman maghrébin* (Rabat, 1979), 39.

to abandon Europe and asks instead: 'Et nous sommes toujours en train de demander: de quel Occident s'agit-il? De quel Occident opposé à nous-mêmes, en nous-mêmes, qui nous-mêmes?'[3] Khatibi and Abdellah Bounfour have elaborated a 'savoir/raison orphelin(e)': 'Qu'est-ce que la raison orpheline sinon le refus pratiqué de l'ethnocide, de la glottophagie et de l'ethnocentrisme. Vigilance donc & toute légitimité 'originelle'.'[4]

In the 'Présentation' for a special issue of *Les Temps Modernes* to which some of North Africa's most influential francophone writers contributed (Khatibi, Bounfour, Abdelwahab Meddeb, Hédi Bouraoui, Tahar Ben Jelloun, Nabile Farès, Mouloud Mammeri), the Maghreb was described very simply: 'Tel écart tourné vers la pensée de la différence, nommons-le Maghreb.'[5] In a lucid description of the issue, Marx-Scouras comments:

Cultural renewal, for these Maghrebi(ne) writers, is a form of deterritorialization from geographic, ethnic and cultural frontiers. Situated between the East and the West, at the intersection of Africa, Europe, and the Middle East, the Maghreb constitutes a privileged geographic and cultural site for the dynamic interplay of different cultural traditions and mixed ethnic groups, of cultural pluralism and multilingualism.[6]

[3] Abdelkebir Khatibi, *Maghreb pluriel* (1983), 14–15.

[4] Abdellah Bounfour, 'La Raison orpheline', *Les Temps modernes*, 33/375 (Oct. 1977), 424.

[5] *Les Temps modernes*, 33/375 (Oct. 1977), 5.

[6] Danielle Marx-Scouras, 'The Poetics of Maghrebine Illegitimacy', *L'Esprit Créateur*, 26/1 (Spring, 1986), 3–10 (pp. 7–8). Other recent articles which approach the area from a number of different perspectives include: Jean Déjeux and Ruthmarie Mitsch, 'Francophone Literature in the Maghreb: The Problem and the Possibility', *Research in African Literatures*, 23 (1992), 33–8; Eric Sellin, 'Francophone Literature of the Maghreb', *Literary Review* (Madison, NJ), 30 (1987), 390–4; Judith Roumani, 'A Literature of One's Own: A Survey of Literary History and Criticism of Maghrebian Francophone Literature', *L'Esprit Créateur*, 26 (1986), 11–21; Hedi Bouraoui, 'The Present State of Francophone Maghrebian Literature: Perspective and Problematics', in Stephen Arnold (ed.), *African Literature/l'État présent* (Washington, 1985), 257–69.

8

ALGERIA

It was Algeria's relative separation from France during the Second World War which stimulated and encouraged writers, intellectuals and publishers to form new groups, and strengthen those which already existed, within the country. The most influential was the École d'Alger which had been set up during the mid-1930s. Earlier groups, made up of the so-called *Algérianistes*, for example, had had quite different concerns. Associated with this group the colonial writers Louis Bertrand, Jean Pomier, and Robert Randau, for example, celebrated the energy and dynamism of the colonial venture. Gabriel Audisio, on the other hand, a major figure within the École d'Alger (he suggested the name), proposed, in his earlier writings, not the re-Christianized North Africa expounded by Bertrand and his followers, but a Mediterranean Africa, a melting-pot of races and cultures. Any writing in French which emanated from this hybrid cultural space would, however, be French. In a somewhat confused argument, Audisio claimed: 'Il n'y a qu'une littérature française à Genève comme au Japon, à Bruxelles comme à Alger; le jour où nous viendrait d'Algérie un nouveau *Discours sur la méthode*, nous ne nous soucierions pas plus de le tenir pour algérien que l'autre pour hollandais.'[1] Similarly, a few years later he argued that 'Il n'y a pas, il n'y a jamais eu de littérature algérienne. Nous entendons exprimer par là qu'il n'existe pas, ou du moins pas encore, une littérature autonome et spécifique dont le caractère soit affirmé par l'existence d'une langue, d'une race, d'une nation proprement algérienne.'[2]

[1] 'L'Algérie littéraire', *Algérie-Sahara*, ii. *Encyclopédie coloniale et maritime* (1948), 246; cited by Jean Déjeux, *Littérature maghrébine* (Montreal, 1973), 18.
[2] 'Les Écrivains algériens', *Visages de l'Algérie* (Paris, 1953), 99; cited by Déjeux, *Littérature maghrébine*, 18.

Most of the writers associated with the École d'Alger were second- or third-generation *pieds-noirs* (of French descent), most notably Emmanuel Roblès, René-Jean Clot, Claude de Fréminville, Marcel Moussy, Jean Pélégri, and Jules Roy. *La Guerre d'Algérie* (1960), by Roy, an anti-colonial pamphlet, was to be particularly influential.

Born in a spirit of resistance, a number of important journals appeared at the end of the war, for example *Fontaine*, edited by Max-Pol Fouchet. Like *L'Arche*, founded in 1944 by Jean Amrouche, under André Gide's patronage, and *La Nef*, founded by Robert Aron, these three journals were later published in Paris. Others remained in Algiers, *Forge, Soleil, Simoun*, gradually including contributions by writers of Muslim origin. The left-wing paper *Alger républicain* was also an important forum.

Crudely, francophone Algerian writing can most usefully be discussed in terms of three phases, before, during the struggle for, and after Independence. It was during the final phase of occupation, particularly during the 1950s, that a number of Algerian writers emerged, forced to use French as their means of expression, although of Arabo-Berber descent. The traditional educational system had been radically altered after the conquest and classical Arabic removed from the syllabus. Advancement depended on success within the French educational system and this meant that the first generations of Algerian writers had little or no knowledge of classical Arabic. Writers such as Jean and Taos Amrouche, Mouloud Feraoun, Malek Ouary, Mouloud Mammeri, and Nabile Farès for whom Berber was the mother-tongue, and Mohammed Dib, Kateb Yacine, and Malek Haddad whose background was Arabic, were all educated in French.

The novels of Mouloud Feraoun and Mohammed Dib, unlike the novels written by French writers living in Algeria before and during the war, are concerned to propose, here and there, a need for quiet and determined resistance, and occasionally to question official discourse and language. A succinct example, which has peculiar critical status because of the frequency with which it has been quoted, is from Mohammed Dib's *La Grande Maison* (1952). The relativity of the French word 'patrie' is exposed in a delightful passage in which the schoolteacher, M. Hassan, is supposed to explain Algeria's relationship with France. The meaning of the French textbook within the Algerian context becomes absurd, even meaningless. One of the schoolchildren has announced, in reply to the question 'Qui d'entre

vous sait ce que veut dire: Patrie?', 'La France est notre mère patrie.'
A little further on M. Hassan reads from the textbook: 'La patrie
est la terre des pères.' He then continues: 'Quand de l'extérieur
viennent des étrangers qui prétendent être les maîtres, la patrie est
en danger. Ces étrangers sont des ennemis contre lesquels toute la
population doit défendre la patrie menacée. Il est alors question
de guerre.' The protagonist is then taken aback: 'Omar, surpris,
entendit le maître parler en arabe. [. . .] D'une voix basse, où perçait
une violence qui intriguait: 'Ça n'est pas vrai [. . .] si on vous dit que
la France est votre patrie.'³ This passage is interesting for a number
of reasons associated with the French educational system and the
policy of assimilation and its paradoxes. Textually this is visible in
the contradiction between the narrator informing us that M. Hassan
spoke in Arabic, but the crucial statement of non-belonging to
France, the direct speech, is in French.

The complexities of the colonial relationship also preoccupied
Jean Amrouche throughout his life. Amrouche, one of the
Maghreb's most influential writers, has been described as both an
Aimé Césaire and a Frantz Fanon of North Africa. Poet, polemicist,
and essayist, Amrouche was born in 1906 into a Catholic family in
Petite-Kabylie. The family was forced to emigrate to Tunisia where
he attended secondary school, before going on the École normale de
Saint-Cloud. Armand Guibert published his first two collections of
poems in 1934 and 1937. Other poems were published in Tunisian
literary reviews. In 1939 *Chants berbères de Kabylie* was published in
Tunis, and in 1944 he launched *L'Arche* with André Gide's patronage. As a schoolteacher at the Lycée Tunis, Albert Memmi
was amongst his pupils. Amrouche travelled widely in Europe
with Guibert and in 1943 was appointed to a post in the Ministry
of Information. He moved to Radio-diffusion française and then
to the Office de la radiodiffusion-télévision française where he was
editor of the radio news. His interviews with Paul Claudel, François
Mauriac, and Gide have been published in audio and written forms.
In 1959 his weekly programme 'Des Idées et des hommes' was
banned and Amrouche removed from his position. He acted
as a mediator between General de Gaulle and Ferhat Abbas, leader
of the Gouvernement provisoire de la République algérienne
(GPRA). Just before he died, in 1962, he was reappointed to ORTF.
His mother's account, *Histoire de ma vie* appeared in 1968. His sister

---

³ Mohammed Dib, *La Grande Maison* (1952), 23.

also writes and has edited a number of records of *Chants berbères de Kabylie*.

About a year after the beginnings of the Algerian war of independence, Amrouche publicly declared his political commitment. He believed that his obligation was to 'expliquer les Algériens aux Français' and equally, 'expliquer aussi les Français aux Algériens'. In a number of articles in the French press, most notably 'La France comme mythe et comme réalité' (*Le Monde*, 11 January 1958), Amrouche described how the colonized of Algeria dreamt of a liberal France while simultaneously experiencing oppression and inhumane treatment. Like Frantz Fanon (*Peau noire masques blancs*) and Albert Memmi (*Portrait du colonisé*), he strongly believed in the specificity of the colonial relationship and that all French people were responsible for that relationship and its enactment in Algeria—and France. Jean Déjeux describes Amrouche's contribution accurately and succinctly:

> Poète en quête de son identité, Amrouche eut avant tout la religion de la poésie. Nous trouvons dans son œuvre de jeunesse une expérience poétique et, en appliquant à l'auteur le mot de René Char, nous pouvons dire que la poésie était pour lui 'la vie future à l'intérieur de l'homme requalifié'. Sa première passion fut cette tragédie du poète déraciné et frustré de son paradis perdu et aspirant à vivre auprès de la source créatrice [. . .] [Ses] poèmes semblent parfois laisser deviner que notre auteur se situait à un carrefour de routes où rythmes ancestraux de la terre natale et reminiscences islamiques de la culture ambiante se croisent avec les évocations chrétiennes.[4]

In an interview with Senghor, he described himself (no doubt describing his interlocutor also) as one of 'les hybrides culturels' in a 'situation de contradiction'.[5] Amrouche corresponded with Jean-Joseph Rabearivelo and shared his anguished sense of cultural bastardy, an experience which later generations (of both North African and Malagasy writers) were to experience so differently. For the latter, hybridity is simultaneously belonging to two or more cultures, and this is often seen as a privileged vantage point and something to be celebrated rather than lamented.

Although the sudden appearance of a francophone Maghrebi literature during the 1950s can largely be accounted for in terms of the number of literate French-educated North Africans, it also took

---

[4] Déjeux, *Littérature maghrébine*, 112–13.
[5] *Afrique-Action*, 13 Feb. 1961; cited by Déjeux, *Littérature mahgrébine*, 113.

place, it must be remembered, within a highly literary culture of both written and oral material in both Arabic and Berber. Mouloud Feraoun's *Le Fils du pauvre, Menrad, instituteur kabyle* (1950) has been marked as the first work of a properly Algerian literature in French. Feraoun's family name was Ait Chaabane but the French administration gave the family the name Feraoun at the end of the nineteenth century when all Kabyle names were 'regularized' (changed). Born in 1913 he did well academically and, in 1935, was appointed schoolteacher in his native village. His first visit to Paris was made in 1949; his correspondence with Albert Camus began in 1951. He started his journal in 1955 (*Journal 1954–1962*), a year after the beginning of the Algerian War. He later became director of various social and educational organizations. He was assassinated in 1962 by a commando of the OAS (Organisation de l'Armée Secrète).

Feraoun's first, largely autobiographical, novel, set in Grande Kabylie, is descriptive of his country and its people, their concerns, the toughness of their lives and the complexities of their philosophical attitudes. The second, *La Terre et le Sang* (1953), is principally about immigrant workers in France. *Les Chemins qui montent* was written at the height of the war which is its concern. His fourth novel, *L'Anniversaire*, remained unfinished but was published in 1972. *Jours de Kabylie* (1954) is a collection of texts and stories of, and descriptions about, his country. He translated part of *Poèmes de Si Mohand* (1960). *Les Lettres à ses amis 1949–1962* was published in 1969.

Some journalists and critics have from time to time expressed an ambivalent, even hostile attitude towards him. Feraoun's concern is to communicate, not obliquely, but rarely overtly. Believing in the complexity of people and experience, both personal and political, he rarely states his position in a straightforward way. He never wholeheartedly denounced the colonial system, for example, although his journal makes it very clear that he was no advocate of it. Thus, his commitment to non-violence and his multi-culturalism have often been discussed rather in terms of 'acculturation'.

It is the phenomenon of acculturation that his novels explore and enact self-reflexively. Written in French, ideas and concepts strange to that language are explored. The Kabyle notions of *nif*, crudely the equivalent of honour, and *sof*, the clan or family, are two important examples. The act of recording in minute detail the manners and customs of his people can be interpreted in a number of ways. That his audience was likely to be largely French or at least French-educated is obvious. It can, therefore, be considered to some extent as 'exotic' literature. When the complexities of the text are taken into account, however, the question becomes less straightforward. Textually, the inclusion of a *kabyle* vocabulary represents a contrast if not conflict. This is equally a theme, explored within the novels. The form within which customs and traditions are revealed also makes a difference. Earlier texts describing the ways of non-French people belonged within ethnographic or anthropological literature. By making not dissimilar information the stuff of novels, the material gains, *de facto*, a certain legitimacy if not status. Nor do questions have to be answered. In Feraoun's novels the problems of acculturation, the importance of tradition but the need constantly to challenge it, the inwardness but strength of the family, the difficulties of immigration, and other subjects are to some extent the matter of the text, but it is the experience of these filtered through individual consciousness, rather than examined analytically or described dogmatically, which is the text's method.

Mouloud Mammeri's work is in many ways comparable. Also of Kabyle origin, his trilogy, *La Colline oubliée* (1952), *Le Sommeil du juste* (1955), *L'Opium et le bâton* (1965), is a historical fresco of Algeria between the Second World War and the War of Liberation. Writing initially for himself and later transforming his notes into his first novel, Mammeri's work is obviously autobiographical. The adolescents of Tasga in *La Colline oubliée* are growing up in a society disrupted by colonialism. They seek escape from the family, society, tradition. Mammeri's novel provoked very considerable debate. Heralded by the French press in Algeria as an accomplished work of 'littérature indigène', it was described as a 'beau roman kabyle' and a 'roman de l'âme berbère'. A year later, however, *Le Jeune Musulman*, 12 (2 Jan. 1953), published an article by an Algerian critic entitled 'La Colline du reniement'. Pointing out that 'les qualités formelles' had been responsible for the critical success the work had enjoyed within the French literary establishment, Mohammed-Cherif Sahli wrote:

La théorie de l'art pour l'art est particulièrement odieuse dans ces moments historiques où les peuples engagent leur existence dans les durs combats de la libération. Une œuvre signée d'un Algérien ne peut donc nous intéresser que d'un seul point de vue: quelle cause sert-elle? Quelle est sa position dans la lutte qui oppose le mouvement national au colonialisme?[6]

---

[6] Déjeux, *Littérature maghrébine*, 186.

Mammeri defended the work claiming that as the novel was concerned with Algerians, it could not but serve the Algerian cause. Further criticism followed however: Mammeri, it was argued, pandered to the tastes of readers of 'regionalist' and 'colonial literature', in its simplistic, folkloric 'vagueness'. Many criticized *La Colline* for its 'selectivity'.

The events of *La Colline oubliée* take place between 1942 and 1944 in Grande Kabylie. The hero of the novel, Menach, falls hopelessly in love with Davda and finally chooses exile. The work is full of dramatic tension—and lyricism. The former is generated by the conflicts between old and young, tradition and new ways, and by the choice between commitment to place and departure (and exile).

In *Le Sommeil du juste* (1955) Arezki, who has embraced the humanism of his Western teachers, gradually realizes, during the course of various adventures, the limitations and falsities of what he has been taught. In a symbolically profane act, having seen for himself the myth of equality and parodying the adage 'all men are equal but some are more equal than others' ('à grade égal, le grade indigène doit obéissance au gradé européen'), Arezki burns all his hitherto treasured books.

That Mammeri's three books form a trilogy is confirmed by the dominant narrative of the third, *L'Opium et le bâton* (1965), in which the protagonist, Bachir Lazrak, at the height of the Algerian conflict, joins the *maqui* and abandons his French girlfriend Claude in favour of Itto, an illiterate Moroccan Berber. Both privately and politically, Bachir frees himself of Western influence and opts for resistance. Mammeri began the book in Morocco, but finished it in Algeria just before the end of the war. Almost all the details are true and the characters based on real people. But Mammeri has described his intention that the book be about the great abstract universals also: the nature of humankind and the nature of human freedom. The title is explained early on: 'Séduire ou réduire, mystifier ou punir, depuis que le monde est monde, aucun pouvoir n'a jamais su sortir de l'opium ou le bâton' (p. 14).

His compatriot Mohammed Dib's trilogy, entitled simply *Algérie*, is constituted by *La Grande Maison* (1952), *l'Incendie* (1954), and *Le Métier à tisser* (1957). The texts cover the years 1939 to 1942. Set in Tlemcen and the countryside round about, they investigate both a real hinterland and a psychological 'hinterland of the mind'. In the first, the adolescent Omar considers the lives of the inhabitants of a large block of flats, and the poverty and despair which dominate.

Some critics, both Algerian and French, accused Dib of depicting Algerians as submissive and without vision. Dib was dismayed. An article in *Progrès* (May 1953), an organ of the Communist Party, argued that it was the writer's duty to show man's strengths and extol the virtues of a working class ready to rise up. The French Communist writer Louis Aragon defended Dib, however.

L'Incendie is concerned with the rural population and their political awakening. The title is metaphorical: 'Un incendie avait été allumé, et jamais plus il ne s'éteindrait. Il continuerait à ramper à l'aveuglette, secret, souterrain; ses flammes sanglantes n'auraient de cesse qu'elles n'aient jeté sur tout le pays leur sinistre éclat.'[7] In a famous passage, the relationship between personal identity and national identity, between the body and the body politic, is made explicit:

Tu te crois peut-être libre de ta personne. Mais ton peuple ne l'est pas. Alors tu n'es pas libre, toi non plus. Car hors de ton peuple tu n'existes pas. Est-ce que ce bras peut vivre hors de mon corps, et pourtant à le voir agir on penserait qu'il est indépendant, ou cette main hors de mon bras, or à voir mes doigts qui attrapent tout ce qu'ils veulent on croirait qu'ils sont indépendants. Tu es comme ça avec tes frères de sang.[8]

The third of the three novels, *Le Métier à tisser* shows the effects of the Second World War and the modernization it brings on Tlemcen and its people, particularly the weavers: 'Nous sommes descendus trop bas. Nous ne pourrions redevenir des hommes par des voies ordinaires; nous nous verrions obligés de boulverser le monde' (p. 76). The fragmentary form and poetic techniques of Dib's later writings represent a break with the quasi-neorealism and *unanimisme* of the trilogy. These, however, belong to a later period.

The Algerian War broke out in November 1954 and from this point on almost all Algerian writing became overtly committed, that is to say that it fought for the cause of liberation, argued for the need for violence, defended the *patrie* or the ancestors, or proposed a vision of a future, liberated, country. Writing also became more diverse, often extending or subverting literary genre or, on the other hand, abandoning more complex literary forms in favour of the direct and polemical.

The war also inspired a great deal of poetry, the novel temporarily taking second place (in terms of genres) (see Denise Barrat, *Espoir*

[7] J.-L. Joubert *et al.* (eds.), *Les Littératures francophones* (1986), 180.
[8] Mohammed Dib, *L'Incendie* (1954), 90.

et parole, 1963). Early on, texts such as Ismail Aït Djafer's *Complainte des mendiants arabes de la Casbah et de la petite Yasmina tuée par son père* (1953) is written in a language of revolt, against poverty, squalor, and sordidness. A more overtly political revolt—and desire for an Algerian nationalist perspective—is expressed in a wide variety of texts by authors of both Maghrebi and European origin. Important in the first group are: Noureddine Aba, Bachir Hadj Ali, Noureddine Tidafi, and especially Malek Haddad and Kateb Yacine. The second group includes Anna Greki, Henri Kréa—and most importantly, Jean Sénac.

Poems such as many of those in Malek Haddad's *Le Malheur en danger*, extend and emphasize the central concern of the passage of Dib's (*La Grande Maison*) mentioned above: 'Chez nous le mot Patrie a un goût de légende . . .'[9]

Poetry which, crudely speaking, belongs within a protest tradition was widely read by a contemporary audience. The degree to which today's readers believe that the poetic text should simultaneously transcend the historical moment and speak in abstract, universal terms will condition present critical attitudes. One interesting difference between protest poetry and novels concerned with the war is bound up with the relative delay, in the case of the novel, in inscribing the experience into that genre.

It is above all retrospectively that the Algerian novel has been concerned with the Algerian War. Although war is present in novels such as those of Malek Haddad (*L'Elève et la leçon*, 1960, *Le Quai aux fleurs ne répond plus*, 1961), it is central, however, in works such as Mouloud Mammeri's *L'Opium et le bâton* (1965), mentioned briefly above, which celebrates the heroism of war.

Kateb Yacine, arguably Algeria's major francophone writer, published his first important work, *Nedjma*, when the war was at its height in 1956. Kateb Yacine was born in Constantine although his birth was registered at Condé-Smendou (now Zirout Youcef). He was born into a large tribe in which endogamous marriages were frequent. His father was a judicial *Oukil* (defence lawyer); he died in 1950. Kateb Yacine was educated first at a Koranic school and then a French school, thus passing into 'la gueule du loup'. During the protests of May 1945 he was at the Lycée in Sétif. He was arrested, aged 16, along with others. As a consequence of this he was expelled

---

[9] Kalek Haddad, *Le Malheur en danger*, quoted in J.-L. Joubert *et al.* (eds.), *Les Littératures francophones*, 184.

from the school. The following year, in 1946, he published his first collection of poems, *Soliloques*. In 1947 he gave a paper in Paris, 'Abdelkader et l'indépendance algérienne'. From 1948 to 1950 he worked as a reporter for *Alger républicain* and mixed in largely communist nationalist circles. In January 1948 his poem 'Nedjma ou le poème ou le couteau' appeared in *Mercure de France*, other poems appeared in *Forge* (1947), *Soleil*, *Simoun*, and *Terrasses* (1950–3).

From 1951 onwards he wandered in France, working in a variety of more or less unskilled jobs. During this period he became increasingly haunted by the idea of writing a book, *Nedjma*. Nedjma was his cousin with whom he was deeply in love but who had married someone else. In 1955 extracts of *Nedjma* and *Le Cadavre encerclé* appeared in *Esprit*. In Paris he worked feverishly on the novel, showing sections to Jean Cayrol at Éditions du Seuil (he has denied its status as a novel).[10] During 1953 he reworked and reshaped his material, working with excitement and passion. Publishers refused his manuscript and it was only after further work on it that it was finally accepted for publication, appearing in 1956.

Kateb Yacine has described his œuvre as an 'autobiographie au pluriel'; this is pre-eminently appropriate for *Nedjma*. The work can be understood as recalling three pasts which constantly interfere and become blurred: childhood memories centred on his mother, recalling his cousin Nedjma, and Algerian history. Nedjma is at the centre: *mère-patrie* and *femme obsédante*. Early on, in a review of 16 August 1956, Maurice Nadeau suggested that the structure of *Nedjma* could best be understood as a universe in which Nedjma ('a star' in Arabic) was positioned at the centre, a sun, attracting, illuminating, even burning, other planets in its orbit: 'Comme tous ces astres sont prisonniers du même mouvement qui, à intervalles fixes, les rend également présents, il s'ensuit, dans une espèce de 'retour éternel', une confusion complète du passé, du présent et de l'avenir.'[11] Déjeux draws on this model and describes *Nedjma* thus:

En simplifiant, on peut donc raconter ainsi cette histoire compliquée comme à plaisir par l'auteur: trois cousins d'une même tribu endogame (Sidi Ahmed, Si Moktar et le père de Rachid) et un quatrième protagoniste, le Puritain, enlèvent successivement une Française, Juive. En séduisant les

[10] See Déjeux, *Littératures maghrébines*, 227.

[11] M. Nadeau, *France-Observateur*, 16 Aug. 1956; quoted by Déjeux, *Littératures maghrébines*, 228.

trois hommes de la tribu de Keblout, elle a fait éclater la cohésion tribale. [. . .] C'est un cercle infernal ou une désertion aussi génératrice de démence.[12]

This is one of the most lucid accounts of the 'story' of *Nedjma*. But the 'story' which can be thus deduced, not to say reduced, is relatively unimportant. What really matters about the text is the degree to which it offers the reader multiple interpretative possibilities. Déjeux, drawing on the interpretative model of his *Anthologie des écrivains maghrébins d'expression française*, continues:

Transposée sur un plan politique [. . .] cette histoire pourrait aussi s'expliquer de cette façon. De jeunes héros sont encerclés par l'oppression coloniale. A peine sortis du collège c'est la prison, le chantier, l'errance pour le travail, la dépersonnalisation. Encerclés aussi en eux-mêmes, obsédés par l'image de Nedjma, mythe de l'Algérie incarnant un passé défiguré et des siècles obscurs, ils la rêvent, vierge, lavée des souillures dont les conquérants successifs l'ont salie au cours des siècles [. . .] Ces jeunes [. . .] débouchent à leur époque, sans modèles paternels mais en se créant un mythe des ancêtres, sur un pays défloré, tragique, déchiré et impuissant à reconstituer l'unité des tribus dispersées. Dans un dernier sursaut historique le pays se redresse pour chasser le dernier occupant agrippé depuis cent trente ans. Et la forme neuve de la nation naît enfin, fruit de la greffe douloureuse.[13]

Formally the text is surprising in its subversion of genre. The influence of Dos Passos, Faulkner, and Joyce suggests itself. Its lexis is diverse and often abstruse. Kateb has drawn on the *ma'na*, popular sayings which convey popular wisdom. Further interpretative potential is offered by the author's emphasis on the role of the unconscious in the writing of the text. This has further encouraged (forms of incoherence within the text suggest the creative contribution of the unconscious) psychoanalytical interpretative methods.

Le Polygone étoilé (1966) is a *montage* of texts belonging to a range of genres (prose fragments, poetry, tales, songs, colonialist writing), written or noted over a ten-year period. 'Characters' from earlier texts reappear, Nedjma most importantly. A polysemic, discontinuous, and disorientating text, it assembles rather than translates or interprets an Algerian experience at a particular historical moment.

---

[12] Déjeux, *Littératures maghrébines*, 228–9.
[13] Ibid. 229. Déjeux's *Anthologie* is also edited by Jacqueline Arnaud and Abdelkebir Khatibi (1964), 2nd edn. (1965), 156.

The final pages, the most lucid and accessible, are autobiographical and conventional although not in the first person. They describe Kateb's father's decision to send his son to a French school:

Pourtant, quand j'ai eu sept ans [. . .], mon père prit soudain la décision irrévocable de me fourrer sans plus tarder dans 'la gueule du loup', c'est-à-dire à l'école française. Il le faisait le cœur serré. [. . .] 'Je ne veux pas que, comme moi, tu sois assis entre deux chaises' [. . .] 'La langue française domine. Il te faudra la dominer, et laisser en arrière tout ce que nous t'avons inculqué dans ta plus tendre enfance.'[14]

Kateb had met Brecht in Paris in 1954, and the title of his play, *Le Cercle des représailles* (1959) testifies to the influence Brecht had had on him.[15] In 1954 his first play *Le Cadavre encerclé* had appeared in the journal *Esprit*. In 1958 the play was staged by Jean-Marie Serreau. The hero of the play, Lakhdar, is surrounded by death: the dead bodies of the victims of a reprisal for an uprising in a Maghrebi town. Lahkhdar, lives and dies torn between loyalty to his community and in revolt against its absolute authority. Powerfully anti-colonialist, it describes the contradiction, dislocation, and disorientation of a community shaped by the all-embracing experience of colonialism.

A volume of plays was published by Seuil with an introduction by the West Indian writer Edouard Glissant. This included *Le Cadavre encerclé*, *La Poudre d'intelligence*, a straightforward comedy written in a direct language and inspired by Maghrebi tales, and *Les Ancêtres redoublent de férocité*, a symbolically complex tragedy.

In 1967 Kateb travelled to Vietnam when the war was at its height. His faith in revolution was strengthened and he returned to an earlier project which became *L'Homme aux sandales de caoutchouc* (1970), a play about Vietnamese resistance inspired by the figure of Ho Chi Minh. The play was performed almost simultaneously in Lyon, in French, and in Algiers in Algerian Arabic. His concern for theatre and commitment to it widened when, in 1972, he became involved in the Groupe théâtral de l'action culturelle des travailleurs. He went on to become director of the theatre in Bel-Abbès. During these years his plays written in Algerian Arabic reached a very wide audience. A growing ironic and satirical mode is apparent in *Nedjma* but is more, and increasingly, important in

[14] Kateb Yacine, *Le Polygone étoilé* (1966), 180.
[15] Lucy Stone McNeece, 'L'Espace du signe: le théâtre francophone de Kateb Yacine', *Revue francophone de Louisiane*, 5 (1990), 16–28.

Kateb's theatre, beginning with *La Poudre d'intelligence*. Later plays, *Mohammed prends ta valise* (1971), a play about emigration which exists in both French and Berber versions, *Saout-en-nisa* (1972), *La Guerre de 2000 ans* (1974), *Le Roi de l'ouest* (1977), *Palestine trahie* (1978), are satires which attack, above all, those contented with the status quo. *La Voix des femmes* (1972) explores the role of women in thirteenth-century Tlemcen society. *La Guerre de 2000 ans* dramatizes a universal fight against oppression. Kateb's desire is to be 'la révolution dans la révolution'—a revolutionary individualist, a nonconformist who fights for a common cause.

Kateb's later plays have not been published. Thus they remain, like oral material, in a state of mobility, constantly shifting and changing in response to contemporary historical circumstance.

This fluidity represents a refusal of the fixed, a refusal of dogmatic assertion, of certainty. Just as Kateb's prose texts combine fragments from numerous genres, so those of writers such as Nabile Farès and Habib Tengour abandon the conventional structuring devices of realism. This tendency, a continuation and extension of Kateb's writing practice, can be read—put very simply—as part of a fascination with contemporary Western intellectual concerns, those of semiology, visible in, for example, the work of the *nouveaux romanciers*, or as a concern to explore an Arabo-Islamic aesthetic, one dependent on pattern, rhythm, and form, rather than the conventions of Western representation. These two are by no means mutually exclusive.

Post-war concerns as they emerge from novels of the 1960s are those of a society emerging from the traumas of war and the shock of independence, the ubiquitous (in francophone writing) theme of the confrontation of old and new (seen in a range of antitheses: old versus young, religion versus the secular, legitimate versus illegitimate, indigenous versus imported, rural versus urban etc.), and, equally ubiquitous (if not constitutive of the definition), identity. Violence dominates the novel of the 1960s: whether linguistic violence or the description of violence, the refusal of taboo or challenge to a range of authorities: religious and secular, the family and the state (where these can be divided).

Mourad Bourboune is best known for his novel, *Muezzin* (1967; *Le Mont des genêts* was published in 1961). The novel's protagonist, *le porteur de la parole*, Said Ramiz is as the title suggests a *Muezzin*, the functionary who calls the faithful to prayer from the mosque's minaret. He is, however, an atheist and, equally inappropriately, has stuttered since birth. His role is to liberate the town by announcing a new Book, an anti-Koran: 'Le Muezzin parle ainsi en phrases populaires et sacrales. En strophes-bidonvilles. Avec une simplicité hermétique accessible au seul commun des mortels.'[16] Like Kateb's notion of 'l'autobiographie au pluriel', Bourboune proposes the notion of living an archetypal life, or in his character's terms: 'J'ai vécu au pluriel.'[17] Similarly, in an interview Bourboune explained: 'Je n'ai d'admiration que pour ceux qui ont su vivre au pluriel [. . .] qui n'ont pas cherché leur seul accomplissement mais qui ont été un point de cristallisation, un drapeau, et qui ont finalement obligé ceux qui les entouraient à être presque aussi grands qu'eux.'[18]

Mourad Bourboune's writings have been less influential than those of Rachid Boudjedra. La Répudiation, in particular, stirred up lively debate. The narrator describes to his French mistress his childhood ('une enfance saccagée'), in particular his father's rejection of his mother, his remarriage to a much younger woman (who becomes his son's lover), and the oppressiveness of the family from which his homosexual brother seeks to escape—and becomes an alcoholic. Algerian history relates symbolically to family relationships. For example his father's rejection of his mother symbolizes the removal of the people from power and the country's abandonment of a revolutionary programme. The text is closely autobiographical: 'dans la mesure où j'ai eu personnellement des problèmes avec mon père quand il a répudié ma mère. J'en ai énormément souffert. Mon père a épousé trois femmes. J'ai une vingtaine de frères et sœurs.'[19]

The family and particularly the rejection of the traditional patriarchal structure is central to Boudjedra's next novel, L'Insolation (1972). Eroticism, ritual violence, and madness all contribute to a sense of revolt and rejection of codes of behaviour. These play an important part in his later novels: Topographie idéale pour une agression caracterisée (1975), L'Escargot entêté (1977), Les 1001 années de la nostalgie (1979), Le Vainqueur de coupe (1981), Le Démantèlement (1982), La Macération (1985). The last two are translated into French from Arabic. Topographie is about an Algerian immigrant in Paris; L'Escargot entêté is about a maniacal bureaucrat; Les 1001 années is a mythical celebration of woman as a means to the rediscovery of a

---

[16] Quoted in J.-L. Joubert et al. (eds.), Les Littératures francophones, 195.
[17] Quoted by Déjeux, Littératures maghrébines, 362.
[18] Le Peuple; quoted ibid. 364.   [19] Déjeux, Littératures maghrébines, 382.

lost identity; *Le Vainqueur* is a textual puzzle about the preparations for an assassination by a nationalist Algerian militant.

Less controversial, but no less influential, are the works of Nabile Farès. Not immediately accessible and apparently more concerned with individual experience, Farès's first novel, *Yahia, pas de chance* (1970), charts the development of an adolescent, his nostalgia for childhood experience—closeness to nature—and the challenge of participating in revolution. The differences between childhood and adult experience, and the problems of identity to which this gives rise (and it is these which constitute the central tension of the novel) are replaced in later works by the tension between loyalty to the homeland and exile. Identity is sought in the past, and access to the past sought by means of incantatory language; possibilities are proposed for the future, cultural differences between places suggest further possibilities. But Farès's writing does not offer easy solutions. His texts are complex and poetically dense. Writing is a quest, not the transcription of truths. Narrative discontinuity and textual pastiche are the formal corollories of this. *Un Passager de l'occident* (1971) and his trilogy *La Découverte du Nouveau Monde*, constituted by *Le Champ d'oliviers* (1972), *Mémoires de l'absent* (1974), *L'Exil et le désarroi* (1976), propose a chaos, a disorder from which coherence can only temporarily be wrested. The notion of identity which emerges from these writings is one of constant metamorphosis; identity is reactive, problematic, provisional. Myth and legend, elemental imagery, that of earth, air, fire, and water, participate in Farès's complex texts suggesting the power of pagan, pre-Islamic structures. Central to his later works, *La Mort de Salah Baye* (1980), *L'État perdu* (1982), is the experience of emigration and exile.

Farès's move from a more personal writing to texts in which the central tension is between home and exile, is similar to the itinerary of Assia Djebar. One of the first Algerian women to write and be heard, Djebar is an important figurehead. She was born in Cherchell, and educated in Blida, Algiers, and Paris. For part of the Algerian war she lived in Tunis; she taught history at the University of Algiers before leaving for Paris.

Her first work, *La Soif* (1957), is a psychological novel, clearly influenced by Françoise Sagan (*Bonjour Tristesse* in particular). Although set in Algeria, Djebar's text is curiously silent when it comes to contemporary historical and political circumstance. It is concerned above all with a young Algerian woman's emancipation as an individual. Djebar was only 20 when the novel was published.

Her second novel, *Les Impatients* (1958), was equally poorly received by Algerian critics largely because of its focus on the cultural problems of a bourgeois family and its growing alienation from tradition. Her third work, *Les Enfants du nouveau monde* (1962), however, is a vast canvas of the Algerian War. More conventional in formal terms than her later works, her concern is for people, and particularly women, and their response to historical circumstance. Similarly, in *Les Alouettes naïves* (1967) it is women's experience, and more importantly women's speech, which she is concerned to transcribe. What matters is the way experience is *told*; it is *la parole féminine* which reveals how women's experience is constructed and thus direct speech constitutes an important part of the text. In the texts which make up *Femmes d'Alger dans leur appartement* (1980), women's conversations, often conversations of a 'mundane' sort, are most of the text. A concern to articulate individual experience—and often autobiographical experience—has gradually been replaced by a desire to give voice to Algerian women who are not in a position to speak. The title of the 1980 collection, that of Delacroix's famous painting of the harem, draws attention to the inability of traditional Muslim women to speak (the veil impedes speech) and to look (beyond the confines of the harem). Assia Djebar's later work does not seek to *interpret* other women's experience, but to allow other women to be heard. This explains her involvement in the audiovisual medium. Her footage *La Nouba des femmes du mont Chenova* won considerable acclaim at the Venice Film Festival in 1979. A similar desire to make heard a *parole féminine* is discernible in her translation work. She has collaborated with a number of contemporary Arabic women writers, most notably the Egyptian, Nawal Saadaoui.

Djebar's most difficult work, *L'Amour la fantasia*, was published in 1985. In part autobiography, it interweaves fragments of Algerian history, seen from a French colonial perspective. Language—in the sense of both *langue* and *langage*—is a central concern. The quest which the text undertakes is for an authentic *parole féminine*, one which articulates Algerian women's experience through the generations. The central paradox which Djebar experiences as a writer and which is dramatized in the written text, concerns the language ('tongue') in which she writes. French has liberated her from the oppression which she associates with Arabic languages and cultures while at the same time severing a tie, an umbilical cord, binding her to previous generations of Algerian women. The imagery which expresses much of this is exclusively concerned with women's experience: 'je recherche, comme un lait dont on m'aurait autrefois écartée, la pléthore amoureuse de la langue de ma mère'.[20] Later in the same text she writes:

Après plus d'un siècle d'occupation française—qui finit, il y a peu, par un écharnement—un territoire de langue subsiste entre deux peuples, entre deux memoires; la langue française, corps et voix, s'installe en moi comme un orgueilleux préside, tandis que la langue maternelle, toute en oralité, en hardes dépenaillées, résiste et attaque, entre deux essoufflements [. . .] Je suis à la fois l'assiégé étranger et l'autochtone partant à la mort par bravade, illusoire effervescence du dire et de l'écrit.

Her 'autobiography' is *de facto* linguistically preoccupied: 'La langue encore coagulée des Autres m'a envelopée, dès l'enfance, en tunique de Nessus, don d'amour de mon père qui, chaque matin, me tenait par la main sur le chemin de l'école. Fillette arabe, dans un village du Sahel algérien.'[21]

Writing by Algerian women distinguishes itself from much recent writing by Algerian men. Works by Djamila Debèche (*Aziza*, 1955), Zoubida Bittari (*O mes sœurs musulmanes, pleurez!*, 1964), and more recently by Aïcha Lemsine and Yamina Mechakra, can be most obviously characterized by their autobiographical preoccupations and concern to write women's history. One of the earliest Algerian (and North African) women writers is Marguerite Taos Amrouche. Her first novel, *Jacinthe noire*, was published in 1957. She was equally concerned, as was Assia Djebar, to act as the spokeswoman for a silent group whose words and worlds might otherwise be lost. Often using her mother as her source, she recorded a large number of Berber songs. She died in Paris in 1976.

The 'documentary' concerns of Algerian women writers have often been used as evidence of a 'literary' weakness. Bouraoui and Brahimi write condescendingly: 'Ces femmes . . . ne *dépassent* pas, dans un premier récit à caractère souvent autobiographique, *le témoignage sociologique*. Celui-ci, *toutefois*, après que des siècles de tradition ont étouffé la parole féminine, nous est précieux.'[22]

It is, not surprisingly, the contemporary Algerian reality which

---

[20] Assia Djebar, *L'Amour, la Fantasia*, 76.
[21] Assia Djebar, ibid. 241 and 243 respectively.
[22] H. Bouraoui and D. Brahimi, in J.-P. de Beaumarchais, D. Conty, A. Rey (eds.), *Dictionnaire des littératures de langue francaise* (3 vols.; Bordas, 1984), 1353; see also Flora Van Houwelingen, 'Francophone Literature in North Africa', in Mineke Schipper (ed.), *Unheard Words: Women and Literature in Africa, the Arab World, Asia, the Caribbean and Latin America*, trans. Barbara Potter Fasting (London, 1985), 102–13.

writers of the 1980s have sought to explore. Emigration and exile is the other major preoccupation. The density and historical strata of Algerian experience are the concern of Tahar Djaout's *Chercheurs d'os* (1984), as the title suggests. It tells of a young man's search for the body of his brother, a victim of the Algerian war. He hopes to bring his brother home to their native village. The journey he undertakes is not only a journey in space but also in time, as he uncovers layers of Algerian history. He is also brought face to face with the realities of contemporary Algeria.

The violence visible in earlier post-war fiction is still very apparent in more recent works, notably those of Rachid Mimouni (*Le Printemps n'en sera que plus beau*, 1978; *Le Fleuve détourné*, 1982, and *Tombeza*, 1984). In the last and the most horrifying, the protagonist is deformed physically and spiritually. Born of a mother who was raped and then rejected by her family, the hero is a monstrous, utterly immoral or amoral figure who attains power through brutish determination. Like many novels of the 1980s, the hero of *Le Fleuve détourné* is displaced: a veteran of the war, presumed dead, returns to his village but can no longer recognize it. The protagonists of Azzedine's novels similarly find themselves *en marge*. The hero of *Les Bandits de l'Atlas* (1983), as its title suggests, is an *hors-la-loi*; the hero of *Les Lions de la nuit* (1985) is a revolutionary preparing for the 1954 uprising. What Azzedine has sought to write is a French which suggests the simplicity or purity of the language of the *fellahs* and the wisdom of ancient Berber tradition which is inseparable from it.

The accessibility of Azzedine's writing marks it out from much of the writing of post-war Algeria. Novels by writers such as A. Meddeb (*Talismano*, 1978), Yamina Mechakra (*La Grotte éclatée*, 1979), Mustapha Tlili (*La Rage aux tripes*, 1975; *Le Bruit dort*, 1978), Mina Boumedine (*L'Oiseau dans la main*, 1973), and Zoulika Boukortt (*Le Corps en pièces*, 1977) are formally and stylistically complex. Techniques exploited by earlier writers are borrowed and developed: narrative discontinuity and textual pastiche; pattern dependent on recurring imagery replacing structure dependent on narrative temporal progression; the dissolution of individual 'character'.

Just as there are those who believe that Algerian writers have a responsibility to write more accessible texts if they are to achieve what is generally posited as their aim, to transform Algeria, so two groups of poets writing after the war can be identified: those whose militancy translates into a simple and direct poetic utterance, and those whose texts are in some sense exploratory, which seek to communicate something *inoui*. Rachid Boudjedra belongs within the first group. The following lines are a literary-historical commonplace: 'La réalité on ne crache pas dessus | On la transforme'. The diction belongs to a colloquial register and the word-order suggests the conversational: 'La réalité? On ne crache pas dessus'.

Equally straightforward is the patriotic poetry fostered by the journal *Promesses*, published after the war by the Ministère Algérien de l'information et de la culture. Mostefa Lacheraf has denounced the 'nationalisme anachronique' and the 'mythes inhibiteurs' of much of this poetry. The simplicity of the poems collected by Jean Sénac (*Anthologie de la nouvelle poésie algérienne*, 1971) is very different.

For Malek Alloula, Algerian poetry is dominated by demagogues. His texts refuse immediate generic identification and are typographically disorientating (in their lack of punctuation, for example). They also extrapolate contemporary concerns for modern mythologies. *Villes et autres lieux* (1979) is in a tradition inaugurated by Walter Benjamin and explores the notion of the modern city.

Situated between the simplicity of the militant poetry of the 1960s and the often obscure poetry of the 1970s, are the linguistically straightforward but poetically dense texts of Mohammed Dib, for example (*Ombre gardienne*, 1961; *Formulaires*, 1970; *Omneros*, 1975, *Feu beau feu*, 1979; *O Vive*, 1987). Dib's later novels, as Charles Bonn points out, are relatively unknown. This he sees as part of a function of a problem inherent in much recent writing from the Maghreb. The difficulty is to do with the absence of what some critics have called 'territoriality'. Just as few critics considered Driss Chraïbi's *Un Ami viendra vous voir* (1967) and *Mort au Canada* (1975) simply because the action does not take place in North Africa, so Mohammed Dib's early trilogy tends to attract far more attention than his later novels (which include *La Danse du Roi*, 1968; *Dieu en Barbarie*, 1970; *Le Maître de chasse*, 1973; *Habel*, 1977; *Les Terrasses d'Orsol*, 1985; *Le Désert sans détour*, 1992). 'Avec *Habel*', Bonn writes, 'l'exil de la parole rejoindra celui, géographique, du lieu (Paris).' Bonn sees the deterritorialization of francophone North African literature, in the case of such writers as Dib as, simultaneously, marginalizing:

C'est en assumant mieux que tout autre cette marge constitutive de l'expérience littéraire en ce qu'elle a de plus affolant que Mohammed Dib est devenu l'écrivain maghrébin le plus grand, mais aussi le plus mal lu: le lieu depuis lequel s'énonce la parole littéraire est innomable. Il est cette 'rive sauvage' qu'annonçait dès 1964 le titre de son roman le plus déconcertant de l'époque. Il est ce 'rien' vertigineux qui récuse toute localisation géographique ou sémantique prédéfinie.[23]

The 'emigration' and 'wandering' of the francophone North African text presents formidable problems for literary historians and critics who seek to define corpuses of texts. What, for example, is the nature of the relationship between Dib's texts and one such as the contemporary French writer Michel Tournier's *La Goutte d'or*? In the latter's text Arabic calligraphy is the central topos which functions as a metaphor for writing, for example.

A further body of texts to which Dib's writing is related is constituted by *beur* literature: writing by second-generation North Africans living in France. Writers such as Nacer Ketanne (*Le Sourire de Brahim*, 1985) and Leïla Sebbar who is half Algerian and half French (although born in Algeria) and therefore not *beur* (*Fatima ou les algériennes au square*, 1981; *Shérazade, 17 ans, brune, frisée, les yeux verts*, 1984), are principally concerned to make the lives of *beurs* the stuff of their fiction. Sebbar, like Assia Djebar, has become increasingly preoccupied by the inability experienced by most members of the immigrant community to make themselves heard and in *Parle mon fils parle à ta mère* (1984) assumes the role of scribe and spokeswoman.

---

[23] Charles Bonn, 'Le Voyage innommable et le lieu du dire: émigration et errance de l'écriture maghrébine francophone', *Revue de littérature comparée*, 1 (1994), 48–59 (p. 59).

9

MOROCCO

THAT a francophone literature emerged both later and less prolifically in Morocco than was the case in Algeria can be explained by a number of differences between the two countries, in particular their relationships with France. The French colonial, and more specifically cultural, influence in Morocco was less marked. Nor was there a significant French colonial literature or body of texts written by Frenchmen *about* Morocco, on which Moroccan writers could draw, or against which they could write, re-forming the Moroccan and the country in a different image. The only notable writers who wrote about Morocco were Maurice Le Glay and François Bonjean. As a French protectorate (1912–56) the indigenous cultures of Morocco were less systematically undermined or destroyed than those of Algeria under French rule. A Berber literary tradition and a secular Arabic tradition survived the period of French occupation.

The advent of Moroccan writing in French can in part be explained by the censorship imposed by the Moroccan state after independence. The case of Mohamed Choukri's autobiography is exemplary and celebrated. Arab publishing houses were unwilling to accept it and it was only in its English adaptation by Paul Bowles that it appeared in print in 1973. The French version, *Le Pain nu* became well-known because it was translated by one of North Africa's best-known and most controversial writers, Tahar Ben Jelloun.

The most important event in the literary history of French writing in Morocco was the founding of the review *Souffles* which allowed Moroccans to become self-conscious in terms of their status as francophone Moroccan writers and to see their writing as constitutive of a francophone Moroccan literature. The figures grouped around the review included Abdellatif Laâbi, the journal's founder, Mohammed Khaïr-Eddine, Abdelkebir Khatibi, Mostafa Nissaboury, and Tahar Ben Jelloun.

The influence of *Souffles* went beyond Morocco itself, altering perceptions throughout the Maghreb. From the beginning Arabic was advocated as the appropriate language of Moroccan literature:

Faut-il l'avouer, cette littérature [en français] ne nous concerne plus qu'en partie, de toute façon, elle n'arrive guère à répondre à notre besoin d'une littérature portant le poids de nos réalités actuelles, des problématiques toutes nouvelles en face desquelles un désarroi et une sauvage révolte nous poignent.[1]

The shift away from writing in French to writing in Arabic has not been as marked as *Souffles* speculated. The nature of writing in French has, however, been quite as revolutionary as the journal projected. The French language, or forms of French, and the genres and conventions of French writing have been fundamentally violated. This, for many, constitutes a more fundamental rejection of the language and culture of France than the use of Arabic. For some who advocate an exclusively Arab Moroccan literature, anything written in what is recognizably a French language belongs not to the literature of Morocco but to the literature of France.

Souffles was concerned not only to debate the future of the country's literature but also to examine and assess the significance of what had so far been written, to propose certain definitions and structures in order to make sense of the founding texts of Moroccan literature. Some texts were denounced as 'folklorique'. Ahmed Sefrioui's tales, for example, *Le Chapelet d'ambre* (1949) and his novel *La Boîte à merveilles* (1954) were seen to belong to writing which was primarily 'ethnographique'. Laâbi was to write à *propos* of this kind of text: 'Elles ne dérangeaient rien. Elles décrivaient une vie quotidienne en hibernation, s'y complaisaient, des *états d'âmes* qu'appréciait beaucoup le public étranger friand d'exotisme et d'orientalisme.'[2] Driss Chraïbi's texts were very differently received. Published in the same year as Sefrioui's novel, Chraïbi's *Le Passé simple* denounces the repressiveness of tradition and the abuse of authority vested largely in the protagonist's father. In his preface to a later novel, *L'Âne*, Chraïbi described the revolt of *Le Passé simple* as

---

[1] J.-L. Joubert *et al.* (eds.), *Les Littératures francophones depuis 1945* (1986), 206.
[2] *Souffles*, 5 (1967), 19.

against the 'sclérose et l'étroitesse de la haute bourgeoisie musulmane traditionnelle'.[3]

Born in 1926 in El Jadida, he was educated at a Koranic school until the age of 10 when he was admitted to the Lycée Lyautey in Casablanca. In 1945 he left Morocco to complete his formal education in Paris where he received his *diplôme d'ingénieur-chimiste*. Shortly before qualifying for a *doctorat dès sciences* he abandoned his studies having lost faith in the methods and purpose of science. In a later novel, *Succession ouverte*, the protagonist comes to a moment of revelation which is in part clearly autobiographical: 'jamais, jamais plus je n'irai à la recherche de cerveaux de vérités écrites, de vérités synthétiques, d'assemblages d'idées hybrides qui n'étaient rien que des idées'.[4] He then travelled widely in Europe and Israel, employed in jobs ranging from night watchman to chemical engineer. His interest in journalism finally culminated in a post at ORTF where he produced a wide range of programmes on topics such as theatre (African and Near Eastern), and on Arab relations with the West. He also wrote plays for ORTF (*Le Roi du monde, La Greffe et les quatre malles*).

Authority and the institutions which give it licence is central to Chraïbi's life and writing: *Les Boucs* (1955), *L'Âne* (1956), *De tous les horizons* (1960), *La Foule* (1961), *Succession ouverte* (1962), *Un Ami viendra vous voir* (1967), *La Civilisation, ma mère!* (1972), *Mort du Canada* (1975), *Une Enquête au pays* (1981), *La Mère au printemps* (1982). In *Le Passé simple* authority is vested in 'le Seigneur', the protagonist's father, and the rebellion which takes place is essentially against the father-figure. The controversy which followed the publication of the novel was as violent as the work itself. The discourses of the two were also similar. Chraïbi was called, for example, a 'bâtard de la pensée'.[5]

The sadomasochism of *Le Passé simple* also dominates *Les Boucs*. Here it is the lives of migrant North African workers in Europe who are at the centre of the novel and it is the society which exploits them which represents the authority against which revolt must take place. Chraïbi's first work denounced the injustices of his home country, the Arab world; his second denounces the West.

Chraïbi's fourth novel, *Succession ouverte* (1962) forms a sequel to *Le Passé simple*. The protagonist hears of the death of his father, 'le

---

[3] Chraïbi, preface to *L'Âne*.   [4] Chraïbi, *Succession ouverte* (1962), 79.
[5] *Démocratie*, 14 Jan. 1957; quoted by Jean Déjeux, *Littérature maghrébine* (Montreal, 1973), 280.

Seigneur' and returns home. But once again he feels the stifling pressures to conform and leaves again for Europe.

Un Ami viendra vous voir (1967) foregrounds what is present but not central to earlier writing: problems specific to women and the forces which contribute to the creation and maintenance of stereotypes, the power of advertising in particular.

In *Une Enquête au pays* (1981) a police investigation takes place, conducted by a Police chief and his Inspector, Ali, in a Berber village in the Atlas mountains. What is revealed are the ways and customs of the people; it is the detail which matters here. Much the same is true of *La Mère du printemps* (1982), an account of the arrival of Islam in Morocco in the year 681. It is the subtle balance of the novel, which conjures up the grandeur of Islam while at the same time mourning the destruction of Berber tradition which accompanied its arrival in the country.

Chraïbi's war against authority finds a corollary in his rejection of conventional and easily accessible forms of writing. His style is often fragmentary and many of his techniques are similar to those of the *nouveau roman*, for example.

A contemporary of Chraïbi, Mohammed Aziz Lahbabi (born in Fez in 1922) has been equally influential in Morocco and further afield. His work has above all been concerned with the nature of the North African personality. His *thèse d'état, De l'Être à la personne* was published by PUF in 1953. Influenced by Bergson and Mounier, his ideas take fuller shape in *Le Personnalisme musulman* (1964). His concern with national culture is visible in his founding of the group Union des écrivains du Maghreb arabe, the Arab review *Afaq*, and his essay *Du Clos à l'ouvert, vingt propos sur les cultures nationales et la civilisation humaine*, published, significantly, in Morocco (1961). He has also published collections of poetry and an anthology, *Florilège poétique arabe et berbère* (1964), later entitled *Douleurs rythmées*. In addition to works written in French, Lahbabi has produced a number of works in Arabic, published in Morocco and the Near East. Admired for his lack of dogma, he has been concerned, above all, to promote openness, both intellectual and practical, and to foster dialogue as a means to understand and respect diverse cultures.

Most francophone Moroccan writers (some of those already discussed are the exceptions) can be viewed as belonging, at least at some stage in their writing career, to the group associated with *Souffles*. What the journal denounced, most importantly, was the universal humanism proposed by Western European discourse. Influenced by such writers as Frantz Fanon, they publicized the Eurocentrism which this disguised. What they committed themselves to was the reconstruction of a national culture.

Originally published only in French, *Souffles* became bilingual in 1968 and also more overtly politically, rather than broadly culturally, concerned. The name of the journal then changed to *Anfas* and was published exclusively in Arabic. In 1972 the review was banned and Abdellatif Laâbi and Abraham Serfaty were considered the appropriate editors to imprison. Much of the discourse of the review whilst published wholly or partly in French, associates the overthrow of a stifling bourgeois Moroccan ideology with the rejection of conventional literary language and forms.

Mostafa Nissaboury's poems (*Plus haute mémoire*, 1968, and *La Mille et deuxième nuit*, 1975) recreate the barrenness of the cultural and spiritual present through the evocation of once rich images of the ancestral past, now deformed and defiled.

For Laâbi, writing is initially both violent, and physical: 'La naissance d'un poème est d'abord pour moi le moment d'étourdissement qui suit une collision. Une collision brutale, avec coupe et blessures, sang, sécrétions, cris, courses, piétinements, mais aussi étincelles, visions chevauchant l'espace-temps.'[6] In *Le Règne de barbarie* a similar description occurs:

> entendez le choc des idiomes
> > dans ma bouche
> la soif des naissances
> entendez le clapotis des sueurs
> > sous mes aisselles
> la course des biceps
> poussé de ma faune intérieure
> > bonds de cavernes
> plume ensanglantée
> > ma tête sur chaque muraille.[7]

Laâbi uses the term 'itinéraire' to describe a written text which transgresses the laws and limits of genre and linguistic convention. His first substantial publication, *L'Œil et la nuit* is described as a 'roman itinéraire'; *Le Règne de barbarie* is similar in its juxtaposition of fragments conventionally associated with different genres: prose poem, poetry, dialogue. Register is similarly mixed.

---

[6] Joubert *et al.* (eds.), *Littératures francophones*, 209.
[7] Laâbi, *Le Règne de la barbarie* (1976), 25.

During his eight years in prison, Laâbi continued to write. *Sous le baillon, le poème*, a collection of poems, was published in 1981, the year after his release. *Le Chemin des ordalies* (1982) is an account of his years in captivity. *Chroniques de la citadelle d'exil* (1983) is a collection of his prison correspondence, not always in conventional letter form. In one of his letters to his wife (12 May 1974) he expresses the central problem faced by all writers but exacerbated by the circumstances in which Laâbi found himself: 'Comment il est difficile d'être poète, c'est-à-dire d'être soi-même, de proposer aux autres une autre forme de compréhension d'eux-mêmes sans leur devenir étranger ou paraître à leurs yeux comme un imposteur?'[8]

Mohammed Khaïr-Eddine is probably the best-known and most notorious writer to have been associated with *Souffles*. His first work, *Agadir*, was published by Seuil in 1967 and, very appropriately, won the Prix 'Enfants terribles', established by Jean Cocteau.

Khaïr-Eddine's family originated in Tafraout in southern Morocco but he was brought up largely in Casablanca. Like Kateb Yacine he was much influenced by Rimbaud. Poems sung by the Egyptian poet, Mohammed Abdulwahab, also made a formative impression. As a young man he went to work in Agadir as a civil servant following an earthquake in which many died; many moved away immediately following the tremor, having lost everything. Part of the difficulty of Khaïr-Eddine's job was establishing who still lived in the area. This experience was later to be part of his text, *Agadir*. In 1965 he left for France and worked in miserable conditions as a labourer in Gennevilliers, outside Paris.

In an article in *Souffles*, Khaïr-Eddine expressed his commitment to a 'littérature sauvage': 'Si la littérature véritable est une remise en cause de toute littérature, elle ne peut être alors que sous la forme d'une subversion à la fois violente et controlée; ceci a été bien compris par les nouvelles promotions des écrivains maghrébins d'expression française.'[9]

His own writing, which includes *Corps négatif* (1968), *Moi l'aigre* (1970), *Le Déterreur* (1973), *Une Odeur de manteque* (1976), *Une Vie, un rêve, un peuple toujours errant* (1978), stages a rebellion against authority (God, the State), and transgresses the conventions of language and form. Khaïr-Eddine describes his approach as 'une guérilla linguistique'. His texts refuse simple categorization; they are an

[8] Joubert *et al.* (eds.), *Littératures francophones*, 210.
[9] Quoted by Déjeux, *Littérature maghrébine*, 409.

amalgam of journalistic report, poetry (of various kinds), and historical, philosophical, or political essay. Laâbi describes the resultant writing, and the ways in which the reader is obliged to read it, thus: 'l'écriture secrète une nouvelle logique d'approche et de perception, de consommation et de restitution du réel [. . .] La lecture est une véritable participation incluant la haine, l'amour, le dégoût, la mutation, la transformation, sans que la lucidité n'en soit pourtant exclue.'[10]

Abdelkebir Khatibi, also an influential member of the group associated with *Souffles*, published his first important text, *La Mémoire tatouée*, in 1971. The tattoo is an important figure in francophone Maghrebi writing and represents a nexus where text and body, calligraphic and corporal, deformation and decoration, meet. Khatibi's well-known gloss on the text is a succinct one:

Comment ai-je délimité le champ autobiographique? En démobilisant l'anecdote et le fait divers en soi, tout en dirigeant mon regard vers les thèmes (philosophiques) de ma prédilection: identité et différence quant à l'Être et au Désert, simulacre de l'origine, blessure destinale entre l'Orient et l'Occident. À l'avant-scène (historique), la question de la maîtrise, de la colonisation et de la décolonisation, dont j'ai vécu de près quelques événements sanglants: bref, comment devient-on un eunuque humilié de l'histoire.

Chemin faisant, une rage intempestive a fait tout vaciller: d'où ce texte, image délabrée d'un tombeau vide. Ce délabrement gardera pour moi la signature d'un mort, d'un adolescent mort.

Et j'aurai jalousement retenu mon être sacrifié à la langue française.[11]

If identity depends on memory, then, as the title of the text suggests, creating/writing/fixing identity in language is a central concern. Oppositions and differences serve as markers: physical/metaphysical, colonizer/colonized, East/West, self/other, female/male.

Vomito blanco (1974) is an essay on the Palestinian question in which religious and racial differences are explored. Khatibi's early interest in semiology is more obviously apparent in *La Blessure du nom propre* (1974). Here the function of signs in koranic belief systems is analysed. *Le Lutteur de classe à la manière taoiste* (1976) uses Taoist, often paradoxical, aphorisms to oppose the dogma of much Arab theological and ideological discourse.

---

[10] *Souffles*, 13/14 (1969).

[11] Khatibi, 'Palimpseste', introduction to later edn. of *La Mémoire tatouée*, quoted by Joubert *et al.* (eds.), *Littératures francophones*, 213.

The titles of *Le Livre du sang* (1979) and *Amour bilingue* rightly suggest the preoccupations of *La Mémoire tatouée*. In the later works it is language or writing and the body or eroticism which reassert themselves as major concerns. Androgyny and incest are associated with textual bilingualism.

In *Un Passager de l'Occident*, Nabile Farès, the Algerian writer, had written: 'Après la décolonisation française de l'Algérie viendra la décolonisation islamique de l'Algérie.' But it was Khatibi, in *Maghreb pluriel* (1983), who proposed deconstruction as a philosophical equivalent of decolonization. For Khatibi and Farès among many, a new culture and society in Maghrebi Africa is conceivable only if decolonization from both Western imperialism and its concomitant idealist metaphysics, and from post-colonial or neo-colonial Maghrebi society which Khatibi characterizes as the area's theological, charismatic, and patriarchal patrimony is achieved. What is proposed by Khatibi (and Abdallah Bounfour) is 'le savoir/la raison orphelin(e)': 'Qu'est-ce que la raison orpheline sinon le refus pratique de l'ethnocide . . . et de l'ethnocentrisme. Vigilance face à toute légitimité originelle.'[12] In *Maghreb pluriel*, Khatibi argues that although a superficial decolonization has taken place, the Maghreb has failed to posit a fundamentally critical discourse which challenges ethnocentrism and imperialism. 'Decolonization of the mind' or 'philosophical decolonization' has still to take place. It is in Derridean deconstruction that Khatibi and a number of other Third World writers have discovered a philosophical equivalent to decolonization.

Khatibi, like Derrida, questions the metaphysical concept of an absolute origin which legitimates identity, meaning, or truth. For the supposedly 'absolute guarantor' or 'universal underwriter' is held to be no more than an ideological invention employed in order to justify a particular practice. Khatibi uses the example of the 'barbarization of the Other', 'barbaros', whereby we attribute to the 'nature' of the Other what is in fact no more than the result of cultural near-sightedness; what is different from ourselves we make inferior. Having rendered the Other 'barbaric', we make legitimate the civilizing mission of colonialism. Identity and meaning are made valid by relegating the unfamiliar and heterogeneous to a position beyond the limits controlled by ideas of origin, unity, homogeneity,

[12] Quoted by D. Marx-Scouras, 'The Poetics of Maghrebine Illegitimacy', *L'Esprit Créateur* 26/1 (1986), 3–10 (p. 5).

and legitimacy. Yet our constant effort to keep the unfamiliar and other beyond these limits is, in a sense, self-defeating. Khatibi recognizes the flimsiness of the separation between inside and outside, same and other. The peculiar status of identity and meaning is related to their dependency on precisely that which is alienated, namely otherness and absence.

Khatibi also attempts to deconstruct the metaphysical premises of generally accepted theories of decolonization. He begins with Fanon's famous appeal to the Third World: 'Allons, camarades, le jeu européen est définitivement terminé, il faut trouver autre chose.' Within the Same–Other dialectic which Fanon proposes, Khatibi suggests that decolonization is the rejection of the colonizing power and one which will supposedly allow the colonized to resume a complete identity defined by something other than the Other. Khatibi recognizes that what is outside and other is *always* present as an inescapable difference to be acknowledged. As Bounfour warns: 'Toute problématique culturelle qui ne remet pas en question la notion d'unité est une problématique ethnocentriste et par conséquent oppressive de tout ce qui se trouve hors d'elle ou à son horizon.'[13] Khatibi is equally interested in what is on the horizon. His purpose in *Maghreb pluriel* is to de-centre, and the Maghreb itself becomes a 'horizon of thought' in relation to ideas of difference and deviation.

In more immediately literary terms, this translates into a particular attitude to the use of French. In *Le Monde* Khatibi claimed that what was important was to:

Briser la syntaxe de la langue française, de rendre celle-ci étrangère à elle-même, tout en introduisant dans ce mouvement critique une parole proprement politique. Et entre ces deux mouvements se glisse un jeu incantatoire qui rappelle fort bien son origine sacrale: le Coran. On a affaire à une espèce de Dieu devoyé qui écrit en versets 'fanoniens'.[14]

There are interesting parallels and differences between Khatibi's project and that of Tahar Ben Jelloun. Born in Fez in 1944, Tahar Ben Jelloun has become one of the best-known North African intellectuals outside the Maghreb. He studied philosophy before training as a teacher and then as a *psycho-sociologue*. At the beginning of his writing career he contributed to *Souffles* and *Intégral*. His first collec-

---

[13] Abdallah Bounfour, 'La raison orpheline', *Les Temps modernes*, 33/375 (1977), 420–32 (p. 421).

[14] *Le Monde*, 17 Dec. 1971.

tion of poems, *Hommes sous linceul de silence* was published in Casablanca in 1971; his second in Paris in 1972. His texts, *Harrouda* (1973), *La Réclusion solitaire* (1976), and *Moha le fou, Moha le sage* (1978), do not belong neatly within generic types or modes. *Harrouda*, a *roman poème* is an amalgam of fragments of text, some belonging to a realistic mode, others a fantastic mode. He has written of the 'irréalisme de l'écriture'. Despite the absence of linear chronology and the text's polymorphism, a central narrative dominates, concerning the character of a prostitute who haunts the collective memory of the people, in particular the urban dwellers of Fass, the transcription of the Arab name for Fez and Tangiers. A semiotic system similar to that of Khatibi emerges. Tattoos, scars, circumcision, and sexual signs have to be 'read' according to what Ben Jelloun describes as a 'lecture déviée' (deviant reading). Deformation of the body, as in Boudjedra's writings, prompts questions about the nature of individual identity and change. The text does not describe the city, it 'reads' the city:

La lecture de Fass devient perte de mots et de pierres. La phrase est une rue tracée au hasard de l'histoire. On traverse la ville en utilisant quelques petits chemins empruntant au langage quelques périphrases. Le texte s'absente. La ville se retire. Les murs voyagent. Rien ne s'accumule. Page du ciel transparent. Les quartiers se superposent sur écran de soleil. Ils disparaissent dans un magma de textes vagues.[15]

The dominant narrative of *La Réclusion* concerns immigrant workers and the forms of violence to which they are subjected. *Moha le fou* uses the popular figure of Moha who opposes the injustices of persecution, torture, repression.

In Tahar Ben Jelloun's later writing, myth and the aleatory play a larger role. Reminiscent of the structure and style of writing of Borges, *L'Enfant du sable* is a strange fable: it is pronounced that Hadj Ahmed's eighth daughter is a boy. She will therefore be brought up as a boy, dressed as a boy, and married to a woman. As in much francophone North African writing during the last decade, the concepts of identity and gender are central. Another obvious example is Abdelhak Serhane's novel, *Messaouda*, published in 1983. The authoritarianism of the protagonist's father, the latter's treatment of his wife, and the former's sexual preoccupations are central concerns of the novel.

In addition to the major writers discussed above, mention should

---

[15] Joubert *et al.* (eds.), *Littératures francophones*, 215.

be made of the poets Mohammed Loakira, Abdallah Bounfour, Mohammed Alaoui Belrhiti, Zaghloul Morsy. Notable too are the writings of Edmond Amran El Maleh (*Parcours immobile*, 1980; *Ailen ou la Nuit du récit*, 1983). He writes as a Moroccan, Jew, and Arab and is concerned with the human archaelogy of his country, uncovering the Arab, Jewish, Phoenician, and French histories of Morocco.

10

TUNISIA

B Y comparison with francophone Moroccan and particularly francophone Algerian writing, Tunisian writing in French is relatively marginal in terms of the country's literary production. The tradition of writing in Arabic was little disrupted by the French presence in Tunisia and, as a French Protectorate, teaching in Arabic continued alongside the introduction of French educational structures. Some schools, the College Sadiki most notably, taught in both languages; many, on the other hand, continued to use only Arabic.

There is, however, a French colonial tradition of writing in French. Georges Duhamel is one of the best-known French writers for whom Tunisia is the locus of much of their work. His widely read *Prince Jaffar* was published in 1946. Earlier texts were written by Charles Boussinot, Charles and Claire Genieaux, and Magali Boisnard. It was not until the second decade of this century that Tunisians first published in French. A small group of writers should be mentioned, including Salah Farhat, Mahmoud Aslan, Mustapha Kourda, Ahmed Chergui, Salah Ettri, Tahar Essafi, Mohammed Nomane.

With the accession to Independence in 1956, the tradition of bilingualism was strengthened by the Tunisian government's decision both to expand education and to teach bilingually throughout the school system. Before Independence the use of French by writers was generally viewed with suspicion. After Independence, and as the first generation of bilingually educated Tunisians emerged from the school system, the question of choice of language was viewed as less politically significant given that the nationalist debate had entered a new phase.

By and large francophone Tunisian writers have published their work abroad although some Tunisian publishers do publish in French. Given the dispersion of Tunisian writers and the large number of their publishers, it is explicable though still surprising that it was only in 1985 that an extensive bibliography (although only of francophone Tunisian poetry) became available, that accompanying Hedia Khadar's *Anthologie de la poésie tunisienne de langue française*. Anthologies such as this allow for, or testify to, the possibility of approaching francophone Tunisian writing as a single homogenous literature; literary traditions are then proposed, sense is made of texts historically. The difficulty is that the very dispersion of francophone Tunisian writers and publishers also suggests the weakness of a Tunisian tradition as there is little sense of writers themselves being familiar with a central canon.

If the broad features of francophone Tunisian poetry are sought, certain observations are likely to be made with increasing frequency and comprehensiveness as more recent poetry is considered. These include formal and linguistic innovation which result from the use of neologism, mixing of register, the inclusion of an Arabic lexis accompanied by notes and glossaries, wordplay, typographic experimentation, and the influence, manifest in a variety of ways, of other Arabic art forms including music, liturgy, and architecture.

The first francophone Tunisian poets, however, display similarities above all as a function of their concern to explore Tunisia's past, thereby contributing to nationalist concerns although their poetry is in no sense militant or recognizably within a protest tradition. Abdelmajid Tlati in *Sur les Cendres de Carthage* (1952), celebrates the beauty of the city's ruins whilst also exploring their contemporary significance and meaning. Claude Benady, notable also for his association with numerous journals, like so many other poets of his generation, celebrates Tunisia's past from outside the country, as an exile looking back in temporal terms and from a distance in space, to his homeland. This spatial and temporal distance may explain the sense of universal significance associated with his poetry (*La Couleur de la terre*, 1951; *Recommencer l'amour*, 1953; *Le Dégel des sources*, 1954): the Other, love, the natural and elemental world.

From the mid-1960s onwards the number of francophone Tunisian poets has grown significantly. Attitudes to French vary widely. Those that can only write in French often express the anguish of a linguistic exile. Those who are *choosing* between a number of languages exploit, often with a degree of defiant pragmatism, the richness and power of their linguistic position. Salah Garmadi, a trained linguist writes: 'Devant toute bouche trilingue [dialectal Arabic, literary Arabic, French] et cousue, je dis "liberté" et "crachez le morceau" en arabe classique ou parlé, en français roté ou éternué: que le mot soit et puis viendront les comptes.'[1]

Hédi Bouraoui settled in Quebec and published his first collection, *Tremblé*, in 1969 and has now produced a considerable œuvre. His poetry begins from an attitude of crisis and attempts to re-create fragments into a significant whole. The historical moment at which he is writing is always obvious in his poetry; he has described his project as one that aims 'faire sauter les barrières culturelles'.[2] Violent eroticism often participates as a liberating, possibly supracultural force.

The difficulty or alleged 'hermeticism' of Bouraoui's texts arises out of the cultural mix on which he draws (the cultural mix *he is*) and the linguistic corollaries of this. His awareness, as a North American, of the situation in Haiti explains its presence in his poems and similarly the importance and liveliness of the North American feminist debate may explain his exhortations to African women. His neologisms suggest the Creole qualities of North American English. Sometimes they are composites (*rirécrire, quoiquiétude*), sometimes puns (*haituvois—aie, tu vois*), sometimes invented verbs based on nouns. Combined with other forms of wordplay, syntactical subversions, and typographical experimentation, Bouraoui's poetry powerfully articulates the chaos of the present and its problems for the future.

Majid El Houssi settled in Italy. His writing is highly personal and emotionally charged and the pain of exile and alienation dominate the poems. These are inseparable from the fetishistic objects which are the tangible loci of emotion—relatives, flowers:

> et j'ai perdu ma feuille de menthe
> ma touffe de jasmin que je portais à
>   l'oreille droite
> le soir
> mes frères mes amis: je ne connais plus
>   leurs noms
> dans mon froid d'absence d'exil
> dans l'invincible jaillissement de la brume.[3]

His litany of loss is physical and tactile, but also cerebral, imaginative, associated with the anxiety and pain of loss of memory, when

[1] *Poésie*, 1/115, (Jan.–Feb. 1984).
[2] Jean-Louis Joubert *et al.* (eds.), *Les Littératures francophones depuis 1945* (1986), 220.   [3] Ibid. 222.

memory is all that can retain the presence of that which is distanced in space and time. The history of Tunisia, present in the name Ifriqiya, the Arabic name for Tunisia and Eastern Algeria, is also explored, in particular the ways of the country's Berber past and its stability. The past is also made present in the religious chants which are woven into his poems.

Very different is the high lyricism of the poetry of Chems Nadir, for a long time associated with the international work of UNESCO. The influence of Saint-John Perse is obvious although the latter's purity contrasts with Nadir's occasional pastiche: the classical is juxtaposed with, for example, either fantasy or the everyday. In *Astrolabe de la mer*, a collection of poetic tales, Nadir draws on oral and written Arabic traditions to explore modern identity. Léopold Sédar Senghor wrote a key preface for the collection. An important world within Nadir's literary one is Mediterranean civilization, its culture and myths, which his poetry celebrates as part of Tunisia's past. His work is not, however, exclusively concerned with distant, apparently abstract culture on a vast scale. The horror of Hiroshima, for example, and its inherent symbolism is cited in a number of poems. There is a lightness and understatement in much of the poetry of Salah Garmadi. He spent a good deal of his life in France, but also published in Tunisia (*Avec ou sans*, 1970; *Nos ancêtres les Bédouins*, 1975) which explains, in addition to the power of his writing, his influence on younger Tunisian poets. Often the paradoxical is dependent on brevity and antithesis, as in the first title mentioned above. Love, similarly, is referred to as 'l'amour présence amour absence'. Wit and irony associated with the contemporary political situation also account for the force of much of his poetry. In *Nos ancêtres les Bédouins* he writes: 'Il est formellement interdit de créer des chefs-d'œuvre et absolument obligatoire d'adorer les chefs d'Etat'.[4] His parody is also directed against the structures of the past: the institution of the French educational system and the teaching of French history, for example. But not all is light touch and wit. Many of the poems of *Nos ancêtres les Bédouins* are hard-hitting political poems which rail against injustice. There is a delight in linguistic pastiche and the parodying of figures drawn from diverse sources, including arabesque architecture, for example, in *Nos ancêtres les Bédouins*.

For Moncef Ghachem the inscription of injustice in texts is central to his poetic project. Social and political anger mixes with tender-

---

[4] 'Jeune dicton en voie de développement'; quoted ibid.

ness for those who suffer as a consequence. And his own suffering is bound up with nostalgia for the time and place of his childhood in his collection *Car vivre est un pays*, whose title exploits a figurative use which points to the inseparability of time (and experience in time) and place (and home).

S. El Goulli's poetry stands out as peculiarly personal, immersed in psychologically charged imagery dependent largely on the elemental. Violence and the disorientation of the self (expressed in the first person) dominate. Ali Hamouda, on the other hand, centres much of his poetry in a sacred woman in *Joues d'aurore* (1970), for example. The 'Terre maternelle' (one of his titles) is often the focus of the poem, the locus of an experience lost but still longed for.[5]

Whether because of his multiple allegiances (or indeed multiple acculturation) to North Africa, Judaism, and French intellectualism, which have nevertheless been contested, or because of the universal dimensions of his work, Albert Memmi remains the best-known Tunisian, if not North African, writer. He has done a great deal to encourage literary and sociological study of Tunisia, the Maghreb, and the post-colonial in general. Born in 1920 in Tunis, Memmi was educated first at a rabbinical school, then that of the Israelite Alliance, and finally the French Lycée in Tunis. Much of his own childhood is described in *La Statue de sel* (1953), his first novel. His university education started at the University of Algiers where he studied philosophy. He then went on to the Sorbonne where he took the *agrégation* in philosophy. He married a Frenchwoman and returned to teach, and to run a psycho-sociological division of the Centre de psychologie de l'enfant in Tunis. It was at this point that he started to write for, and then to edit, the literary page of the Tunisian journal *L'Action*. In 1956 he returned to Paris with his family.

In France he quickly became involved in wide-ranging, often interdisciplinary, posts and projects, almost always associated with the psychological, sociological, literary, or more broadly cultural, and these often within a colonial or post-colonial context. At Éditions Maspero he became editor of the Domaine maghrébin series devoted to North African culture. His own writings include novels, poems (later in life), essays, and articles in a wide range of

---

[5] Alain Montadon, 'De la poésie tunisienne francophone contemporaine', in *Lendemains: Études comparées sur la France*, 17 (1992), 68–74.

journals and newspapers: *l'Action, l'Arche, Cahiers internationaux de sociologie, l'Esprit, Les Lettres françaises, Les Temps modernes, Le Monde,* etc. His anthologies of North African writing, *l'Anthologie des écrivains maghrébins d'expression française* and *l'Anthologie des écrivains français du Maghreb* (1969), have been enormously influential in terms of what is generally understood as the canon of francophone Maghrebi writing and in terms of the notion of tradition bound up in this.

It is above all as a theoretician of alienation that Memmi's contribution can best be understood, although Jean Déjeux proposes 'domination' as a major preoccupation (see *Littérature maghrébine,* pp. 304 ff.). Memmi's notion of alienation is close to that of Jean-Paul Sartre and it was the latter who contributed an influential *Precédé* to Memmi's *Portrait du colonisé* (1957). The *Portrait* followed by *Portrait d'un juif* (i and ii, 1962 and 1966), *l'Homme dominé* (1966), *Juifs et Arabes* (1975). It was this last that provoked a long, bitter, but illuminating debate with the Moroccan writer Abdelkebir Khatibi.

La Statue de sel remains his best-known novel. A first-person narrative, *La Statue* recounts the story of a life from childhood to adulthood. The protagonist's experience of discovering his fundamental and 'unalterable' (the etymology is relevant) difference and the exclusion which results from this, which is the base note of the *récit*. The stages of alienation move from an original authentic self (and its spiritual, religious, and cultural allegiances) and language ('le patois tunisois') to a point of recognition that assimilation must always be problematic. The French betrayal of North Africa during the Second World War and the impossibility of being accepted in France in the way that Memmi, like so many others from the French territories, had been led to expect, induced perpetual psychological crisis, to bastardy not by birth but by assimilation: 'l'impossibilité d'être quoi que ce soit de précis pour un juif tunisien de culture française', in Albert Camus's words which were to become the preface for a later edition of 1966. The novel ends with the narrator fleeing to Argentina. This may be the novel's ending, the structure being carefully crafted, but it is clear that it is no conclusion.

Agar (1955) is also obviously and polemically autobiographical. It is about a mixed marriage and the interplay of dominance and dependence. The protagonist of the novel, a Tunisian doctor, returns to Tunis, his home city, with his wife who is a French Catholic. While the mixed marriage and the children which will issue from it represent an attempt to replace cultural alienation with cultural *métissage*, the marriage is subject to social pressures which it cannot stand. Memmi argues, in the preface to the 1963 edition, that the failure of the marriage should not lead the reader to a pessimistic interpretation of the novel: 'Loin de décrire une fatalité, *Agar* énonce en vérité les conditions d'une libération.' He describes the book as 'un essai de dévoilement des conditions négatives' of a successful mixed marriage and 'la fraternité entre les peuples'.[6]

It was not until 1969 that Memmi published his third novel, *Le Scorpion*. Here the dependence experienced by the dominant is proposed and explored in a 'confession imaginaire' which constantly questions its own language and the possibility of gaining access to the complexities of human experience through language. The protagonist, a Jew living in Tunis, undertakes to sort his brother's papers. His brother Emilio/Émile is a writer who has disappeared in mysterious circumstances. The text is made up of fragments of Emilio's writings, the narrator's discourse, and those of others (Marcel, Bina, J.H.), and includes photographs and drawings. Different levels of 'truth' are suggested and the polyphonic structure suggests the multiplicity of individual identity. Themes and characters from Memmi's earlier writing further enrich the significance of the text.

During the mid-1970s it became increasingly clear that Memmi's position *vis-à-vis* Palestine was alienating him from other North African intellectuals. His relationship with Tunisia, as a North African Jew living in Paris, is a complex one. He himself believes that Tunisia remains central to his writing but it is interesting that in a rare interview where he speaks openly about these complications, he refers to Tunisia in terms of a 'terreau' rather than a 'patrie'. Tunisia, he explained, matters in terms of both his 'inspiration' and his 'palette' (the painterly term is significant) and he adds: 'mon terreau est là, et se retrouve pratiquement dans tous mes livres'.[7]

Memmi has often emphasized the coherence of his œuvre, arguing that whether essay or fiction, the autobiographical is always crucial, the essential point of authentication of any idea: 'C'est donc ma vie, mon expérience vécue qui donne son unité à mon œuvre.'[8] This is perhaps least true of his novel *Le Désert*, published in 1977, the most historical of his texts. The novel is about Jubair Ouali El-Mammi, exiled prince and supposed author of *La Chronique du*

[6] Preface to *Agar* (1963), 16–17.

[7] Albert Memmi, *La Terre intérieure: Entretiens avec Victor Malka* (1976), 12–13.

[8] Joubert *et al.* (eds.), *Les Littératures francophones*, 226.

Royaume-du-Dedans (parts of which are included in *Le Scorpion*). The events of the story take place in the fourteenth century. The text has, in common with his other work, a concern to explore the nature of power (in terms of the group) and identity (in terms of the individual and his relationship with the group). At the end of an eventful life El-Mammi asks, at the novel's revelatory climax: 'Ai-je tenté, sérieusement, de reprendre le royaume de mon père? N'ai-je pas agi, plutôt, comme si le seul royaume à conquérir était celui de soi-même?'[9] Similarly in *Le Scorpion*, Émile, fascinated by Rousseau, writes: 'son système éducatif s'obstine à partir de l'individu seul et nu; sa vie privée même porte la marque de cette distance d'avec la société qui l'entourait, dont il aurait voulu ardemment faire partie et dont finalement il ne fut jamais' (p. 40). As Isaac Yétif, one of the most interesting commentators on Memmi, has written, all Memmi's writing could be entitled 'à la recherche d'un *moi* perdu'.[10]

Memmi's preoccupations with identity are also visible in the rare francophone Tunisian publications of the 1950s and 1960s. Hachemi Baccouche published *Ma foi demeure* in 1958, and a historical novel, *La Dame de Carthage*, in 1961. The first explores the possibility of a dual allegiance, in the post-Independence period, to Tunisia and France.

Francophone Tunisian writing which concerns the experience of North Africans living as immigrants in France can be regarded as a distinct type of writing. Many of these texts concern the lives of students or manual workers living in relative poverty, generally in urban centres. Notable examples of this kind of writing are Moncef Metoui's *Racisme, je te haïs* (1973) and Slaheddine Bhiri's *L'Espoir était pour demain* (1982).

Of the novels concerned with contemporary Tunisia which have also been published in Tunisia, Gilbert Naccache's is one of the most interesting and complex in terms of its relationship with *le vécu*. The text is a pastiche made up of a novel written while the author was in prison, an account of the experience of imprisonment, political tract, and autobiography. The last is an account of childhood and the young author's decision to stay in Tunisia whilst cultivating a marginal and critical position in terms of the dominant social, political, and cultural climate.

If Naccache's concern is above all to explore the apparent but

[9] Memmi, *Le Désert* (1977), 177.
[10] Quoted by Jean Déjeux, *Littérature maghrébine* (Montreal, 1973), 329 n.

perhaps misleading antithesis between freedom and confinement, Mustapha Tilli's concern is parallel. In *La Rage aux tripes* (1975), *Le Bruit dort* (1978), *Gloire des sables* (1982), what is central is the relationship between home and exile, between integration and alienation. In all three novels the protagonists are living in New York, apparently well-integrated into a society regarded as a *meltingpot*.[11]

While the term 'melting-pot' has entered the French language, the notion of the *bâtardise* is a French parallel. New York is the locus of 'la bâtardise'—and a city, like most, in which so many groups are in one sense or another marginal: many racial and sexual minorities of one kind or another (Blacks, Jews, homosexuals, etc.). The degree to which these novels can be read as Tunisian literature is therefore less obvious than for other francophone Tunisian texts where the locus of the action is Tunisia and the characters Tunisian. In each of Mustapha Tilli's novels, however, an event triggers a loss of balance and the hero confronts the precariousness of his supposed security in New York. In *La Rage aux tripes* the hero is an Algerian who chooses revolutionary action as the solution to his problems of identity. He leaves for Palestine. The narrator interrogates himself in the second person. Further technical interest derives from a blurring of past and present.

Le Bruit dort has two main characters, Albert Nelli, a French Jew, and Adel Safi, a Tunisian. The first, a writer, dies; writing has failed to provide solutions. Adel Safi leaves for Cambodia. In terms of form the novel has been compared to Memmi's *Le Scorpion* because of the parallels in the texts' construction. Both are composites and both are self-reflexive in their questioning of language and writing. Youcif Muntasser, the hero of *Gloire des sables*, like the hero of *La Rage aux tripes*, is an Algerian. Two narrators question and reveal the character of Youcif, a complex, awe-inspiring, but ultimately tragic figure, possessed by occult forces.

Hélé Béji has also written a number of important francophone Tunisian texts. *Désenchantement national* (1982) is a polemical and outspoken essay on decolonization and political propaganda, in which, like most of Memmi's writing, the autobiographical is overt and inseparable from the argument. *Œuil du jour* (1985) is a highly poetic conjuring of Muslim women's tradition. Proustian in the complication and evocation of its language, *Œuil du jour* crystallizes,

---

[11] For a wide range of literary-critical texts which focus on the city, see Université de Paris, *Paris et le phénomène des capitales littéraires* (2 vols.; Paris, 1984).

in the woman narrator's grandmother, a woman's way of seeing and living, from which the narrator herself has been severed. Comparable in many ways to the writing of Assia Djebar, Hélé Béli's text reveals the complexities of women's liberation and the losses which are inevitably involved. There is also perhaps, a nostalgia which prejudices certain feminist questions.

The narrator of Souad Guellouz's *La Vie simple* (1975) is an illiterate young woman who tells of a friendship between two women who belong at opposite ends of the social scale. Similar in some ways to Mariama Bâ's *Une si longue lettre*, the text suggests, although not simplistically, that modernity offers women liberation. *Jardin du nord*, on the other hand, could be read as the second part of a diptych. Here it is the past which offers Sofia a richness which modern life, in its emphasis on conformity, denies. Sofia re-creates her childhood in all its subtleties within a family concerned not simply to reflect the influence of Europe as it makes its presence felt in Tunisia, but to guard against losing touch with the ways and customs of tradition, which will protect the family against some of the dangers of (post-)colonization in all its complexity.

Francophone Tunisian writing is itself marginal within a society in which the principal literary tradition is one of writing in Arabic, a tradition which, of course, was relatively little disturbed under the Protectorate and which has continued since Independence. Those Tunisian writers living in exile, however, of which there are large numbers, have tended to write in French or English rather than Arabic. Many exiled writers have moved to French-speaking countries. A large number of francophone North Africans, including Tunisians, live in Quebec, for example.[12] These texts have a complex status, 'belonging' to the literature of the host nation, as well as to myriad other literatures: that of the author's origins, both Tunisia or North Africa, for example, or the Jewish diaspora, or North African women's writing, to cite the most obvious. As the city becomes a recognized point in common in literary and other cultural manifestations so, as most immigrants live within the city, immigrant writing may become more and more associated with that context.

The multiplicity of Tunisian origins, of people, of language, renders the notion of *bâtardise* relevant to much francophone Tunisian writing and indeed francophone North African writing gener-

---

[12] A fascinating bibliography is Denise Helly and Anne Vassal, *Romanciers immigrés: biographies et œuvres publiées au Québec entre 1970 et 1990* (Quebec, 1993).

ally. But that bastardy, in part influenced by deconstruction and the questioning of simple antitheses, suspicion regarding the possibility of completeness, of total recuperability in language and writing, is seen more and more as a privileged status, allowing a fuller and more varied approach to the exploration of contemporary experience both political and personal, public and private, and in that (deconstructed) no(wo)man's land in between.

11

EGYPT

THAT French travel writers had constructed an Egypt in French was a *donné* to which the first francophone Egyptian writers responded. Their desire was, above all, to explore and explain their country in greater depth and more accurately. It was largely for a French audience that they sought to set the record straight. *Romans de mœurs* and transcriptions of oral material are the dominant genres during the first quarter of the century. Albert Adès and Albert Josipovici draw on pan-Arabic legend in their *Livre de Goha le simple.* Out-el-Kouloub's writing (*Harem*, 1937; *Le Nuit de la destinée*, 1954; *Hefnaoui le magnifique*, 1961) draws on her own childhood experience growing up in an old aristocratic Muslim family, and on the oral tradition. Although of Lebanese nationality (see Chapter 12), Andrée Chedid's novels are often set in Egypt, the country of her birth: *Le Sixième Jour* (1960), *Nefertiti et le rêve d'Akhnaton* (1974).

More overtly militant and angrier in their denouncing of the misery of the lives of so many in Egypt are the texts of Albert Cossery: *La Maison de la mort certaine* (1944). The year after its publication he left Egypt for France. Distanced from his native land, his writing became more complex formally and in terms of tone. Sometimes militant but also celebratory of Egypt's past, his later writing includes: *Les Fainéants dans la vallée fertile* (1948), *Mendiants et Orgueilleux* (1955), *La Violence et la dérision* (1964), *Un Complot de saltimbanques* (1976).

The salon poetry practised in francophone Egypt during the first quarter of the century was academic and of little interest. During the 1930s, however, francophone Egyptian poetry, largely due to Georges Henein (*Le Seuil interdit*, 1956), developed surrealistic practices. Advertised by the journal *Part du sable* (later a publishing house of the same name), these activities were to have a profound effect on writers such as the young Edmond Jabès, Marie Cavadia, Horus Schenouda, and Joyce Mansour, author of a number of erotic and violent collections: *Cris* (1953), *Déchirures* (1955), *Les Gisants satisfaits* (1958), *Le Bleu des fonds* (1969), *Ça* (1970).

It is Albert Cossery, however, who has been proposed by a number of critics as Egypt's most important francophone writer. In a recent lucid article on francophone Egyptian writing, J.-F. Fourny concludes, providing insights not only into Cossery's writing, but into francophone Egyptian—if not North African—if not indeed francophone literatures generally:

What the novels of Albert Cossery show us is nothing less than the contemporary juxtaposition of slices of history, both modern and premodern, of elements belonging to the Middle Ages and to the nineteenth and twentieth centuries. History has not ended, for the world is not homogeneous; the two have not stopped beginning anew, somewhat like what would happen if all the phases described in *L'Histoire de la folie* or *Les Mots et les choses* [Foucault] were suddenly to surface in order to coexist for a few minutes, one right next to the other. And it would also be a great injustice to Albert Cossery if we didn't recognize in his positions the marks of literary and philosophical nobility that are his, those of the refusal of history and of the great human temptation of sleep and forgetting.[1]

[1] J.-F. Fourny, 'Laziness and Technology According to a Storyteller in Cairo', *Yale French Studies*, 82/1 (1993), 158–71 (p. 171).

12

LEBANON

THE French presence in the Lebanon begins with the Crusades. The French language, however, in an already polyglot country, became important only in the sixteenth century when François I signed agreements with the Ottomans (1535) allowing the entry of traders and missionaries who were to act as the purveyors of French culture and, most importantly, of the language.

Michel Misk is generally cited as the first significant francophone Lebanese writer. His initial collection of poetry was published in 1874. Like much of the writing which belongs to the first period of francophone Lebanese literature, resistance to the Turks is a central concern. *Antar*, by Chekri Ganem, was performed at the Paris Odéon and met with great success. The play, in verse, is about Arab resistance to the Turks. Between 1920 and 1943, the period of the French Mandate and the second of the four periods of francophone Lebanese literature generally proposed, most writing is preoccupied with the nature of the Lebanese nation. *La Revue phénicienne* (founded in 1920) explored and celebrated Lebanese antiquity. The third period of Lebanese writing belongs to the years from 1943 to the outbreak of war in 1975. This is the period in which Lebanese writing is most varied and open to foreign influence. Since the mid-1970s problems of Lebanese nationalism have once again dominated writing.

At the end of the nineteenth century it was Paris which was the centre of a liberationist francophone Lebanese writing concerned to encourage the independence of the country from the Ottomans. The French language was thus the language of Lebanese nationalism and militancy. Najib Azouri's important essay on Arab nationalism, *Les Pays arabes aux Arabes*, was written and published in French in 1905. In 1908 the journal *La Correspondance arabe* was founded and published in Paris. Similarly, in 1911 the *Revue islamique* and *Temps* were founded in Paris by Khaïrallah T. Khaïrallah, author of *La Syrie* and *Le Problème du Levant* (both 1912). *Caïs* (1921), also by Khaïrallah, is an illustrated tale, an adaptation of *Madjnoun Laïla* ('The Madman of Laïla') an Arabic 'Romeo and Juliet'. Most literary texts of the first period proposed above (*c.*1875–1920), draw on Arab tradition and stand in relationship with the 'exotic' texts by French (travel) writers: Chateaubriand, Lamartine, Nerval, Gautier, Flaubert.

Chekri Ganem (1861–1929) wrote in a number of genres: *Ronces et fleurs* (1890), poems; *Ouarda, fleur d'amour* (1904), a play; *Un quart d'heure des mille et une nuits* (1908), a play; *Daad* (1908), a novel; and *Antar* (1910/1921), a play. Two other influential writers of the first quarter of the century were Jacques Tabet (1885–1956) and Jean Bechara Dagher (1874–?). Their writing, like that of their less well-known contemporaries, consists of novels, *romans de mœurs*, transcriptions of myths and legends, nostalgic and melancholic poetry written by the Lebanese poet in exile.

The Turkish occupation came to an end in 1920, the date of the French Mandate and the creation of Grand-Liban. A modern constitution was adopted and French became the second (after Arabic) official language. It was also at this point that intellectuals divided, roughly speaking into two groups: those who wanted a return to Lebanon's historical roots, a reconnection with the country's Phoenician past, and those who wanted to create a modern state, recognizing the status of Lebanon under the mandate. Charles Corm (1894–1963) became an influential figure advocating the first. A prolific writer, he founded *La Revue phénicienne* in 1920 which became the forum for discussion by a whole generation. Most of the significant francophone poets of the period were associated with the journal and many were published by the publishing house which developed alongside the periodical: Hector Klat (1888–1977), Élie Tyane (1887–1957), Michel Chiha (1891–1954). These writers explored the rich Phoenician past inspired by Corm's seminal *La Montagne inspirée* (1934) which became something of a manifesto.

Farjallah Haïk's trilogy, *Les Enfants de la terre* (*Abou-Nassif*, 1948; *La Fille d'Allah*, 1949; *La Prison de la solitude*, 1951) is a detailed account of life in a Lebanese village. The violence and brutality of much of Lebanon's past is described in Laurice Schehadé's *Journal d'Anne* (1947). The most outstanding poet of the period is Georges

Schehadé. His plays *Monsieur Bob'le* (1951) and *L'Émigré de Brisbane* (1965) gained international recognition. His *Poésies*, published in 1952, was much admired by contemporary French poets including André Breton, René Char, and Saint-John Perse.

More classical, Fouad Gabriel Naffah's *La Description de l'homme, du cadre et du lyre* (first published in Beirut in 1957 and then in Paris in 1963) is a long dialogue of initiation. Violence, which is even more important in francophone Lebanese literature than in most modern literatures, recurs in much of the poetry of Nadia Tuéni (*L'Âge d'écume*, 1966; *Juin et les mécréantes*, 1968; *Poèmes pour une histoire*, 1972). The violence of Lebanon's past and present and a profound desire never to betray a place and people that have suffered so much, are central to the poetry of Vénus Khoury-Ghata (*Terres stagnantes*, 1968; *Au sud du silence*, 1975; *Les Ombres et leurs cris*, 1980). She is also a novelist, and *Vacarme pour une lune morte* (1983) shares similar concerns to his poetry.

Although the novel has been an important genre for the exploration of contemporary political and social questions, an important literature of ideas, of essays and articles, also exists. Salah Stétié (*Les Porteurs du soleil*, 1972) argues for the contribution poetry can make in the formation of a modern Arab identity. Selim Abou's essay on Lebanese bilingualism has also been influential, as has his text, *Liban déraciné* (1972), a series of accounts by Lebanese exiles living in Argentina. The composite text is described as an 'ethnopsychanalyse des autobiographies'.

Exile and its emotional corollaries are the central themes isolated by Salah Stétié, critic and historian of francophone Lebanese poetry: 'Peut-être l'exil n'est-il, au niveau profond, que la vocation, assumée par le poète, de cette terre, la sienne, le Liban—qui est seuil entre deux mondes, lieu de départ à la fois et point de nostalgie.'[1] He has also written a number of collections of poetry (*La Mort abeille*, 1972; *L'Eau froide gardée*, 1973; *Fragments: Poèmes*, 1978).

The war is central to one of the Lebanon's most important writers, Andrée Chedid (in particular *Cérémonie de la violence*, 1976) and to Nohah Salameh's *Les Enfants d'avril* (1980). Chedid has published some twenty collections. Among the most important are *Textes pour la terre aimée* (1955), *Contre-chant* (1969), *Visage premier* (1972),

---

[1] Jean-Louis Joubert *et al.* (eds.), *Les Littératures francophones depuis 1945* (1986), 246.

Fraternité de la parole (1976), *Épreuves du vivant* (1982). Simple in their language, her poems are concerned with both the small and large events of human existence, ranging, for example, from friendship to death.

The tragedy of the Lebanese war, but also the need for hope is evoked in the poetry of Élie Maakaroon's *Terre qui brûle* (1975) and Claire Gebeyli's *La Mise à jour* (1980) and *Papier de guerre lisse* (1981). Since the end of the troubles, the possibility of making the war central to writing has become evident. Amin Maalouf, recent winner (1993) of the Prix Goncourt, for his extraordinary novel *Le Rocher de Tanios*, explained in a lecture that the immediate horror of the troubles made it impossible for him to write about it, but now that relative calm has been established he is considering exploring various possibilities for a novel about the war. Clearly this is a feeling he shares with a number of Lebanese contemporaries in Paris, where he now lives, and in the Lebanon and elsewhere, most notably in North and South America.[2]

Guide to Further Reading

Unless otherwise stated place of publication is Paris.

Algeria

Novels

The first generation of Algerian novelists and novels includes: Mohammed Dib (beginning with *La Grande Maison*, 1952), Mouloud Feraoun, whose first novel was *Le Fils du pauvre* (Algiers, 1950), Mouloud Mammeri, beginning with *La Colline oubliée* (1952), and Algeria's most famous novelist Kateb Yacine, of greatest renown his early novel *Nedjma* (1956). Rachid Boudjedra, whose novel *La Répudiation* was published in 1969, went on to produce an important œuvre. Assia Djebar, one of Algeria's most important woman novelists published her first novel, *Les Alouettes naïves*, in 1967. Leïla Sebbar, beginning with *Shérazade* (1982), explores the difficulties experienced by a 'génération franco-maghrébine'.

---

[2] 'Rencontre avec Amin Maalouf', Maison Française d'Oxford, 10 Nov. 1994.

Poetry

Originally a militant *poésie engagée*, Algerian poetry after Independence becomes more concerned with social criticism and the difficulties experienced by the individual rather than the country. Jean Amrouche contributed early on, beginning with *Cendres* (Tunis, 1934). Malek Haddad's first collection was published in 1956 (*Le Malheur en danger*). An important group of poets made their debuts in the 1960s: Noureddine Aba, *La Toussaint des énigmes* (1963), Mohamed Dib, *Ombre gardienne* (1961), Nabile Farès, *L'Éxil au féminin* (1966), Jean Sénac, *Matinale de mon peuple* (1961). Two notable poets from the later period are Malek Alloula (*Villes et autres lieux*, 1979) and Rabah Belamri (*Le Galet et l'hirondelle*, 1985).

Theatre

Known for their novels and poetry respectively, Kateb Yacine, beginning with *Le Cercle de représailles* (1959) and Noureddine Aba, beginning with *L'Aube à Jérusalem* (Algiers, 1979) are also Algeria's most important playrights.

Morocco

Novels

From the earlier generation Driss Chraïbi (*Le Passé simple*, 1954) and Ahmed Sefrioui (*Le Chapelet d'ambre*, 1949) stand out as particularly important. Tahar Ben Jelloun is undoubtedly Morocco's most controversial novelist and essayist. *Harrouda* (1973) is his first novel. Mohammed Khaïr-Eddine, beginning with *Agadir* (1967), is also important.

Poetry

Many of Morocco's well-known novelists are also poets: Tahar Ben Jelloun (*Le Discours du chameau*, 1974), Mohammed Khaïr-Eddine (*Soleil arachnide*, 1969), Abdellatif Laâbi (*Le Règne de barbarie*, 1980).

Tunisia

Novels

Tunisia's best-known novelist (and major essayist and critic) is Albert Memmi. His first novel, *La Statue de sel*, was published in

1953. Two major voices who emerged a little later are Salah Garmadi (*Le Frigidaire*, Tunis, 1987) and Fawzi Mellah, beginning with *Le Conclave des pleureuses* (1987).

Poetry

Tunisia's major poets are (in chronological order of first publication, in brackets): Salah Garmadi (*Avec ou sans*, 1970), Hédi Bouraoui (*Éclate module*, Montreal, 1972), Majid El Houssi (*Imagivresse*, Padua, 1973), Amina Saïd (*La Métamorphose de l'île et de la vague*, 1985).

Theatre

Tunisia has produced relatively few playrights. Fawzi Mellah is Tunisia's best-known dramatist (beginning with *Néron ou les oiseaux de passage*, 1973).

Tales from the Maghreb

Three North African writers in particular have published substantial contributions in this field. They are: Mirida N'Ait Attik (*Les Chants de la Tessaaout*, Casablanca, 1965), Nacer Khemir (*Les Contes de l'ogresse*, 1975), Mouloud Mammeri (*Poèmes kabyles anciens*, 1980), Rabah Belamri (*Les Graines de la douleur*, 1982).

Secondary Material

Three invaluable bibliographies exist: Jean Déjeux, *Bibliographie méthodique des œuvres maghrébines de fiction* (Algiers, 1920–78) and the more selective descriptive bibliography by Tahar Bekri, *Littératures du Maghreb* (1989). Jacqueline Arnaud and Françoise Amacker, *Répertoire mondial des travaux universitaires sur la littérature maghrébine de langue française* (1984) is, obviously, a bibliography of secondary material.

Studies of North African Writing

Jacqueline Arnaud is also the author of a major study, *Recherches sur la littérature maghrébine de langue française* (1986; first edition, 1982). Other important critical texts include Jean Déjeux, *Littérature maghrébine de langue française* (Sherbrooke, Quebec, 1980; first edition 1973), and Jacques Madelain, *L'Errance et l'itinéraire: Lecture du roman maghrébin* (1983).

Egypt

Novels

Andrée Chedid, who is Lebanese but was born in Egypt, writes about the country of her birth (see e.g. *Le Sixième Jour*, 1960). Albert Cossery's novels employ a simple language to tell of the country's misery (*La Maison de la mort*, 1944, is characteristic).

Poetry

Joyce Mansour (*Le Seuil interdit*, 1956) and Georges Henein (*Le Signe le plus obscur*) are arguably the country's most important poets. Andrée Chedid (see Novels, above) is also a major poet (*Cérémonie de la violence* is perhaps her most famous collection).

Secondary Material

J. J. Luthi, *Introduction à la littérature d'expression française en Egypte* (1974) is the standard introduction. There are studies of both Chedid and Henein (see above) in the Seghers 'Poètes d'aujourd'hui' series, by J. Izoard (1977) and Alexandrian (1981), respectively.

Lebanon

Novels

The Lebanon's most celebrated novelist is undoubtedly Amin Maalouf, winner of the Prix Goncourt in 1993 for *Le Rocher de Tanios*.

Poetry

Poetry is the country's most important genre. Georges Schehadé has published a large œuvre (*Poésies*, 1952). Also notable are Vénus Khoury-Ghata (an early collection is *Terres stagnantes*, 1968); *Vacarme pour une lune morte* (1983) is from the later period. Salah Stétié (*La Mort abeille*, 1972) is one of a significant number of poets living in exile for whom the experience of exile is central to their poetry.

Theatre

Schehadé (see Poetry, above) has also contributed a number of important plays, e.g. *Monsieur Bob'le* (1951) and *L'Émigré de Brisbane* (1965).

Secondary Material

The Standard introduction is S. Khalaf, *Littérature libanaise d'expression française* (1974).

Studies of a more theoretical kind and books and articles relevant not only to North Africa and the Near East but to other areas also, are to be found in the Select Bibliography at the end of the book.

PART IV SUB-SAHARAN AFRICA AND MADAGASCAR

13

SUB-SAHARAN AFRICA

'COLONIAL', 'African', 'Negro', 'Neo-African', 'Negro-African', 'Black', 'Negritude', 'Senegalese', 'Cameroonian' (and other national appellations), 'Third World', 'Post-colonial', 'Sub-Saharan': the continuing proliferation of appellative terms (further complicated by the number of languages in which these may be written: English, French, Portuguese, and numerous African languages most obviously), testifies to the complexities of any literary history of the area and generates complex problems for criticism. The range of combinations of these terms is also consonant with the protean and hybrid nature of the field. A large number of origins and traditions for these literatures, some regressing ever further into history, can equally be proposed.

It is now widely known that the assumption that African literature (as opposed to African literature in the European languages) began as a consequence of European influence is erroneous. Numerous typologies for a wide range of oral genres have been defined: panegyric and historical poems constituting the two major historical genres; proverbs and riddles making up two of the most important philosophical ones. Oral traditions undoubtedly represent the most significant source for much African literature in the European languages (most importantly francophone, anglophone, and lusophone). And whilst the oral traditions now compete with, and are threatened by, writing (to which they also continue to contribute), ever cheaper modern technologies, tape-recordings, radio, film, and video, for example, have also offered exciting possibilities for the traditional performed arts and modern variants.[1]

[1] For an introduction to African oral literature see Ruth Finnegan, *Oral Literature in Africa* (Oxford, 1970).

African written traditions are less directly related to modern written traditions but they are, of course, traditions which long predate
the arrival of Europeans in Africa. From the eighth century BC the
Semitic kingdom of Saba in south-west Arabia spread its influence as
far as the high plains of Ethiopia. It was at this point that syllabic
writing was introduced. In West Africa, from the fourteenth century
onwards, Timbuktu became an important cultural centre where
educated men of different races met and wrote in Arabic, and generally in verse, poems, and theological and legal tracts. At the end of
the eighteenth century the Peuhl leader Ousmane dan Fodio led a
holy war against the Hausa emirs. The zealous followers of the
Prophet realized the potential of translating the Holy Book into the
languages of the people they were seeking to convert to Islam. This
realization brought about the birth of what became known as *ajami*
literatures; an Arabic word meaning 'foreign' and designating works
in non-Arabic languages transcribed in Arabic script.

Whilst West African literature in Arabic script, like the *guèze*
literature of Ethiopia, was devotional and moralizing, the literary
destiny of East African literature was very different. There a
syncretic *métisse* (cross-race) Swahili society developed. Significant
literary texts appeared from the beginning of the eighteenth century. Written in Arabic script, it remained predominantly a literature of epic poems (*utendi* or *utenzi*). At the end of the eighteenth
century sovereignty disputes between the governors of Mombasa
and the sultans of Oman encouraged the birth of protest literatures.
Throughout the nineteenth century two traditions, one religious,
the other secular, coexisted. The secular literature chronicled major
events affecting Swahili society. Later, this included attempts to
resist German invasion, for example.

On the whole the colonizers promoted Swahili literature. They
encouraged the use of the Latin alphabet and provided the means
to publish Swahili texts. Numerous English and German linguists
collaborated with Africans in transcribing and translating large
numbers of classical texts into the European languages.

Ethiopian and Muslim written literatures were restricted to relatively small numbers of people in relatively small areas of Africa.
Arabic and Muslim invasions were followed by the European invasion and it was this last which was to prompt the birth of African
literatures in the European languages. Two parallel traditions, one
associated with the British and Protestant colonial project, the other
Latin and Catholic (French, Portuguese, and Spanish), can usefully

be distinguished. The first considered the provision of a translated Bible a priority. Protestant English missionaries throughout a wide area (and some Americans in the south, and Germans in the East, Togo, and Cameroon), studied local languages, transcribed them, taught them, and translated the Bible and other edifying texts such as Bunyan's *Pilgrim's Progress*. Africans were also encouraged to write (again, only certain kinds of text), and to transcribe oral material, providing this did not conflict with the Protestant ethic. The degree to which missionaries could control writing varied from area to area. Among the most important and diverse literatures in an indigenous African language is that of the Xhosa.[2]

Where the colonial culture was predominantly Latin and Catholic the aim was to assimilate an élite into the metropolitan culture; few efforts were made to study local African languages, to transcribe them, or to encourage Africans to express themselves in them. Written literatures from these areas appeared, therefore, later than in those areas colonized by Protestant powers, and were written in the European languages.

These were greatly stimulated towards the end of the nineteenth century by a revival in Europe of interest in indigenous African culture. In France the purveyors of information about African culture were colonial administrators, ethnologists, or social anthropologists and later, writers and scholars. The ideas which stimulated this climate of interest were heterogeneous, paradoxical, and often contradictory. Various assaults on the primacy of Western civilization, its arid rationalism, and dehumanizing technological materialism, were being made. The exclusive claim to knowledge made by rational and scientific thinking was challenged by such writers as Henri Louis Bergson (who emphasized the importance of intuition, for example). Freud followed with his claims for the importance of the subconscious and these ideas seemed compatible with ethnologists' claims for a 'primitive thought', characterized as prelogical and participatory.

It was during the first half of the nineteenth century, however, that the first important works of African ethnology and linguistics were published in French. Baron Roger, a Frenchman, published *Fables sénégalaises recueillies dans l'Ouolof* in 1828 and David Boilat, a Senegalese *métis*, published *Esquisses sénégalaises* in 1853, followed by

---

[2] For an account of this literature see A. C. Jordan, *Towards an African Literature: The Emergence of Literary Form in Xhosa* (Berkeley, 1973).

a *Grammaire de la langue ouolof* (1858). The number of similar publications which appeared from the beginning of this century is much greater. The Malian interpreter Moussa Travele, for example, published three important works: *Petit dictionnaire bambara–français et français–bambara* (1913); *Proverbes et contes bambara* (1923); *Manuel français–bambara* (1929). Other comparable publications were to follow, written by colonials, Europeans, and assimilated Africans.

The great European Africanists emerged at the end of the nineteenth century and their writings were to make a profound impression on the first generation of African writers to be the products of the French educational system. Leo Frobenius's *Histoire de la civilisation africaine* was published in French in 1936 (published in the original in 1898). Jean Paulhan's *Hain-Tenys mérinas* (1913), Malagasy texts which he transcribed and translated into French, and *Expérience du proverbe* (1925), based on his thesis prepared under the direction of Lévy-Bruhl, and Maurice Delafosse's *L'Âme nègre* (1922) were also significant publications which contributed to the refutation of the notion that Africa (and Madagascar) had neither long histories nor rich cultures. Marcel Griaule's work with the Dogons was also important in this respect. Publications such as the *Journal de la Société des africanistes* (1944–7) were equally influential. Léopold Sédar Senghor, for example, contributed some early articles to this review.

F. V. Equilbecq was one of the first French colonial administrators to document a significant amount of African oral material. In 1913 he published translations of transcriptions he had collected during his travels in Senegal, Upper Volta, Niger, and Guinea together with an essay in which he distinguishes various genres. *Aux lueurs des feux de veillée: Essai sur la littérature des noirs, suivi des contes indigènes de l'ouest afrique* was followed by two further volumes, published in 1915 and 1916. A recent edition, *Contes populaires d'Afrique Occidentale, précédé d'un Essai sur la littérature merveilleuse des Noirs*, with an *Avant-propos* by R. Cornevin (Paris, 1972), testifies to its continuing importance. Blaise Cendrars's *Anthologie nègre*, published in 1919, went to a second edition in 1921 and was republished in a revised form in 1947.

French interest in Africa was also satisfied and stimulated by 'colonial literature'. This literature was defined and documented in particular by Marius and Ary Leblond (most importantly *Le Roman colonial*, 1926), also authors of their own colonial novels, and Roland

Lebel (*Histoire de la littérature coloniale en France*, 1931). Its defining characteristic according to its supporters depends on a difference proposed between 'colonial' and 'exotic' literature. The latter, writers such as Lebel argued, consists of writings about Africa written by French travellers who are concerned to compare the 'exotic' locus with a place of reference (France) and who delight in the superficial characteristics of the foreign place. Paul Morand's *Paris–Tombouctou* (1928) is often cited as the archetype. 'Colonial literature' or *colonialisme littéraire* (to use Lebel's expression), displayed a strict allegiance to the broader field of the *sciences coloniales*, those branches of study—political, economic, geographical, sociological, ethnographic, and so on—pertaining to the colonial project. Metropolitan writers who wrote about Africa, and 'colonial writing', remained distinct, the latter fostered by its own periodicals, published both in Africa and France. The most important are publications such as *L'Afrique française*, first published in 1891, which included brief bibliographical details about colonial writings, and in particular about letters, and *La Vie*, published by Marius and Ary Leblond in 1912, which in a section entitled 'La Vie des Colonies' published articles noting and commenting on new publications. The most significant publication was, however, *Outre-mer* (1929–37). The large amount of space devoted to colonial writing is explained by its broad intentions, stated in the preface and short section 'Notre programme', published in the first issue. Its objective, it was stated, was to: 'répond incontestablement aux nécessités de la politique coloniale de la France [. . .] Nous avons conquis le sol, nous l'avons aménagé, nous y faisons régner l'ordre et la paix, nous parvenons à tirer sérieusement parti de ses ressources; *il nous reste à conquérir définitivement les âmes.*' What was stressed was the contemporary

nécessité pour les représentants de la race parvenus à un degré supérieur de civilisation de porter tout leur effort sur l'étude attentive des caractéristiques des races moins évoluées, de se rendre compte le plus exactement possible des réactions, souvent si imprévues, que produisent sur elle les mesures prises à leur égard, de comprendre, en un mot, et dans le sens le plus général du terme, l'âme indigène.

C'est à cette œuvre indispensable que la Revue 'OUTRE-MER' se propose de collaborer.[3]

In addition to colonial periodicals, colonial writers also enjoyed the support of various organizations, for example their own Associa-

---

[3] *Outre-mer*, 1 (1929), 3–5.

tion des écrivains de la mer et de l'outre-mer, founded in 1926, and the Académie des sciences coloniales, founded in 1922. Numerous literary prizes were also available: Le Prix de littérature coloniale, Le Prix triennal de littérature coloniale, two prizes awarded by the Comité national des conseillers du commerce extérieur, and a number of more specific prizes.[4]

Colonial literature was defined by characteristics extrinsic and intrinsic to its constituent texts. That it was into this literature that the first texts by Africans writing in French were assimilated is made clear by Lebel's definition: 'La littérature coloniale: celle-ci doit être produite, soit par un Français né aux colonies ou y ayant passé sa jeunesse, soit par un colonial ayant vécu assez longtemps là-bas pour s'assimiler l'âme du pays, soit enfin par un de nos sujets indigènes, s'exprimant en français bien entendu.'[5]

A particular attitude was also required of the 'colonial writer' if his writing was to conform to the definition proposed by Lebel:

L'esprit colonial est une affirmation de l'énergie morale. La littérature coloniale, fille de cette résolution saine, s'affirme en réaction contre le décadentisme. [. . .] Elle [la littérature coloniale] montre le rayonnement de la force française, la puissante beauté de la Plus Grande France. Abandonnant, d'autre part, les utopies où se complaisait l'ignorance, elle se charge de vérité ethnique et s'attache à l'étude de problèmes psychologiques et sociaux d'où dépend la conduite des affaires politiques. Non seulement elle chante la gloire de l'Empire, mais elle participe aux tâches impériales.[6]

In another work, L'Afrique occidentale dans la littérature française (depuis 1870), Lebel argued:

Les ouvrages modernes revêtiront un intérêt ethnographique et traduiront la psychologie des races; dans le domaine colonial, cette curiosité naturelle prend une signification plus précise: c'est l'expression du besoin de la connaissance intime du pays et de ses habitants, utile à notre domination, aux fins vers lesquelles tend notre effort civilisateur, et, d'autre part, utile à l'œuvre d'enseignement qu'il importe de poursuivre auprès du public. Les écrivains coloniaux, observateurs avertis, curieux du fonds réel, des mœurs et du caractère des noirs, conféreront à leurs livres une valeur de documentation qui, sans nuire à leur charme, en accroîtra l'intérêt [. . .] Ainsi apparaîtront des œuvres spécifiques consécutives au progrès matériel et

---

[4] For a contemporary list see ibid. 240–3.
[5] R. Lebel, Histoire de la littérature coloniale en France (Paris, 1931), 85.
[6] Ibid. 212–13.

social de la colonie, reflétant une volonté de recherches utiles et de rééducation impérieuse, et qui pourront dépasser le domaine purement littéraire.[7]

This emphasis on the documentary and factual characteristics of colonial writing was summed up by Lebel in what he described as 'la formule même de la littérature coloniale, qui tend à répandre sous la forme d'un récit objectif, un enseignement exact qui a la connaissance utile du monde noir.'[8]

Early works of an anthropological nature by Africans were quickly annexed by colonial literature. Lebel's anthology, *Livre du pays noir* (1928), includes writings by Ahmadou Mapaté Diagne (*Les trois volontés de Malic*, 1920), Bakary Diallo (*Force Bonté*, 1926), René Maran (*Batouala*, 1921, and its sequel *Djouma, chien de brousse*, 1927). These texts are often cited as the founding texts of francophone African writing. Francophone Senegalese literary histories (Diagne and Diallo are both Senegalese) can cite earlier examples. 'La relation d'un voyage du Sénégal à Soueira', published in 1850 in *La Revue coloniale*, by Léopold Panet, a *métis sénégalais*, and *Esquisses sénégalaises* (Paris, 1853; republished, Karthala, 1983), by a *métis* Catholic priest, are two early examples.

Diagne's *Les Trois volontés* is short and written for a specific purpose: as a French reader for primary school children. Diallo's *Force-Bonté*, on the other hand, is an autobiographical novel written, as the preface by Jean-Richard Bloch is very concerned to point out, not by a schoolteacher or civil servant, but by a Fula shepherd boy, conscripted into the *tirailleurs sénégalais*. Despite the brutality that he both witnesses and suffers, the narrator retains an unequivocal belief in the future of French involvement in Africa.

It was only with the patronage of colonial administrators, school teachers, missionaries, and journalists that Africans in Africa had access to publication. In France, however, views about the nature of the African, and the consequences of these new ideas for colonial politics, created a new climate for publications by Africans. Lucie Cousturier's reports were influential and Maurice Delafosse maintained in his work *Les Nègres* that Negros had reached the necessary degree of civilization to establish stable states, entirely comparable to oriental and European states of the same period. André Gide's

---

[7] Lebel, *L'Afrique occidentale dans la littérature française (depuis 1870)* (Paris, 1925), 225–9.

[8] Ibid. 219.

Voyage au Congo (1927) and *Retour du Tchad* (1928), and Paul Morand's *Magie noire* (1928), also altered opinion. It may well be that Gide's desire to journey to Africa was stimulated by René Maran's *Batouala: véritable roman nègre*. Although the work is not mentioned in Gide's *Journal* it is unlikely that he would not have read or at least heard discussed, a work which had won the Prix Goncourt the year after Proust's *A l'ombre des jeunes filles en fleurs*. Maran was a West Indian who went to Africa as an administrative officer in the Oubangui-Chari region of French Equatorial Africa. Both prefaces, the first written in 1920 to accompany the first edition, the second to accompany the 1937 edition, emphasize the documentary importance which the author attributed to the text: 'Il n'est, à vrai dire, qu'une succession d'eaux fortes. Mais j'ai mis six ans à le parfaire. J'ai mis six ans à y traduire ce que j'avais, là-bas, entendu, à y décrire ce que j'avais vu. [. . .] J'ai poussé la conscience objective jusqu'à y supprimer des réflexions [. . .] Ce roman est donc tout objectif.[9] Maran also situated the novel very precisely: 'Ce roman se déroule en Oubangui-Chari, l'une des quatre colonies relevant du Gouvernement Général de l'Afrique Equatoriale Française. Limitée au sud par l'Oubangui, à l'est par la ligne de partage des eaux Congo-Nil, au nord et à l'ouest par celle du Congo et du Chari [. . .][10]

Maran's *Batouala* provoked a controversial debate and was harshly criticized.[11] The importance of Maran's paratextual material, the prefaces most obviously, should be emphasized. Much of the controversy which surrounded publication of the book was aroused by these rather than the text itself. Similarly, Maran's subtitle, a further aspect of the paratext which the author exploited, distanced the text from 'colonial literature' and encouraged the reader to approach it as belonging to a new genre, that of the *roman nègre*. Having won the Prix Goncourt, the most prestigious prize for the French novel, it became clear that writing by Africans or those of African descent was no longer to be controlled exclusively by the colonial institution. One of the interesting linguistic (as opposed to straightforwardly political) consequences of this, was that the language of the text no longer had to testify to the writer's successful assimilation.[12] In other words there was room for a language which

[9] René Maran, *Batouala: véritable roman nègre* (definitive edn., Paris, 1938; first published 1921), 9–10.   [10] Ibid. 14.

[11] For a discussion of reactions to *Batouala* see R. Fayolle, '*Batouala* et l'acceuil de la critique', *Actes du colloque sur la critique et réception de la littérature française* (Paris, 1978), 23–9.

[12] See Conclusion also.

was not simply 'correct' French. Maran, for example, in the direct speech of his novel, transcribed the 'local' French of the region in which the book is set. Many reviewers objected to this *petit nègre*. It was only, however, in direct speech that Maran's language departs from standard French. Gradually, however, the language of the French African novel was to change more radically, culminating, many would argue, in the 'revolution' of Ahmadou Kourouma's language (in *Les Soleils des indépendances*, 1968; see above).

The colonial institutions gradually lost their monopoly on African literature as African writers (often supported by prominent metropolitan French writers) formed groups (mainly in Paris) and founded periodicals, most notably: *La Revue du monde noir*, first published in 1931, *Légitime defense* (1932), and *L'Étudiant noir* (1935).

The importance of creating a forum for black intellectual and artistic expression was made clear in the opening number of the *Revue*. The editors, Dr Sajous, a Liberian who had spent a great deal of time in the West Indies, and two Martinican sisters, Paulette and Andrée Nardal, wrote in a prefatory piece, 'Ce que nous voulons faire': 'Donner à l'élite intellectuelle de la Race noire et aux amis des Noirs un organe où publier leurs œuvres artistiques, littéraires et scientifiques.'[13] The *Revue*'s attitude to colonialism was essentially reformist. Paulette Nardal, in an article entitled 'Eveil de la conscience de race', published in the sixth issue, made clear her view that the exploration and development of race consciousness did not require a rejection of 'la culture latine et le monde blanc en général'.[14] It was the journal's belief in a synthesis between Negro-African and European culture which encouraged the appearance of *Légitime Défense* edited by three former contributors to the *Revue*. Appearing within months of the *Revue*'s demise, their concerns were not with a world-wide 'Negro nationalism' but with the position of the assimilated black French-speaking West Indian. More influential, in terms of the development of African literature in French, was the review *L'Étudiant noir*.[15] The journal was the corporate publication of the Association des étudiants martiniquais en France. It

[13] Paulette and Andrée Nardal, 'Ce que nous voulons faire', *Revue du monde noir*, 1 (Nov. 1931), 1.

[14] Paulette Nardal, 'Eveil de la conscience de race', *Revue du monde noir*, 6 (Apr. 1932), 31.

[15] *L'Étudiant Noir*, Paris (Mar. 1935). For a long time supposedly *introuvable*, the journal has given rise to extraordinary speculation on the part of a number of early critics. The record has been set straight in the theses of M. Steins and J. Costissela in particular.

contained three particularly important articles by Senghor, Aimé Césaire, and Léonard Sainville.

Senghor's text 'L'Humanisme et nous: René Maran', is an important early statement of ideas which were to be developed into his earliest conceptions of Negritude: 'L'humanisme doit aboutir à la découverte et la connaissance de soi, à "l'humanisme noir" dans notre cas, que je définirais volontiers: un mouvement culturel qui a l'homme noir comme but, la raison occidentale et l'âme nègre comme instruments de recherches; car il y faut raison et intuition.'[16] In 'Nègreries: jeunesse noire et assimilation', Césaire argued for the need for authenticity: 'la jeunesse noire ne veut jouer aucun rôle; elle veut être soi'. He concludes: 'Elle [la jeunesse Noire] veut avoir ses poètes, ses romanciers, qui lui diront à elle, ses malheurs à elle, et ses grandeurs à elle; elle veut contribuer à la vie universelle, à l'humanisation de l'humanité; et pour cela, encore une fois, il faut se conserver ou se retrouver: c'est le primat de soi.'[17]

L. Sainville's article, 'Un livre sur la Martinique', discusses Lafcadio Hearn's *Esquisses martiniquaises*, a work he much admires and proposes as an example of a properly Martinican literature. Detailed descriptions of daily life, of work, festivals, and traditions guarantees the authenticity of 'une bonne littérature nègre'.[18] Although not mutually exclusive, these three articles can be seen to represent two approaches to African writing (or Negro-African writing as it was seen until rather later). The positions of Senghor and Césaire were to develop into the poetic theories associated in particular with Negritude, and Sainville's into a predominantly political and ideological theory of writing more relevant to the novel.

African poetry in French emerged within the context first of Léon-Gontran Damas's *Poètes d'expression française 1900–1945* (1947), and, a year later, with Senghor's *Anthologie de la nouvelle poésie nègre et malgache de langue française*, prefaced by Sartre's influential text 'Orphée noir' and with Senghor's introduction. Damas's introduction to his own book was more prescriptive than descriptive: 'De plus en plus, Politique et Littérature s'entrepénètrent et leur synchronisme se fait de plus en plus apparent dans les œuvres des représentants de la nouvelle école.'[19] One of the most surprising features of Damas's anthology is the difference between the excited

---

[16] *L'Étudiant Noir*, 3.   [17] Ibid. 4.   [18] Ibid.

[19] L.-G. Damas, *Poètes d'expression française 1900–1945* (Paris, 1947), 16.

polemic of the introduction and the considerably less revolutionary tone of almost all the poems included. The coherence of the anthology was explained in a number of ways: as the product of a 'culture franco-indigène', as 'poésie coloniale d'expression française' and 'poésie indigène d'expression française', and as constituting a 'mouvement poétique d'outre-mer'. It was above all the context of French colonialism which provided the focus for the anthology; neither race nor colour are referred to as significant. Indeed the anthology includes poems by poets of various colours, including white.

Senghor's markers are racial and Sartre's text, unlike Damas's, depends on constant references to the oppositions between black and white. In a typically complex and often elliptically argued essay, Sartre offered a wide range of sometimes complementary, sometimes contradictory definitions and descriptions of Negritude. The relationship between Negritude and (Negro-)African literature, was also proposed in a number of, at times, mutually exclusive configurations. Rather than clarifying Negritude, these paradoxes in Sartre's polemic stimulated secondary discourses surrounding (Negro-)African literature. Quotations from the essay were incorporated into a wide range of discussions to become the touchstones for relatively distinct approaches to literary texts. For example, the paradoxes of an anti-French literature written in French to which Sartre pointed, have been seen by some critics of (Negro-)African literature as paramount.[20] A further instance of the essay's legacy can be seen in discussions of the relative significance of race and class in considering the Black writer's allegiances. This question was greatly to influence later discussion of the context in which francophone (Negro-)African literature should be considered. Two schools of thought emerged, one emphasizing the cultural (and racial), the other class, situating (Negro-)African literature within the context of the literature of the proletariat. Negritude's historicism, which Sartre also emphasized, was seen by later critics as a crucial point of departure for any discussion of the literature associated with it. The versatility of Negritude, not as a literary doxy belonging to a particular historical moment, but as an adaptable literary-critical trope, was guaranteed, to a large extent, by the multiplicity of meanings with which Sartre invested it in his seminal essay. In addition, in emphasizing Negritude (in one instance) as a socio-political force or ideol-

[20] See e.g. Bernard Mouralis, *Les Contre-littératures* (Paris, 1975).

ogy, Sartre assured its place within political (as well as cultural and literary) debate.[21]

The word 'Négritude' first appeared in Aimé Césaire's long poem, *Cahier d'un retour au pays natal* (1939 in the Parisian journal *Volontés*, 1947 in book form):

> Ma négritude n'est pas une pierre, sa surdité
>   ruée contre la clameur du jour
> ma négritude n'est pas une taie d'eau morte sur l'œil mort de
>   la terre
> ma négritude n'est ni une tour ni une cathédrale
>   elle plonge dans la chair rouge du sol
> elle plonge dans la chair ardente du ciel
> elle troue l'accablement opaque de sa droite patience [. . .][22]

The meaning of 'Negritude' within the complex poetics of the *Cahier* cannot be simply defined. But what is proposed is a state of being, a particular consciousness.

Thus, while Negritude often emerges from a poetic text as an essence, a fixed Black ontology, the history of the term bears witness to the fact that there is no stable, original, and base doctrine to be unproblematically discovered, and in relation to which all other definitions can be seen as simple derivations, extensions, or perversions. Commentaries on Negritude are often drawn to investigate its 'origins', that is to say the moments of its initial articulations in the texts of Césaire and Senghor in particular.[23] The quest for synoptic sense, based on their texts, and the abundance of widely differing commentaries subsequently produced on those canonical texts, itself testifies to a history of the continuous adaptation and transformation of those origins. Thus Negritude cannot now be understood independently from the numerous commentaries to which it has given rise, and in which it is now diversely embodied. The most significant, both because of its seminal status, and because of its complexities, is Sartre's 'Orphée noir'.[24]

---

[21] For a discussion of Negritude as a literary-critical trope, see my *Negritude and Literary Criticism: The History and Theory of 'Negro-African' Literature in French* (Greenwood, Westport, Conn., 1996).

[22] Aimé Césaire, *Cahier d'un retour au pays natal* (Paris, 1947; bilingual edn., 1971), 117.

[23] See e.g. I. Kimoni, *Destin de la littérature négro-africaine ou problématique d'une culture* (Kinshasa/Sherbrooke, 1975).

[24] Two works which exploit the term but which are fundamentally different are, e.g. Julio Finn, *Voices of Negritude* (London, 1988), an essay and anthology of poems

The 'prise de conscience nègre' of the 1930s and 1940s was manifest both in discourses associated with Negritude and in a desire to distance (Negro-)African writing from the colonial institution. Thus the primary material, and most particularly poetry written during the first half of the century, is intimately bound up with an illustration and exploration of *l'âme nègre* and the secondary material, prefaces, introductions, and articles emphasize, first and foremost, the need to foreground *l'âme nègre* within secondary discourses, thereby denying the status of the literature as 'colonial' literature and instead emphasizing its affiliation to a *culture nègre*.

The African poetry of the first half of the century is thus predominantly protestatory and celebratory. Both types were represented in Senghor's *Anthologie*, which included only three poets from Black Africa: Senghor himself, Birago Diop, and David Diop. Railing against the injustice and suffering of history, in particular the experience of slavery and colonization, African poetry also expresses the dignity, richness, and order of the pre-colonial past. Among the most violent in its rejection of the colonial experience is that of David Diop (described by Gerald Moore as the 'Maiakovski de la révolution africaine'):

> A coups de gueule de civilisation
> A coups d'eau bénite sur les fronts domestiques
> Les vautours contruisaient à l'ombre de leurs serres
> Le sanglant monument de l'ère tutelaire.[25]

The repetition of the violent 'à coups de', ironically associated with the notion of 'civilisation', and linked by the inhuman and animal 'gueule', epitomizes much of Diop's work in which irony and violence (both in terms of imagery and linguistic strategies which subvert established codes concerning, for example, register) dominate. Diop's titles are unambiguous in terms of their relationships with the poems: 'Défi à la force', 'Le Temps du martyre', etc. A refusal of European stereotypes is also often violent. Diop's 'je déchirerai les rires Banania sur tous les murs de France' is an obvious example. Nor are poetic acts of violence individually authenticating, but

translated from French, Portuguese, and Spanish; and l'Harmattan's *Dictionnaire de la négritude*, ed. by Mongo Beti and Odile Tobner. Entries begin with 'ABERNATHY, Ralph David', the Baptist minister and friend of Martin Luther King, continue with 'ABOLITIONISME' and end with 'ZOLOUSE (or ZULUS)'.

[25] David Diop, in L. S. Senghor, *Anthologie de la nouvelle poésie nègre et malgache de langue française* (1948).

rather undertaken on behalf of the group. Implicit in a number of
Diop's poems is an indictment of the manner in which the Negro
has been deprived of individuality. It is simply in the name of 'le
Nègre' with a capital 'N' that Diop pleads:

> Souffre, pauvre Nègre! . . .
> Le fouet siffle
> Siffle sur ton dos de sueur et de sang [. . .]
> Souffre, pauvre Nègre! . . .
> Nègre noir comme la Misère![26]

The ellipsis suggests the inexpressible and the use of capitals preceded by the article suggests, by typographical similarity, the
synonymity of 'le Nègre' and 'la Misère'. Often Diop's poetry is
strikingly direct; 'Défi à la force' is a simple poem:

> Toi qui plies toi qui pleures
> Toi qui meurs un jour comme ça sans savoir pourquoi
> Toi qui luttes qui veilles pour le repos de l'Autre
> Toi qui regardes plus avec le rire dans les yeux
> Toi mon frère au visage de peur et d'angoisse
> Relève-toi et crie: NON![27]

Bernard Dadié's famous poem/prayer, 'X', also proposes total identification with a universal 'Noir':

> Je vous remercie mon Dieu, de m'avoir créé Noir,
> d'avoir fait de moi la somme de toutes les douleurs,
> mis sur ma tête,
> le Monde.
> J'ai la livrée du Centaure
> Et je porte le Monde depuis le premier matin.[28]

Where Diop celebrates, rather than laments Africa, it is sometimes
an individual that he describes. His first wife was Virginie Camara
and 'Rama Kam' was dedicated to her:

> Me plaît ton regard de fauve
> Et ta bouche à la saveur de mangue

---

[26] Diop, in *Coups de pilon*, cited in J.-L. Joubert *et al.* (eds.), *Les Littératures
francophones depuis 1945* (1986), 23.

[27] Diop, cited in John Reed and Clive Wake (eds.), *French African Verse*, with
English translations (London, 1972; repr. 1980), 26.

[28] B. Dadié, *Légende et poèmes: Afrique debout! Légendes africaines. Climbié. La Ronde
des jours* (1966), cited in J.-L. Joubert *et al.* (eds.), *Littératures francophones*, 23.

Rama Kam
Ton corps est le piment noir
qui fait chanter mon désir
Rama Kam
Quand tu passes
La plus belle est jalouse
Du rythme chaleureux de ta hanche
Rama Kam
Quand tu danses dans la lueur des nuits
Le tam-tam Rama Kam
Le tam-tam tendu comme un sexe de victoire
Halète sous les doigts bondissants du griot
Et quand tu aimes
Quand tu aimes Rama Kam
C'est la tornade qui tremble
Dans la chair de nuit d'éclairs
Et me laisse plein de souffle de toi
O Rama Kam![29]

The inversion with which the poem opens disrupts familiar French syntax suggesting translation from another language. The creation of rhythm implied by the tam-tam and the rhythm of Rama Kam's hips are associated not semantically, but through the syllabic rhyming and rhythmical association of her name, 'Rama Kam' and the 'tam-tam', an African drum. African flora ('mangue', 'piment noir'), fauna ('la panthère'), and weather ('la tempête'), a word belonging to African lexis ('Dyoudoung'), and an important cultural figure ('le griot') combine to celebrate both Rama Kam and Africa, and suggest their interdependence. A less erotic celebration of Africa is associated not with a lover, but with another female figure, in 'X':

Afrique mon Afrique
Afrique des fiers guerriers dans les savanes ancestrales
Afrique que chante ma grand-Mère
Au bord de son fleuve lointain.[30]

Diop was born in France and his poetry conjures an Africa from which he has been alienated but to which he returned. Diop's influence has been enormous; he is often referred to as the greatest francophone African poet. He is the only poet of the older generation represented in Présence Africaine's *Nouvelle somme de la poésie du*

---

[29] Diop, 'Rama Kam', *Coups de pilon* (1956), 25.   [30] Ibid. 21.

monde noir.[31] Equally violent, in its imagery and the understatement of its everyday register, is much of Yambo Ouologuem's poetry. 'Quand parlent les dents nègres' begins conversationally: 'Les gens me croient cannibale | Mais vous savez ce que les gens disent'. The penultimate section is bitter in its sarcasm:

> Les couteaux faisant défaut
> Ce qui s'explique chez des végétariens
> Occidentaux
> On se saisit d'une lame Gillette
> Et patiemment
> Crisss
> Crasss
> Floccc
> On m'ouvrit le ventre.

The poem ends triumphantly, but also absurdly and on a note of anticlimax:

> Une plantation de tomates y fleurissait
> Irriguée par des ruisseaux de vin de palm
> Vivent les tomates.[32]

Although less violent than Diop, both A. Kanie and F. N'Dinsouna write simple but powerful poetry. Kanie's poems are often condensed narratives which end ironically:

> J'irai là-bas, bien loin là-bas
> Au pays des Blancs
> J'irai boire bien loin là-bas
> A la source des Blancs
> C'est à la source
> Que l'eau est pure . . .
> [. . .]
> J'en ai assez de traîner ma botte
> Dans la boue des routes
> De brousse
> J'irai là-bas auprès des Blancs
> Forger la clé qui ferme ou brise
> Les prisons![33]

As an allegory of assimilation (the narrator intends to 'drink at the

---

[31] *Nouvelle somme de la poésie du monde noir*, special issue of *Présence africaine* (1966).

[32] Y. Ouologuem, in *French African Verse*, pp. 152–4.

[33] A. Kanie, 'Envol', in Reed and Wake (eds.), *French African Verse*, 42.

font of knowledge of the White Man'), the ending suggests not mimicry but triumphant deceit. An *imitation* key is not going to be made, but rather a *forgery*.

The structure and functioning of N'Dintsouna's poems are sometimes similar. 'A L.A.' begins:

> Ils m'ont dit
> Tu n'es qu'un nègre
> Juste bon à trimer pour nous
> J'ai travaillé pour eux
> Et ils ont ri
> [. . .]
> Ils m'ont dit
> Tu n'es qu'un sauvage
> Laisse-là tes totems
> [. . .]
> Va à l'église
> [. . .]
> Et ils ont ri
> Alors ma patience excédée
> Brisant les nœuds de ma lâche résignation
> J'ai donné la main aux parias de l'Univers
> Et ils m'ont dit
> [. . .]
> Meurs tu n'es qu'un traître
> Meurs . . . pourtant je suis une hydre à mille têtes.[34]

Paulin Joachim and Malick Fall (see below), writing slightly later, are two poets working within what can crudely be described as the protest tradition.[35]

Francophone Africa's best-known poet internationally is Léopold Sédar Senghor. His collection *Chants d'ombre*, written before the war and published in 1945, is also often nostalgic in tone. Senghor went to Paris as a student, passing the *agrégation* in 1935. He taught until 1939 when he was called up. Imprisoned by the Germans in 1940 he was released two years later because of poor health. He entered Senegalese politics first as a *député* (1945). In 1947 he founded the Bloc démocratique sénégalais. In 1960 he was elected President of Senegal.

The Africa from which he individually is exiled is also an Africa

---

[34] N'Dintsouna, ibid. 44.
[35] See e.g. the poems selected by Reed and Wake, ibid. 118–24 and 170–4 respectively.

from which Africans have been alienated by the vicissitudes brought by colonialism:

> Comment oublier l'éclat du soleil, et le rythme du
>   monde la nuit le jour
> Et le tam tam fou de mon cœur qui me tenait éveillé
>   de longues nuits
> Et les battements de ton cœur qui à contretemps
>   l 'accompagnaient
> Et les chants alternés. Toi la flûte lointaine qui
>   répond dans la nuit
> De l'autre rive de la Mer intérieure qui unit les
>   terres opposées.[36]

Senghor's private elegiac and lyrical voice gives way, in *Hosties noires* (1948) to an indignant, public poetry: 'l'Europe qui enterre le levain des nations et l'espoir des races nouvelles'.[37]

The principally personal lyricism of *Chants d'ombre* and the denunciation of the West in Senghor's second collection of poems, *Hosties noires* (1948), are in marked contrast. The latter describes the experience of the *tirailleurs sénégalais*:

> Ils sont là étendus par les routes captives, le long des
>   routes du désastre
> Les sveltes peupliers, les statues des dieux sombres drapés
>   dans leurs manteaux d'or
> Les prisonniers sénégalais ténébreusement allongés sur la
>   terre de France.[38]

Senghor's two volumes of memoirs, *Plume raboutée* (1978) and *A rebrousse-temps* (1982) are fascinating but little known. His later collections, and *Nocturnes* (1961) in particular, combine the personal and the public. The personal is most immediately identifiable in terms of locus; Joal, Senghor's place of birth, becomes a metaphor for the ordered, peaceful world of pre-colonial Africa, close to Senghor's Negritude:

> Toi, seigneur du Cosmos, fais que je repose sous Joal-Ombreuse
> Que je renaisse au Royaume d'enfance bruissant de rêves.[39]

Senghor's use of the *verset* encourages comparison with Claudel and

---

[36] L. S. Senghor, 'Qui m'accompagnent koras et balafong', *Poèmes* (Paris, 1964; repr. 1984), 43.

[37] Senghor, 'Luxembourg 1939', ibid. 66.

[38] Senghor, 'Assassinats', ibid. 77.   [39] Ibid. 200.

Saint-John Perse. But this should not obscure relationships with other traditions which Senghor's poetry establishes. The poet's knowledge of Wolof, Serer, Bambara, and Peuhl. In the 'post-face' to *Éthiopiques* (1956), entitled 'Comme les lamantins vont boire à la source', Senghor stresses the important influence of his local oral tradition: 'j'ai surtout lu, plus exactement écouté, transcrit et commenté des poèmes négro-africains'.[40] His debt to the poetess Marône is also made clear: 'La grande leçon que j'ai retenue de Marône, la poétesse de mon village, est que la poésie est chant sinon musique—et ce n'est pas là un cliché littéraire.' In a footnote he adds: 'J'ai découvert le génie de Marône au cours d'une enquête que j'effectuais sur la poésie négro-africaine de tradition orale. Auteur de quelque 2.000 chants gymniques, elle avait étendu sa gloire aux limites de l'ancien Royaume de Sine (Sénégal).'[41] Nor should the influence of his own translations of African poems be ignored.[42]

Birago Diop, one of only three African poets represented in Senghor's *Anthologie*, is best known for his *Contes*. Many of his poems, however, successfully conjure the Africa of his ancestors and assert the primacy of traditional African values:

> Ceux qui sont morts ne sont jamais partis:
> Ils sont dans le Sein de la Femme,
> Ils sont dans l'Enfant qui vagit
> Et dans le Tison qui s'enflamme
> [. . .]
> Écoute plus souvent
> Les Choses que les Êtres,
> La Voix du feu s'entend,
> Entends la Voix de l'Eau
> Écoute dans le Vent
> Le Buisson en sanglots,
> C'est le Souffle des Ancêtres.[43]

Less descriptive, but equally evocative of the African past, in this case the Somalian past, is William J. F. Syad's poetry (particularly the poems of *Khamsine*, 1959, prefaced by Senghor). He writes both in French and English; his later work is more philosophical and polemical (*Cantiques*, 1976); the early collection contains poems in which delicate images, often of small things experienced close at

---

[40] Senghor, *Éthiopiques* (Paris, 1956), 107.   [41] Ibid. 121.
[42] Senghor, included at the end of *Poèmes*.
[43] B. Diop, 'Souffles', in Reed and Wake (eds.), *French African Verse*, 20.

hand, are associated with the large abstracts of Time and History. 'Hier' is characteristic of much of this early work:

> Une oreille
> Penchés
> Vers des siècles
> somnolents
> sur le chemin
> obscur de temps
> Oh! Naftaye
> tu m'as conté
> le passé de ma culture
> Pensée ivre de ma race
> Somale
> Et comme
> ce sable fin
> au creux
> d'une main
> tu glissais
> dans le passé
> où l'esprit
> seul
> peut glaner.[44]

An œuvre comparable to Senghor's in size and complexity is that of the Congolese poet Tchicaya U Tam'si. Accused of hermeticism by many, the poet has often reiterated his conviction that his poetry can and should be read literally: 'M'accuser d'hermétisme, c'est presque vouloir me censurer. Si on a une lecture littérale de ce que j'écris, on comprend ce que je dis.' In the same article, he describes succinctly and not reductively, his ambitious poetic project: 'Je veux créer un nouvel imaginaire, une terre nouvelle où intégrer tous les éléments syncrétiques [. . .] Ma poésie est comme le fleuve Congo, qui charrie autant de cadavres que de jacinthes d'eau.'[45] His first collection, *Le Mauvais sang* (1955) was followed by *Feu de brousse* (1957) and *A triche-cœur* (1958), *Épitomé* (1962), *Le Ventre* (1964), *Arc musical* (1970), *La Veste d'intérieur* (1977) and *Le Pain ou la cendre* (1978). There is a heteroclite quality about Tchicaya's poetry which draws on, subverts, and cleverly combines elements from diverse traditions and creates emotional correlatives which range from the euphoric to the morbid. His poetry is not simply characterized. The

---

[44] Syad, 'Hier', ibid. 96.
[45] Tchicaya U Tam'si, quoted by Alain Rouch and Gérard Clavreuil, *Littératures nationales d'écriture française* (1986), 125.

pure self-centred and self-preoccupied emotion of Paul Verlaine's 'Il pleure dans mon cœur comme il pleut sur la ville', with its simple poetic strategy dependent on simile, is parodied and subverted in Tchicaya's sonnet, 'Il pleut mon Dieu il pleut toute la ville est salé', where suggestions of the power of the modern State ('Je plaide ce faux crime | que je n'ai pas commis'), create an atmosphere of angst: 'J'ai froid mon Dieu dehors il fait si frais si frais'.[46] This effect which might be described as a modernized 'pathetic fallacy', is often highly affective: 'Ça y est ce sont bien les tracteurs qui s'engueulent sur ma savane. | Non c'est mon sang dans mes veines! | Quel mauvais sang!' or again in 'Heure de vie': 'j'ai bien pensé ainsi | certains jours où le désarroi | pesait sur mes épaules | comme mille wagons chargés | de tout le poids du monde.'[47]

Tchicaya rejected what he regarded as the restrictive prescriptions of Negritude and few of his poems are immediately identifiable as African or Congolese. One exception is 'Natte à tisser':

> il avait l'âme mure
> quand quelqu'un lui cria
> sale tête de nègre
> [. . .]
> sale tête de nègre
> voici ma tête congolaise
> c'est l'écuelle la plus saine.[48]

Tchicaya's poetry is generally cited as the most important contribution to francophone African poetry since Negritude. His violence emanates from myriad elements of his poetry: imagery, syntax, register, mixed emotional correlative, unexpected juxtaposition, rupture, severance. All these are features of the post-modern, but there is never a sense that these are being used gratuitously or for spurious effect.

Tchicaya has also published other works. His edition of African tales, *Légendes africaines* (1967) is evidence of his fascination with them. His play *Zulu* testifies to his preoccupation, as for African theatre generally, with the figure of Chaka. More innovative is his play *Le Destin glorieux du maréchal Nnikon Nniku*, a black comedy about dictatorship. A number of novels and short stories appeared later (see below).

---

[46] Tchicaya U Tam'si, 'Il pleut mon Dieu . . .', in *French African Verse*, 46.
[47] Tchicaya U Tam'si, 'Le Signe du mauvais sang', ibid. 52.
[48] Tchicaya U Tam'si, 'Natte à tisser', ibid. 90.

Joseph Bognini's poetry is more readily accessible although some of his poems suggest the form of the riddle, and are puzzling for that reason. 'Devine', as its title suggests is playful:

> —Devine ce qu'est le temps
> et dis-moi ce gue tu penses?
> —nuages roses sur le tapis de l'Océan.[49]

Equally light-hearted in tone is Malick Fall's 'poem of assimilation' (this could be proposed as a genre within (Negro-)African poetry in French):

> J'allais à l'école les pieds nus et la tête riche
> Contes et légendes bourdonnant
> Dans l'air sonore [. . .]
> [. . .]
> Tu vas à l'école en compagnie d'Homère
> Des vers d'Éluard ou des contes de Perrault
> N'oublie pas Kotje à l'orée du sanctuaire.[50]

The confrontation of cultures comically exposed in 'Écoliers' becomes more problematic in 'Intentions' where a collision of cultures suggests a destructive, if not nihilistic, absurdity:

> J'édifierai une cabane
> Un ascenseur en coin
> [. . .]
> Je raserai toutes les cases
> Alentour
> Les tombes les fétiches le mil
> Et le riz
> [. . .]
> Et je te dirai
> Monsieur
> Prenez place
> Dans le royaume détragué
> Des fous du village.[51]

Francis Bebey's poetry also dramatizes the double-perspective of Black and White, European and African:

> Un jour, tu apprendras
> Que tu as la peau noire, et les dents blanches,

---

[49] J. Bognini, 'Devine', Ce dur appel de l'espoir (1960), 64.
[50] M. Fall, 'Écoliers', in Reed and Wake (eds.), French African Verse, 118.
[51] Fall, 'Intentions', ibid. 120.

Et des mains à la paume blanche,
[. . .]
Mais si jamais tu apprends
Que tu as du sang rouge dans les veines,
Alors, éclate de rire.[52]

E. B. Dongala's 'Prière et repentance d'un petit chrétien' is reminiscent of Malick Fall's comic poems:

seigneur
pourquoi as-tu fait ce matin
si gris si triste
est-ce par ce que j'ai péché
[. . .]
seigneur
[. . .]
je reconnais mon irrèparable mon impardonnable mon mortel
péché
[. . .]
mais eux seigneur tous ceux qui n'ont rien fait
rends-leur ce soleil brillant qui fait la joie de leur vie
[. . .]
et donne à maman ce soleil qu'elle désire tant pour sa récolte de manioc
mais moi ne me laissez pas vivre
car j'ai séché le cours de catéchisme dimanche.[53]

Lamine Diakhaté and A. Y. Diallo bave both written elegiac poems which lament the disappearance of pre-colonial Africa: 'SHANGO, dieu d'IFE redonne à mon Continent | la sérenité des premiers âges', Diakhaté pleads.[54] In 'Le Remords' allegiance is pledged: 'Afrique, mère aimée | ton enfant prodigue | trop tôt entêté s'enlise dans la boue des mares sournoises. | Vole à mon secours. [. . .] | je resterai fidèle jusqu'à la fin des jours!'[55]

Although the poetry of Tchicaya U Tam'si and Jean-Baptiste Tati-Loutard is widely read and both have gained international reputations, African poetry (often published in small editions) has become increasingly overshadowed by the novel. A number of more recent poets have, however, found audiences. Jean-Marie Adiaffi (*D'éclairs et de foudres*, 1980), a leading Ivory Coast writer associates dream-states with sincerity and honesty, vital to constructive human inter-

[52] F. Bebey, 'Un jour tu apprendras', ibid. 136.
[53] E. B. Dongala, 'Prière et repentance d'un petit chrétien', ibid. 144–6.
[54] L. Diakhaté, 'Homme vieux au visage de songe', ibid. 168.
[55] A. Y. Diallo, 'Remords', ibid. 180–2.

action. Véronique Tadjo (*Latérite*, 1984) strives for a simplicity and lack of pretension in writing for both adults and children. Paul Dakeyo, who founded Éditions Silex in Paris where he now lives, has published a number of collections of poems (*La Femme où j'ai mal*, 1989) and edited anthologies, including an important anthology of South African poetry in French translation (*Aube d'un jour nouveau*, 1981).

A major forum for the discussion of African poetry in French has been the journal *Présence Africaine*. This periodical, first published in 1947, was to constitute a major focus for the exchange of ideas— political, sociological, historical, literary, and so on. Alioune Diop provided the impetus for the founding of the journal, first produced by André Gide, Jean-Paul Sartre, Albert Camus, Michel Leiris, and various others. A publishing house of the same name, the first to be dedicated to Black culture, emerged alongside the journal. Two important Congrès des écrivains et artistes noirs, in Paris in 1956 and Rome in 1959, were also largely organized by Présence Africaine.

Among the important non-literary works which appeared under the auspices of Présence Africaine was Cheikh Anta Diop's *Nations nègres et culture* (1955). A Senegalese linguist and ethnologist, he argued that the unity of African civilization was based on its origin, Egyptian civilization, which was essentially Negro (*nègre*):

En disant que ce sont les ancêtres des Nègres, qui vivent aujourd'hui principalement en Afrique noire, qui ont inventé les premiers les mathématiques, l'astronomie, le calendrier, les sciences en général, les arts, la religion, l'agriculture, l'organisation sociale, la médecine, l'écriture, les techniques, l'architecture; que ce sont eux qui ont, les premiers, élevé des édifices de 6 000 000 tonnes de pierre (*Grande Pyramide*) en tant qu'architectes et ingénieurs—et non seulement et tant qu'ouvriers; que ce sont eux qui ont construit l'immense temple de Karnak, cette forêt de colonnes, avec sa célèbre salle hypostyle où entrerait Notre Dame avec ses tours; que ce sont eux qui ont sculpté les premières statues colossales (*Colosses de memmon*, etc.), en disant tout cela on ne dit que la modeste et stricte vérité, que personne, à l'heure actuelle, ne peut réfuter par des arguments dignes de ce nom.[56]

Présence Africaine has also published and continues to publish numerous influential political texts. Among the earlier texts are Mahjemout Diop's *Contribution à l'étude des problèmes politiques en*

[56] C. A. Diop, *Nations Nègres et culture*, cited in J.-L. Joubert *et al.* (eds.), *Littératures francophones*, 24–6.

Afrique noire (1958), Albert Tevodjere's *l'Afrique révoltée* (1958), and Mamadou Dia's *Réflexions sur l'économie de l'Afrique noire* (1960). In the collection 'Leaders Politiques', the publishing house produced *Nation et voie africaine du socialisme* (1961) by Senghor and, the following year, *Expérience guinéenne et Unité africaine*, by the Guinean Head of State, Sekou Touré, with a preface by Aimé Césaire. The SAC (Société Africaine de Culture) also publishes its conference proceedings with Présence Africaine. Among the most important publications from the 1960s and 1970s are those on *Les Religions* (Abidjan, 1961), *L'Art nègre* (Dakar, 1966), *Les Perspectives nouvelles sur l'histoire africaine* (Dar es Salaam, 1965), *Le Théâtre négro-africain* (Abidjan, 1970), *Le Critique africain et son peuple comme producteur de civilisation* (Yaoundé, 1973).

Whilst poetry was an important genre early on, and possible for journals such as *Présence Africaine* to support, it was not until the 1950s that the African novel in French existed as a significant corpus of texts. Bakary Diallo's *Force-Bonté* (1926) was briefly discussed above. Ousmane Socé's *Karim: roman sénégalais* was published in 1935. Frequently dismissed as a 'colonial novel', *Karim* can also be seen as an early example of an African *roman de mœurs*, as its subtitle indicates. The confrontation of traditional values with the pragmatism of modern capitalist (and colonial) economy, although not central to the novel, nevertheless justifies its consideration as a prototype for what was to become an important genre. His second novel, *Mirages de Paris* (1937) was the first of a genre of francophone African autobiographical novels written in exile.[57]

Doguicimi (1938), by Paul Hazoumé is generally regarded as the first historical novel. It is a serious work set in the Kingdom of Abomey in the nineteenth century. Félix Couchoro's novels (beginning with *L'Esclave*, 1929) are *romans feuilletons*, often ignored by literary critics. They are of considerable historical interest as Couchoro wrote for both a European audience and a readership in Dahomey (since 1975, Benin). Appearing first in *Présence Africaine*, Abdoulaye Sadji's *Nini, mulâtresse du Sénégal* (1947), like *Karim* published a little more than a decade earlier, is an urban *roman de mœurs*, an implicit indictment of colonialism, but more explicitly, a criticism of his compatriots' willingness to abandon their culture and be assimilated into the largely chimerical colonial culture. *Maïmouna*

---

[57] For a discussion of francophone representations of Paris, see my 'Mirages de Paris . . .', in M. Sheringham (ed.), *Parisian Fields* (London, 1996).

(1957) describes the protagonist's attraction to the city and the disillusion she later experiences. Seydou Badian, a Malian writer, in *Sous l'orage* (1957) explores the confrontation of values between two generations focused on the question of arranged marriages. A similar theme characterizes Francis Bebey's *roman de mœurs*, *Le Fils d'Agatha Moudio* (1963). Malick Fall's *La Plaie* (1967) is comparable to Sadji's *Maïmouna*. The novel is set in the city where the protagonist begs and steals to survive. Temporarily handicapped he inspires pity, but once well again is treated with contempt.

One of the first kinds of novel to constitute a significant type was the *roman de formation*, the autobiographical novel in which the protagonists leave their village or country drawn to the attractions of the city, or Europe. The seminal text is by the Guinean, Camara Laye, entitled simply, *L'Enfant noir* (1953), which won the Prix Charles-Veillon. In many ways an ambiguous text, *L'Enfant noir* has been extolled—and vehemently denounced. To some extent differences of opinion can be explained in terms of whether the work is either self-conscious even ironic, or naïve in its evocation of an idyllic Africa, long since destroyed by colonialism.[58]

The subtitle of Aké Loba's novel of the same type also suggests the appropriateness of the term *roman de formation*: *Kocoumbo: l'étudiant noir* (1960). At once falling within this genre and within the genre of the philosophical novel, Cheikh Hamidou Kane's novel, *l'Aventure ambiguë* (1960) dramatizes the opposition between mysticism and scientism. In parallel with this antithesis are the confrontations of Cartesian rationalism and the religious life, Islam and Catholicism, mysticism and materialism, Africa and Europe, etc. An Islamic mysticism permeates the closing scenes of the novel in which the protagonist Samba Diallo is mysteriously killed by his double (thus constituting, rather, a suicide?). The exploitation of the legendary couple, hero and anti-hero, belongs within the oral tradition: Samba Gueladio Diegui and Doungourou, Silamakan and Poullori. Bernard Dadié's *Climbié* (1956) is another example of an early *roman de formation*, set entirely in the Ivory Coast. The protagonist passes through the French educational system and into the colonial administration.

These early novels were criticized by contemporary readers and

---

[58] A recent study of Camara Laye's writing which considers previous critical responses is Ada Uzoamaka Azodo's *L'Imaginaire dans les romans de Camara Laye* (New York, 1993).

have since been more harshly dealt with by those who regret their focus on an individual and the novelist's failure to denounce, on a broader level, the colonial system, its violence and fundamental and inescapable contradictions and absurdities, at least for the African if not also for the colonizer. These are the concerns of two early Cameroonian novelists, Mongo Beti (Alexandre Biyidi) and Ferdinand Oyono, and one of the most overtly committed African novelists and film-makers, the Senegalese Sembène Ousmane. Alexandre Biyidi, using first the pseudonym Eza Boto, published *Ville cruelle* in 1954 in which a young boy first discovers the dangers of the city. This was followed by three novels published in the name he now uses, Mongo Beti: *Le Pauvre Christ de Bomba* (1956), *Mission terminée* (1957), *Le Roi miraculé* (1958).

In *Ville cruelle* a peasant travels to town to sell his cocoa and is badly treated by the colonial administrators. The novel's greatest strength lies in its ability to describe a banal character (Banda), living a banal life within a banal society (located in the town of Tanga), during the 1930s. The banality is dependent on the sterility of life within colonial structures. The three novels Beti published in 1956, 1957, and 1958 complement one another to fulfil his aim of exploring modern African identity tending towards assimilation and alienation among the young, and towards a repressive and inflexible conservatism among the old.

In *Le Pauvre Christ de Bomba* the irony emanates from the naïve account of Père Drumont's attempts to Christianize the people of Tala provided by the diary kept by the priest's cook. The latter is devoted to his master and describes events which are at times brutal, at times simply absurd, without judgement or emotion, except occasional (misplaced) sympathy for the Père. The narrative technique which introduces a wide discrepancy between the reader's perspective—based on, for example, the direct speech reproduced in Denis's journal—and his own response which he describes in the first person. The discrepancy arouses the reader's critical faculties which are thus perfectly controlled, but not dictated to, by the author.

Le Roi miraculé takes place in 1948 and the Catholic priest is apparently more successful than Père Drumont in *Le Pauvre Christ*. But the conversion of the village chief leads to his repudiation of his many wives, the first step in a chain of events encouraging rapid social disintegration. Père le Guen is sent away by the colonial officials.

Beti has also written a number of other texts including an important essay, *Main basse sur le Cameroun* (1972) and later novels, *Remember Ruben* (1974), *Perpétue ou l'habitude du malheur* (1974), *La Ruine presque cocasse d'un polichinelle* (1979). These novels form a trilogy covering the period 1938 to 1970 in a country in central Africa. The transition from colonial rule to independence and the forms of political power which operate after independence provide the focus for the novels. They are, however, very different in style and *La Ruine*, in particular, distinguishes itself from the earlier two in its epic, picaresque, and comic dimensions. It is, in addition, the only novel by Beti in which revolutionary action is successful.

Ferdinand Oyono's *Une Vie de boy* is comparable in technique to Beti's *Le Pauvre Christ*. Again, it is a journal written by a naïve 'boy' that constitutes the text. Here it evokes not so much irony arising out of a double perspective, but more a method which allows for the straightforward description of the events of lives (those of his employers) which the reader then interprets as mediocre, petty, and narrow. In *Le Vieux nègre et la médaille* it is the eponymous protagonist who caricatures himself. Dazzled by the colonial way of doing things he lives to impress the colonial hierarchy. Decorated, finally, by the Governor himself, he is imprisoned later the same day, unrecognized by the police. Oyono's third novel, *Chemin d'Europe* (1960) provides an acute insight into acculturation. The hero (or anti-hero) of the novel has become an archetype of the Cameroonian, and indeed the African, novel: the *picaro*, severed from his own cultural traditions but unable fully to be assimilated into Western culture. Oyono's writing has attracted considerable critical attention.

Ousmane Sembène's *O pays, mon beau peuple!* (1959) is often cited as the first of a genre of militant African novels in French. By a Socialist Realist, Sembène's novels are accurate in their detail. A former docker (his *Le Docker noir* (1956) is highly autobiographical) and trade-unionist, he fought as a *tirailleur sénégalais* during the Second World War. His writing testifies to his experience of war, workers' strikes, poorly paid and despised employment, and organizations such as the CGT (Confédération général du travail) and the PCF (Parti communiste français). The son of a fisherman, he was obliged to leave school after an altercation with the head (a European). He was called up in 1942 and returned to Dakar in 1946. The following year he travelled to Marseilles. During the 1950s he published his first literary works but decided, not very many years later, that the cinema 'était la meilleure école du soir'. He travelled to the USSR to study cinema at the Gorki Studios and produced his first film, *Borrom Sarret*, in Senegal in 1963 (see below).

The title of a later text, *Les Bouts de bois de Dieu* (1960), is a direct translation of a metaphor simply for people. The novel concerns the strike of 1947/8 during the construction of the Dakar–Niger railway line, but the focus is on the wives of the strikers. The solidarity of all those involved is convincingly conveyed by the epic, optimistic language of the novel:

Les pagnes, les camisoles, les mouchoirs avaient été lavés. C'était une multitude colorée; qui défilait maintenant sous un ciel clair que les coups de vent de la veille avaient nettoyé du moindre petit nuage. Entre Rufisque [*c*.20 km from Dakar], la dernière halte, et Dakar, l'air marin venu de l'Atlantique apporta sa fraîcheur. La colonne avait engraissé, des femmes des villages, des Rufiquaises s'étaient jointes à celles de Thiès, des hommes aussi qui avaient grossi l'escorte et marchaient en arrière-garde ou sur les bas-côtés de la route. Les femmes chantaient, riaient, plaisantaient.[59]

The rightness of the people's action is light-heartedly confirmed by the sky, like the women, having cleaned up for the occasion. Women dominate the scene as in many stories of dramatic social change within the oral tradition. The structure of the work is complex: like the railway, the narrative penetrates different areas: Dakar, Bamako, Thies. Encouraging a rejection of colonial subservience and optimistic on the whole in their endings, Sembène's novels are equally critical of the reactionary and stifling forces of tradition. The *retour aux sources*, proposed by many of the writers associated with Negritude and Senghor in particular, is presented as regressive and escapist. This is very obvious in the stories which make up *Voltaïque* (1962) and in his novel *L'Harmattan* (1964) which takes place on the eve of the 1958 referendum. His later novels, *Vehi-Ciosane* and *Le Mandat* (1965), *Zila* (1973), *Le Dernier de l'empire* (1981) are discussed below.

Novels which convey a strong sense of African mysticism suggest a closer relationship with oral traditions than most of the novels descibed above. Camara Laye's fantastic and oneiric work, *Le Regard du roi* (1954), which is also reminiscent of Kafka and Julien Green, describes the odyssey undertaken by Clarence, a White man, who sets out to discover the *réalité profonde* of Africa, represented by a

---

[59] Sembène Ousmane, *Les Bouts de bois de Dieu* (1960), cited in J.-L. Joubert *et al.* (eds.), *Littératures francophones*, 45.

mysterious king, whose gaze he must attract. A comparable novel is Olympe Bhêly-Quenum's *Un Piège sans fin* (1960) which is also suffused with African mysticism and occultism. His later novel, *Le Chant du lac* (1965) is similar in atmosphere. Writing very much within the tradition of David Ananou and Félix Couchoro, Bhêly-Quenum's works associate a bleak and pessimistic vision of Dahomey (now Benin) with the notion of Christian (Catholic) suffering and redemption.

Initiated by Europeans in the nineteenth century, the transcription and translation of oral material is less automatic than the terms suggest. The *conte*, the major oral genre to have become an integral part of African literature, has relatively specific functions and has to be understood within a particular social context. Both its function and context are alienated by transcription and translation. Recounted after sunset, the experience of listening unifies a group and illustrates certain values and attitudes. History, philosophy, and religion can all be told in the tale. Animal stories can be characterized according to the animal concerned: the hare, the hyena, the crocodile, the elephant, the spider. Simple moral lessons and social satire are the main functions of many animal tales. The choice of tale depends, if told orally, on contemporary events and characters. The reactions of the listeners—and their interjections—affect the performance. Tone of voice, gesture, whether the tale is told rapidly and succinctly or drawn out and embellished, these are some of the many variables involved in the telling.

The written text can, to some extent, find equivalent techniques to create similar effects: punctuation and repetition will obviously control, to some extent, the pace of the tale. The myriad techniques of poetry—rhyme, rhythm, alliteration, etc.—may all be exploited. But a good deal is simply changed. One of the most serious differences between the tale told and the tale transcribed is that what might be called the hypogrammatic feature of the oral tale is lost. The term derives from the French linguist Riffaterre who uses it to explain one of the fundamental features of poetry which depends on a recognition of difference between *two* patterns of words. All sorts of other questions come into it. The point to be made here is that the reader (as opposed to the listener familiar with a whole tradition) will be unaware of the hypogrammatic features of the tale. The listener, on the other hand, identifies the often small but subtle and crucial differences between the way the story is being told this time and the way they have heard it told in the past. The degree to which

the teller can depart from the tradition is, of course, socially moni-
tored. If the difference is too great, the audience can object. The
differences introduced will be explicable in terms of making the tale
relevant and appropriate according to the moment at which it is
told.

Whether the written *contes*, which constitute a major genre
within modern African literature, should be regarded as forming a
separate genre, rather than being seen as a transcription and translation of particular oral 'texts' is, therefore, a complex question. What
is clear is that a spectrum exists with something close to exact
transcription and translation at one end, and at the other texts
inspired by, but developments and transformations of, oral texts.
There are also written texts whose form is reminiscent of an oral
historical account. *Cette-Afrique-là* (1963) by the Cameroonian writer
J. Ikelle-Matiba, recounts the transition from German to French
colonial rule in his country. Nazi Boni's novel, *Crépuscule des temps
anciens* (1962) is a chronicle of three centuries of history in the
Bwanu region (in Upper Volta, now Burkina Faso), although the
arrival of Europeans is privileged. *La Légende de M'Foumou Ma
Mazono* (1954) by the Congolese writer Jean Malonga and *Soundiata
ou l'Epopée mandingue* (1969), by the Guinean, Djibril T. Niane, both
base their texts on transcribed oral history. A. Hampaté Bâ's *Kaidara*
(1969) and *l'Éclat de la grande étoile* (1974) are bilingual texts, published in both Peuhl and French. Bâ also writes as a historian
(*L'Empire peul du Macina* (1955, 1962, 1984) based on fifteen years of
research). Most important, in his view, is his record of the teachings
of Tierno Bokar, 'le sage de Bandiagara', his spiritual master (*Tierno
Bokar, le Sage de Bandiagara, essai* (1957), reissued in a reworked
edition in 1980, *Vie et enseignement de Tierno Bokar, le Sage de
Bandiagara: essai*.

As a novelist, to appeal to one of the broadest generic terms, Bâ
has made a major contribution to African literature with *L'Étrange
destin de Wangrin: Les Roueries d'un interprète africain* (1973). As the
subtitle indicates, language is central to the *récit*, transcribed by Bâ
and supplemented by accounts Bâ solicited from *griots* and others.
As a colonial interpreter Wangrin has access both to the colonial
language and its numerous registers from *le français* 'couleur vin de
Bordeaux', spoken by the colonial administrators, to 'le français des
tirailleurs', but also to Arabic and various African languages
(Bambara and Peuhl in particular). Knowledge of these languages
put Wangrin in an immensely powerful position, controlling the

flow of information between diverse cultural groups. He exploits his position to full advantage, while initially delighting in tricking the wealthy to benefit the poor. However as he forgets his duty to the gods and to his tradition, his fortunes turn. He becomes the lover of 'Madame Blanche Blanche' whose name says it all, and gradually turns to drink. Although he maintains a certain dignity in his acceptance of his destiny, Wangrin is a tragic figure. *L'Étrange destin de Wangrin* is as formally deceptive as its eponymous anti-hero is deceiving; it evades obvious generic characterization just as Wangrin evades obvious roles, or slips deceitfully from one to the next. The language of duplicity—and the duplicities of language—are often described and enacted by means of analogy with animals and animal tales.

Equally experimental and innovatory in formal literary terms are some of Boubou Hama's texts. In addition to historical and political writings, Hama has published a *récit* (*Magie de la forêt vierge*, 1932), a *roman autobiographique/essai* (*Kotia-Nima*, 1969) and numerous *contes*, beginning with *Les Baobabs merveilleux* which appeared in 1971 (in collaboration with Andrée Clair). A fourth generic term associated with another group of his texts is *récit initiatique*. *Le Double d'hier rencontré demain* (1973) and its sequel *Aujourd'hui n'épuise pas demain* (1973; both subtitled *récit initiatique*) stage three 'characters': Bi (who represents/is yesterday), the Master-Initiator Bi-Bio (Bi's double), and Souba (who represents/is tomorrow), the initiate.

Souba also represents Africa and the allegory suggests that it is only by retaining a proper understanding and respect for Africa that the best of what the West has to offer can be appropriately assimilated.

Two of the best-known *conteurs* who write/translate into French are Birago Diop and Bernard Dadié. Diop, a colleague of Senghor, Césaire, and Damas, publicized early on the wealth of oral material on which modern African writers might draw. His *Contes d'Amadou Koumba* (1947), *Les Nouveaux Contes d'Amadou Koumba* (1958), *Contes et Lavanes* (1963), *Contes d'Awa* (1977), are all important texts, as are *Légendes africaines* (1954) and the *contes* of *Le Pagne noir* (1965), both by Bernard Dadié.

Very different, particularly for the European reader unfamiliar with the history, are the direct transcriptions of historical *récits*, recorded, transcribed, and translated. The Soundiata legend has been recorded (1966) and published by Massa Makan Diabaté,

L'Aigle et l'Épervier ou le Geste de Sunjata (1975) and by Camara Laye who noted it in 1963 and published it in 1978 (*Le Maître de la parole / Kouma Lafolo Wpiima*, 'history of the first words'). The extraordinarily long genealogies are fascinating but highly confusing. The same is often true of the narratives, subnarratives, and parallel narratives.

Very much more immediately accessible are the songs and poems which have been translated into French. Pacéré Titinga, whose native village, Manega (Burkina Faso) is at the centre of his work which is not so much 'based on' the oral tradition but as closely as possible, a transcription into a written form. 'A la limite', he explains, 'si je réussis mon œuvre, celle-ci n'est plus mienne, mais celle des griots eux-mêmes.'[60] The Cameroonian writer Patrice Kayo is similarly committed to a local literature, in his case bamiléké (West Cameroon); (see, for example, *La Sagesse bamiléké*, 1964; *Chansons populaires bamiléké*, 1968; *Chansons populaires bamiléké*, 1983; among a number of similar works), although he has been equally committed to establishing Cameroonian literature as a national literature, as director of *Cameroun littéraire*, editor of *Ozila*, and author of, for example, *Anthologie de la poésie camerounaise de langue française* (1977) and *Panorama de la littérature camerounaise* (1978).

All oral forms of expression are not only vocal but theatrical. That is to say they draw on expressive means exploited in theatre: facial expressions, gesture, sensitivity to the audience's response and degree of participation, and so on. Social and religious rituals are equally theatrical: ceremonies associated with marriage and death, most obviously; moreover certain kinds of psychiatric or religious therapy may also depend on adherence to a strictly predetermined sequence of verbal utterances and physical movements. In storytelling, above all, the divide between the *performance* of an oral tale— the term pre-empts the point that a story is never simply 'told'—and theatre becomes most blurred. The teller of the tale will in turn become the various characters involved. In different parts of Africa different theatrical traditions developed. Two of the most studied are the phenomenon of the *mvet* in Cameroon, and the *koteba* in Mali. The former is a professional who masters not only storytelling, but also singing, instruments, dance, and mime. The 'text' which is then performed dramatizes the conflict between the *Majona*, the mortals, and the *Ekang*, the immortals. The Malian

---

[60] Pacéré Titinga, cited in Rouch and Clavreuil, *Littératures nationales*, 31.

koteba is a dramatic sequence performed annually by young people. Largely improvised, certain 'types' of sketches are performed, associated with 'the jealous husband', 'the tax collector', 'the unscrupulous marabout', and so on.

African theatre changed fundamentally after the arrival of the European missionaries who introduced a theatre in which a stage, painted scenery, and payment were constituent parts of the whole. The function of this theatre was essentially pedagogical. A little later, from 1930 onwards, the École William Ponty in Dakar, Senegal, which educated Africans for the colonial administration, made theatre an important educational focus. Pupils would document interesting or amusing happenings from village life which were then dramatized. From these unpromising origins and stimulated by the Concours théâtral interafricain, organized by Radio France Internationale, and by European interest (Jean-Marie Serreau's productions of Aimé Césaire and Kateb Yacine, and Peter Brook's version of Birago Diop's *L'Os* for example), francophone African theatre has developed. Whilst Aimé Césaire's plays are probably the most staged in Africa, influential African playwrights have also emerged. Like Césaire who bases many of his plays on the lives of important Black heroes (the Haitian Roi Christophe, and Patrice Lumumba, for example), one strand of francophone African theatre can be defined by its focus on an African hero from history. Thus Chaka (the Zulu warrior who inspired the South African writer Thomas Mofolo's novel written in Lesotho) has inspired plays by Abdou Anta Kâ, Seydou Badian, Djibril Tamsir Niane, Charles Nokan, Tchicaya U Tam'si, Senouvo Agbota Zinsou, and of course, even earlier, Senghor's dramatic poem, 'X'.

Nokan has a particular vision of the social function of literature. It should represent, and be accessible to, ordinary people. His theatre is thus didactic and formally schematic. *Ier Soleil noir point* (1962) exploits a rhetoric reminiscent of Paul Claudel's theatre. A similar tone characterizes the composite text, *Violent était le vent* (1966), generally classed simply as a novel. *Les Malheurs de Tchako* (1968) belongs within that tradition which dramatizes Chaka's amazing contribution to African history. It was followed in 1971 by *Abraha Pokou ou Une grande africaine*. It may well be that harsh judgements of Nokan arise out of a critical evaluation of his texts rather than from actual performances of his plays.

Lat Dior, who fought against the French invasion of Senegal, is central to plays by Amadou Cissé Dia. The last King of Dahomey,

Behanzin, is the main character in Jean Pliya's *Kondo le requin* (1966) which won the Grand Prix littéraire de l'Afrique noire the subsequent year. It was followed by the equally historical *Les Rois d'Abomey* (1972) and *La Secrétaire particulière* (1973), a satire on bureaucracy.

Simon Kimbangu ou le Messie noir (1972), by Elebe Lisembe, explores the eponymous hero's resistance to the colonial order. Equally historical are Cheikh A. Ndao's *L'Exil d'Albouri* (1967) and Bernard Dadié's *Monsieur Thôgô-Gnini* (1970) and *Béatrice du Congo* (1970).

Distinct from theatre which draws on heroic conflicts in history, is a theatre of satire. The three butts of the satire which stand out most obviously are the reactionary forces of tradition, the comic and pathetic mimicry of colonial ways, and the aberrations of post-colonial Africa. This last group is particularly well represented by Congolese and Cameroonian playwrights, for example, *La Marmite de Kola M'Bala* (1966) and *Oracle* (1969) by Guy Menga, and *Trois prétendants, un mari* (1975) and *Le Train spécial et Son excellence* (1978) by Guillaume Oyono-Mbia, and Sony Labou Tansi's *La Parenthèse de sang* (1981) and *Je soussigné cardiaque* (1981). Oyono-Mbia's *Trois prétendants*, a comedy which focuses on the implications of the marriage dowry, won the Prix El Hadj Ahmadou Ahidjo in 1970 and always attracts a large and appreciative audience when performed in the Cameroon. While on a British Council Scholarship at the University of Keele, Oyono-Mbia was awarded a major prize for his play, *Until Further Notice*, in the African theatre competition organized by the BBC African Service. Performed at the Edinburgh Festival in 1967, the play dramatizes the period which precedes the drama, as a village awaits the return of a young couple who have been studying in Europe. Oyono-Mbia has also written a French version, *Jusqu'à nouvel avis*, first recorded by the French services of the BBC. He has continued to write both in French and English. His *Excellency's Special Train* (1969) is a radio play first broadcast by the BBC. *Notre fille ne se mariera pas* was first performed in the same year. Three collections of short stories which he began in 1964 were published in 1971–2, entitled *Chroniques de Mvoutessi*. Central to all his work is the comedy arising out of the conflict between traditional values and those of a modernized, 'educated', Westernized, and urbanized people. As a bilingual writer his work has a peculiar national status in the Cameroon as his work is accessible both to the anglophones of Western Cameroon and the francophones in the east. Among a number of playwrights to have appeared in recent years are Maxime N'Debeka, Senouvo Agbota Zinsou, Ahmed Tidjani Cissé, and Werewere Liking.

Sony Labou Tansi is the founder (in 1979) of one of the most important African troupes, the Rocado Zulu Theatre in Brazzaville, which he directs. In addition to producing works by Congolese playwrights, he has staged Aimé Césaire's *La Tragédie du Roi Christophe*. In recent years it is his own plays which the troupe has performed (*La Parenthèse de sang*, 1981; *Antoine m'a vendu son destin*, 1986; *Qui a mangé Madame d'Avoine Bergotha?*, 1989). In addition to Sony Labou Tansi's troupe a number of other African companies have travelled widely both in Africa and beyond: L'Ensemble Koteba, directed by Souleymane Koly, and the Théâtre Ki-Yi, directed by Werewere Liking, are both based in Abidjan as is the Compagnie du Didiga, directed by Bernard Zadi Zaourou. The Théâtre de la fraternité, directed by Pierre Guingané, is also based in Abidjan. The Théâtre Nyogolon in Bamako is another that is established on the international scene.

Francophone African theatre is accessible only to a minority in many areas of Africa. In a number of countries theatre in African languages is developing. Alongside this development is the phenomenon of *théâtre total* which stages dance, song, and the recitation of traditional tales, for example. Nor is African theatre solely the preserve of the literate educated. *La cantate*, in Togo, combines the performance of songs sung in Ewe, accompanied by dance, and telling oriental or biblical stories, for example *Ali Baba et les quarante voleurs* and *Isaac et Rebecca*. Also in Ewe (but also in French and English) and originating in neighbouring Ghana, the concert or concert party is an improvised play, usually a picaresque tale. One well-known example is *Francis le Parisien* by the Happy Star Concert Band in Lomé (collected and presented by Noble Akam and Alain Ricard (1981)). Certain obviously modern aspects of the concert party are immediately apparent: the music, which is an indispensable element, is produced on electric instruments; the players speak at a microphone placed centre-stage; the performance is staged in particular venues and the spectators pay. On the other hand it is the narration which is the focus of the spectacle and the performance, like the telling of tales, can only take place at night.

The Africanization of francophone African theatre can be explained in terms of the control gradually assumed by African writers and directors, rather than missionaries or colonial administrators or teachers in part concerned to prepare pupils for a place within colonial structures. A similar shift of control is represented by the gradual emergence of African publishers and the integration of francophone African texts within the newly developing African educational systems after Independence. The emergence of an African literature controlled by Europeans and largely read and written about within non-African literary institutions is thus giving way to, or competing with, an African literary institution represented by African publishing houses, African school syllabuses, and African critics.

The first publishing house, however, Éditions CLE (Yaoundé), was founded in 1963 through the efforts of German and Dutch Protestant missionaries. Les Nouvelles Éditions Africaines (Dakar, Abidjan, Lomé) was founded at Senghor's request in 1972. CEDA (Centre d'Editions et de Diffusions Africaines) began publishing in Abidjan in 1974 followed by numerous small presses with limited distribution, such as Éditions Jamana (Mali) and Éditions Sopecam (Cameroon).

In Paris, a market dominated by Présence Africaine found rivals both in new companies and new series: l'Harmattan, Karthala, Silex, and Hatier's influential 'Monde noir poche' series, for example. CLEF (Club des Lecteurs d'Expression française) which receives support from the French state, has also grown in importance.

In addition to the market controlled by these publishing houses is the market for 'popular' fiction, produced in extremely cheap editions and sold in the streets. In Cameroon, for example, the significantly named Éditions du demi-lettré, founded by Desiré Naha, has published numerous novels in French. Similarly, in Zaïre, writers such as Zamenga Batukezanga have produced a large number of short novels—almost one a year since 1971—for a very large market. Concerned to explore certain contemporary problems, the generation gap, the failure of traditional marriage, and so on, Zamenga Batukezanga's writing has largely been dismissed by critics. Whatever else it may represent, it testifies to the existence of a large reading public in the country, anxious to read works of fiction about contemporary society.

Poetry, although less important than the novel, also continues to reach a significant public, in part due to the success of poetry readings and performances. During the post-Independence period the kinds of poetry being written has multiplied. This is clearly visible in the large number of anthologies published over the last three decades. Some are limited by a national focus and these naturally invite the reader to consider the homogeneity of *La Poésie camerounaise* or *Poésie du Sénégal* (edited by Babacar Sall), for example. Sall's 'Avant-propos' is typical in the way in which it invites the anthology to be approached:

Dans Poésie du Sénégal, le lecteur trouvera, entre autres, des poèmes qui parlent du pays et de ses habitants, des poèmes qui portent des noms communs de personnes et de choses, des poèmes qui sont des lieux de mémoire, et qui ne sont en réalité que prétextes pour découvrir le paysage intérieur des poètes.[61]

Beyond national trends or characterizations, poems can be crudely grouped. A militant, readily accessible poetry continues to be written after Independence, and to denounce colonialism and its myriad legacies. Most strongly in Guinea and Congo-Brazzaville, the singing of an idyllic Africa is replaced by a vision of poetry summed up thus: 'la poésie doit avoir pour but la vérité pratique'. Most Congolese poetry—J.-B. Tati-Loutard constitutes an exception as is discussed further below—is *engagée*. The Cameroonian poet Paul Dakeyo writes a militant poetry, but one which is not without a certain lyricism:

> Le vent humide, les cris d'oiseaux
> Me parviennent comme autant
> D'inquiétudes
> Dans la nuit essentielle
> Le feu, l'enfant, l'école, l'homme.[62]

More violent in its militancy is Pacéré Titinga's poetry. Titinga, originally from Upper Volta, won the Grand Prix littéraire de l'Afrique noire in 1983 for his collection, *Poèmes pour Angola* (1982).

A further type of poetry suggests the mysterious powers of language. A number of poets from Zaïre, in particular, for example Nzuji Mukala and Pius Ngandu Nkashama, are peculiarly linguistically preoccupied. This is rather different, however, from the hermeticism of V. Y. Mudimbé: 'La savane est une suppuration offerte au soleil. Que s'y perpétuent les délices des bébés . . .'[63] Mudimbé, an academic philosopher as well as a poet and novelist,

---

[61] Babacar Sall, *Poésie du Sénégal* (1988), 3.
[62] P. Dakeyo, in J.-L. Joubert *et al.* (eds.), *Littératures francophones*, 62.
[63] V. Y. Mudimbé, *Déchirures*, cited ibid. 63.

began his writing career with an influential collection of essays which strike at the core of the problem of Western *versus* African discourses:

Le discours africain, expression d'une autre idéologie, est, dans son principe même, récusé par l'idéologie dominante et, d'entrée de jeu, considéré comme 'scientifiquement' irrecevable. Le discours 'occidental', par contre, même aberrant (pour mémoire, les thèses du primitivisme, par exemple), possède des privilèges de légitimation qui souvent proviennent de critères externes au discours lui-même.[64]

His poems, *Déchirures* (1971), *Entrailles précédé de Fulgurances d'une lézarde* (1973), *Les Fuseaux, parfois* (1974) have a philosophical dimension. *Les Fuseaux*, in particular, dramatizes the tensions between body and mind in verse and prose poems. Antonin Artaud's writing, which he cites, has been a strong influence.

Hieratic and oratorical, Théophile Obenga's writing is strongly influenced by Cheikh Anta Diop's researches into the Egyptian origins of Black Africa. His poetry is suggestive of liturgy: 'Gloire à toi | Dame de la danse et de l'amour | Dame noire aux cheveux tressés | Dame toujours nouvelle d'encens nouveau.'[65] Rooted in the Congo, and dominated by a preoccupation with time, identity, and the landscape, J.-B. Tati-Loutard's poetry is at times hermetic, at times easily accessible: 'Baobab! je suis venu replanter mon être près de toi | Et mêler mes racines à tes racines d'ancêtre.'[66] Tati-Loutard rejected what he saw as the easy but restricting prescriptions of Negritude, first on the grounds that it limited the writer's freedom, the 'libre expression des tempéraments', and secondly because of its spurious homogeneity based on 'l'âme noire': 'Dans leur phobie de ne pas pouvoir dire autrement que l'Européen ou l'Asiatique . . . [les jeunes Africains] usent leur force à cultiver une différence convenue, alors qu'il suffirait d'ôter l'écran de la race pour libérer leur tempérament.'[67]

Although less prolific, Noël X. Ebony, who died tragically in 1986, has also written poems representative of the high point of contem-

---

[64] Mudimbé, cited in J.-P. de Beaumarchais, D. Conty, A. Rey (eds.), *Dictionnaire des littératures de langue française* (Bordas, 1984), 1579.

[65] T. Obenga, 'Stèles pour l'avenir', in J.-L. Joubert *et al.* (eds.), *Littératures francophones*, 63.

[66] J.-B. Tati-Loutard, 'Baobab' ('Retour au Congo'), *Les Racines congolaises* (1978), 43.

[67] Tati-Loutard quoted by R. Chemain and A. Chemain-Degrange, *Panorama critique de la littérature congolaise contemporaine* (1979), 19.

porary francophone African poetry. His collection, *Déjà vu* (1983) embraces the *retour aux sources* of Negritude, an explicit emphasis on the oral tradition, a certain militancy, and a degree of internationalism in its referents, in short a highly wrought poetic *bricolage*.

The novel of the 1960s is best characterized in terms of its growing diversity. Whereas major novels of the 1950s could, without enormous reduction, have been divided into groups, after Independence the novel displaces poetry as the major genre, and diversifies. Olympe Bhêly Quenum's *Un Piège sans fin* (1960) and *Le Chant du lac* are equally complex in interpretative terms. Typical of a new complexity (although from the late 1960s), is Yambo Ouologuem's *Le Devoir de la violence*. Awarded the Prix Renaudot in 1968 amid considerable controversy, the most sustained element of *Le Devoir* is its attack on a romanticized pre-colonial Africa simplistically appealed to by the Negritude apologists unwilling to identify either the political complexities of pre-colonial Africa or contemporary ideological complexities. Formally as innovative as its argument, *Le Devoir* stimulated considerable controversy, not only because of its polemic, but also because of accusations of plagiarism. It may well be that this is an accusation which betrays its own Eurocentrism, given the irrelevance, the total meaninglessness, of plagiarism within the oral tradition on which Ouologuem draws quite as much as he does on European and American writers. The sex and violence of *Le Devoir* is equally central to his later texts, *Lettre à la France nègre* (1969) and *Les Mille et une bibles du sexe* (1969), published under the pseudonym Rodolphe Utto. *Lettre à la France nègre* is dedicated 'à toutes les victimes de l'antiracisme' and this is consonant with the shock-tactics which operate at every level of his texts: linguistic (syntactic), thematic (violent sadism), ideological (pandering to what might be hypothesized as the archetypal European's secret desires for a barbaric African discourse). Ouologuem's texts are reminiscent of Lautréamont's, apparently revelling in profanation, but in a more extreme way than Lautréamont's, foregrounding the problems of limitation and restriction—in terms of just what can be written—imposed on African writers by the political and historical context in which they write.

Ahmadou Kourouma's *Les Soleils des indépendances* (1968) may, equally, be remembered not for the ideological controversy which it excited, but because of its innovatory language. The opening lines are well-known: 'Il y avait une semaine qu'avait fini dans la capitale Koné Ibrahima, de race malinke, ou disons-le en Malinke: il n'avait pas soutenu un petit rhume . . .'[68] Suggesting direct translation from the Malinke, idiom, in terms of both language and style, the narration of *Les Soleils* does not imply the perspective of the ethnographer or the outsider. It is the reader who is distanced by the language which is no longer strange to the context it describes. Nor is this linguistic method separable from other aspects of the novel. The 'contamination' or 'bastardization' of the narrator's language by the hero's has a parallel in the Malinke hero's gradual decline and ultimate failure in the post-colonial culture in which he is obliged to live. Fama, the novel's hero, is a Malinke prince who gradually discovers that there is no place for him in the newly independent country. The action takes place in two imaginary countries, Côté des Ebènes, and la République socialiste Nikinai. What are criticized are totalitarian regimes in which the individual loses both identity and freedom. Salimata, the hero's wife, is as powerless in the newly independent society as within traditional structures. The sterility of the couple symbolizes the failure of independence, suggesting the human unhappiness which accompanies the failure to find just political solutions. Kourouma's play, *Tougnantigui ou le diseur de vérité* (1972) is concerned with similar themes. Although diversity is the major characteristic of the francophone African novel after Independence, certain preoccupying themes dominate. *Les Soleils* is an indictment of post-Independence Africa and its inability to find coherence and meaning. Alioum Fantouré's *Le Cercle des tropiques* (1972) is a political novel which explores autocratic and dictatorial methods of government by means of a hallucinatory account by an ordinary citizen. *Le Récit du cirque* (1975) is also an exploration of power but here the novel is more complex. The action takes place in a theatre where a classical play is about to be performed. This is interrupted by a member of the audience who suggests that a quite different performance should be staged. The text is thus highly self-reflexive, probing difficult questions about *engagement* and African writers' responsibilities in terms of politics and ideology, as well as literary accessibility. *L'Homme du troupeau dans le Sahel* (1979) takes place in the Sahara during the Second World War. The journey undertaken by a group of men charged with looking after the beasts is also the allegorical journey which Africa will embark on some twenty years later. The epic tone of the novel reflects both the

---

[68] A. Kourouma, *Les Soleils des indépendances* (Montreal, 1968; Paris, 1970), opening page.

theme of the journey (reminiscent of Saint-John Perse's *Anabase*) and the seriousness and dangers of political expediency which the allegory suggests.

Mongo Beti's *Perpétue* (1974) is also a criticism of political structures, in this case the one-party state. Fantouré's *Le Récit du cirque* (1975) also concerns a one-party state. Other novels seeking to expose the shortcomings and injustices of post-Independence Africa include (among many), Pierre Bamboté's *Princesse Mandapu* (1972), Antoine Bangui's *Prisonniers de Tombalbaye* (1980), Ibrahima Ly's *Toiles d'araignées* (1982), Mandé-Alpha Diarra's *Sahel, sanglante sécheresse* (1981), V. Y. Mudimbé's *Le Bel immonde* (1976), Tierno Monénembo's *Crapauds-brousse* (1979), and Henri Lopès's short stories, *Tribaliques* (1971). Formerly Prime Minister of the République Populaire du Congo, his novel *La Nouvelle Romance* (1976) deals not only with political corruption and compromise but also with the relationship between politics and tribalism. Both works explore the position of women in African society. *Le Pleurer-Rire* (1982) exploits the 'esthétique du grotesque' in a pastiche which suggests the fragmentation and lack of order and direction of a post-Independence African state. It is also self-reflexive and self-parodying in interesting and significant ways. *Le Chercheur d'Afrique* (1990) explores the possibilitites of discovering the past both as an individual (identity) and a group (history).

Three novels which explore different forms of commitment are Emmanuel Dongala's *Un Fusil dans la main, un poème dans la poche*, V. W. Mudimbé's *Entre les eaux*, and Williams Sassine's *Saint Monsieur Baly*, all published in 1973. In the first the protagonist returns to Africa from university in France and decides to join the freedom fighters of South Africa. In Mudimbé's *Entre les eaux* the protagonist is torn between his vocation as a priest and revolutionary action. In *Saint Monsieur Baly* a schoolteacher retires but decides to open a school for deprived children.

Ousmane Sembène's novels of this period, *Le Mandat* (1966) and *Xala* (1973), were both made into films by Sembène himself. His novel *Le Dernier de l'empire* (1981) is also concerned with a (not so) fictional African state, Sunugal. Satirizing Senghor's Negritude ('Authenegrafricanitus'), it explores power and the relationships between class (as it emerges in a modern society) and caste, or traditional social hierarchies.

Much influenced by Latin-American writers, particularly Gabriel Garcia Marquez, Sony Labou Tansi has written a number of novels

(*La Vie et demie*, 1979; *L'État honteux*, 1981; *L'Anté-peuple*, 1983; *Les Sept solitudes de Lorsa Lopez*, 1985). Drawing on a vast lexis (obscure French words, African words, witty neologisms), exploiting digression to a fantastic and comical degree, Sony Labou Tansi's writing is immensely entertaining but also serious. Dadou, for example, the hero of *l'Anté-peuple*, reflects in prison:

On est en prison parce que d'autres, là-bas, chantent les plats et les chansons. On est en prison, simplement parce que, là-bas, des gens parlent de foot-ball. Et il faut bien qu'ils parlent. Sinon le monde s'arrêterait. Pour qu'ils parlent en paix, d'autres gens doivent être sur la natte, en prison, écrasés. Mais il n'y a pas d'écrasants. Il n'y a pas d'écraseurs.[69]

The social condition is an unjust one. It is not simply a matter of individual moral aberration.

Mongo Beti who published nothing for a long period (1958–72) returned to writing with a pamphlet on his country during the immediate post-Independence period: *Main basse sur le Cameroun* (1972). Nor is Beti's long silence uncommon. Seydou Badian published nothing for fifteen years (*Le Sang des masques* came out in 1976), and Ahmadou Kourouma for almost twenty. Beti's later novels, *Remember Ruben* (1974), *Perpétue ou l'Habitude du malheur* (1974), and *La Ruine presque cocasse d'un Polichinelle* (1979), also concern the political and social conditions of Cameroon during the same period. Central to both *Les Deux mères de Guillaume Ismaël Dzwatama futur camionneur* (1982) and *La Revanche de Guillaume Ismaël Dzwatama* (1984) is the relationship between Africa and Europe explored through mixed marriages. Olympe Bhêly-Quenum's *L'Initié* (1979) combines an exploration of a mixed marriage with an exploration of the possibilities of combining European and traditional medicine. Tingo, the protagonist, who has studied in France, returns home with his French wife.

The length of Ahmadou Kourouma's silence as a novelist is mirrored in the time-span of *Monné, outrage et défis* (1990). It concerns the 120-year reign of Djigui, King of Soba, during which he resists and then co-operates with the colonial forces.

Tchicaya U Tam'si's novels of the 1980s (*La Main sèche*, 1980; *Les Cancrelats*, 1980; *Les Méduses ou les Orties de mer*, 1982; *Les Phalènes*, 1984) are remarkable both for the time-spans which they often embrace (*Les Cancrelats* and *Les Phalènes* both cover fifty years, from

[69] Sony Labou Tansi, *L'Anté-peuple* (1983), 77.

the turn of the century to the eve of Independence), for their poly-phonic narrative techniques, and for the absence of straightforward chronology. Realism and the fantastic, the natural and the super-natural, are interwoven in rich and complex texts which constantly question the significance of happenings in a society in which every-thing is changing fast.

Massa Makan Diabaté's writing is equally difficult but for very different reasons. It is the *tone* of his novels which is responsible for a fundamental ambiguity. According to Diabaté, 'ce sont des livres d'inspiration religieuse'. But the novels' humour renders this prob-lematic. Yet *Comme une piqûre de guêpe* (1980) which dramatizes an initiation ceremony, suggests that a grotesque parody of the sacred is always so close to the genuinely sacred that it may be safer to exploit humour in any attempt to suggest the sacred. Beneath the caricature and the absurdity of Diabaté's world is a profound respect for African tradition. From a literary-historical point of view Diabaté's novels are also interesting in terms of the relationships they establish with earlier African novels (in the case of *Comme une piqûre*, the *romans d'initiation* of the 1950s, most obviously Laye's *L'Enfant noir* and Kane's *L'Aventure ambiguë*).

It was only during the 1970s that francophone African women writers emerged. The way was no doubt prepared by influential francophone African spokeswomen, for example, Thérèse Kuoh, founder of the Union des femmes africaines et malgaches, Agnès Diarra, Arame Diop, and Awa Keita. *Femme d'Afrique* (1976), Keita's autobiographical and political novel, was awarded the Grand Prix littéraire d'Afrique noire. Nafissatou Diallo's *De Tilène au plateau* (1975) is, equally, an autobiographical text. *Le Fort maudit* (1980) concerns the destiny of Thiane, ultimately a slave. Aminata Sow Fall's *Le Revenant* (1976) and three years later, *La Grève des bâttu*, can be described as a *roman de mœurs* and a *roman social* respectively. *L'Appel des arènes* (1982) is more didactic, concerned with the prob-lems of cultural alienation and the role of education. Mariama Bâ's texts are more obviously those of a woman writer. *Une si longue lettre* (1979) explores the problems and unhappiness of polygamy. *Un chant écarlate*, Bâ's second novel, was only half written when she died in 1981. It was published posthumously, in its incomplete form. A number of influential essays have also been published by women. Awa Thiam's *La Parole aux négresses* was published in 1978 and is based on recordings of conversations with women. More influential is Catherine N'Diaye's *Gens de sable* (1984) which, perhaps influenced by Roland Barthes's *Mythologies*, explores various aspects of Senegalese life.

Production by women during the 1980s is marked by a shift away from autobiographical or documentary texts towards something apparently more fictional, although writers such as Nafissatou Diallo draw on history and legend. Calixthe Beyala's *C'est le soleil qui m'a brillée* (1987) is a militant feminist novel which exposes the injustices of the patriarchy. More formally innovative is Véronique Tadjo's fragmentary novel *A Vol d'oiseau* (1986), which attempts to recapture moments of a failed love affair. Werewere Liking is one of the most prolific francophone African women writers. She has published poetry (beginning with *On ne raisonne pas le venin*, 1977), essays (*Du Rituel à la scène chez les Bassa du Cameroun*, 1979, and *Une Vision de Kaydara*, 1984), a *récit-essai* (*A la rencontre de . . .*, in collaboration with Manouna Ma Njock), plays which are subtitled *théâtre-rituel* (beginning with *La Queue du diable*, published in *Du Rituel*), and prose works described as *chant-roman* and *conte initiatique*. Werewere Liking's concern to find appellative terms for her texts which distinguish them from Western texts and suggest relationships with indigenous forms is not an easy and isolated gesture, but reflects a sustained concern to write an *African* literature. The language of her texts is complex, requiring a knowledge of both the French language and culture, together with African mores and francophone African diction.

Much of what is important in Liking's project is revealed by an approach which takes account of her status as a francophone *woman* writer. She can, alternatively, be seen as one of a group of African writers for whom questions of literary form and philosophy are intimately bound up. Williams Sassine (in *Le Jeune homme de sable*, 1979), V. Y. Mudimbé (in *L'Écart*, 1979) and Jean-Marie Adiaffi (in *La Carte d'identité*, 1980) explore the nature of human existence and individual identity and personality, in novels which abandon any kind of realism in favour of formal and stylistic complexity. Boubacar Boris Diop's *Le Temps de Tamango* (1981) is set in the year 2063. The protagonist, a scientist assisted by a novelist, attempts to reconstruct the events of the 1970s in his country. The contradictions and paradoxes of history which are encountered suggest the complexities of historiography and the impossibilities of gaining full access to the past. Certain interesting parallels with Henri Lopès's *Le Chercheur d'Afriques* (1990) suggest themselves (see above). More technically straightforward are Mbwill a Mpaang Ngal's novels,

Giambatista Viko (1975) and *L'Errance* (1979) in which the nature of the modern African novel, its language and philosophy, and the comparative cultural values of European and African civilization, are the ambitious themes. Both novels explore the relative significance for the assimilated or partly assimilated African, of African and European imaginative discourse, philosophy, and religion. This takes the fictional form, in the earlier work, of a narrative which recounts the experiences of an African intellectual who, in the hope of achieving literary acclaim, writes a novel based on material from the oral tradition. The work is judged to be a sacrilege by African elders and the protagonist is compelled to undergo an initiation in order to be cured of his 'alienation'. Ngal's novel serves as a timely warning at a point in African literary history when the idea of reconnecting with tradition, while at the same time not wholeheartedly rejecting 'modernity' or Western traditions, lies at the centre of many writing projects.

The oral tradition is a resource to be exploited, a library to be made available, but the relationship between African oral discourse in African languages and written European discourse in European languages is an immensely complex one. Symbiosis of some kind suggests itself as the alternative either to participating exclusively within an oral culture on the one hand, or being assimilated into a written European culture on the other. But for symbiosis to be satisfactory in aesthetic, political, literary, and moral terms, it needs to be something more than a ludic post-modern pastiche—rather, an intelligent sensitivity to the subtleties of each tradition and the meaning of hybridity and *métissage*.

Significant numbers of African authors are also writing in African languages. Wolof, which has a standardized orthography and grammar, and is the most important language of Senegal, is widely used in novels and films particularly. Most writers and film-makers—Ousmane Sembène is the most obvious example—produce versions in French as well, allowing their works to reach an international audience.

A further recent kind of fiction which can be identified as a distinct type is one in which Paris is the locus (and is frequently where the author lives) for an exploration of the complexities of internaticnalism, immigration, and cultural, ethnic, or linguistic hybridity. Published in 1987, Pius Ngandu Nkashama's *Vie et mœurs d'un primitif en Essonne 91000*, concerns an initiative, in the Parisian suburbs, to set up an African co-operative movement. Among a number of novels all published in 1988 are: Doumbi-Fakoly's *Certificat de contrôle anti-sida*, Yodi Karone's *A la recherche du cannibale amour*, Bernabé Laleye's *Mangalor*, Blaise N'Djehoya's *Le Nègre Potemkine*. Paris was also the place of exile for (among a larger number) three important poets: Paul Dakeyo, Maxime N'Debeka, and Mukala Kadima-Nzuji.

The complexities of African writing and the African writer's position, also serve as reminders that literature cannot be discussed as a completely separate area of human activity. As Edward Saïd has forcefully argued, 'most modes of writing [and, it could be added, oral genres] about men and women in history are, in fact, tangled up together'. He goes on to point out that their separation is often carried out: 'on professional, even epistemological grounds in order to accomplish social goals of one sort or another, and that criticism if it is to be criticism and not only the celebration of masterpieces, deals with the separations, the entanglements'.[70]

It is only within relatively stable and powerful intellectual (and often academic and pedagogical) contexts that there is sufficient consensus for the canonization of 'masterpieces'. Francophone African literature is read and criticized by significant numbers of readers on three continents (in Africa, Europe, and North America) and there is no obvious consensus about the context or field within which francophone African literature (only one of a number of areas that were proposed at the beginning of this chapter) should be read and studied. Nor, therefore, is there agreement about the canon of African literature, although in several African countries a growing consensus about the great works of that country's literature (often embracing texts in a number of languages) is emerging with the appearance of anthologies and school textbooks. But it is nevertheless unlikely that the 'separations' and 'entanglements' of which Saïd speaks will be overlooked. It is these, of course, which make the study of African literature capable of so richly illuminating the complexities of the literary text *qua* cultural product. Diglossia, *métissage*, hybridity: these characterize most francophone writing but within the multiplicities and vastness of an essentially abstract space— African literature—their meaning is always complex, and always

---

[70] Edward Saïd, *Beginnings* (New York, 1975; repr. 1985), p. iv (preface to Morningside edn.).

intellectually exciting. Even the geographic boundaries in Africa (and this is not the same for the Caribbean islands, for example), are in the main artificial, and invented by Europeans.

Homogenization, and the quest for a fixed literary canon, is often a response to fear. What is to be hoped is that there is sufficient confidence and freedom for the diversity and hybridity of African literatures to be celebrated and studied in all their complexity, and not reduced either by narrow publication programmes or by restrictive institutional and pedagogical practices.

14

MADAGASCAR

The sections devoted to Malagasy poetry in French in the two anthologies which were first to attract attention to Black francophone writing (Léon-Gontran Damas's seminal *Poètes d'expression française*, 1947, and Léopold Sédar Senghor's influential *Anthologie de la nouvelle poésie nègre et malgache de langue française*, 1948, introduced by Sartre's famous essay 'Orphée noir'), are both of a length comparable to the sections devoted to the whole of Black Africa. The year Damas's anthology was published was the year in which tensions on the island came to a head. Between 10,000 and 80,000 people (depending on the source) were killed in the anti-colonial uprising of 1947. The island's three best-known poets, Jean-Joseph Rabearivelo, Jacques Rabemananjara (imprisoned for alleged involvement in the uprising), and Flavien Ranaivo, were writing during a period of turmoil and one in which the discovery and defence of Malagasy culture was part of a growing nationalism. All were concerned with Malagasy literary traditions and Rabemananjara's poetry became increasingly militant. For the editors of the anthologies mentioned above, Malagasy literature in French was pioneering. As is obvious from the length of the section devoted to Madagascar here, Malagasy literature in French has become increasingly marginal since the intense programmes of *malgachisation* which followed Independence.

The vast island of Madagascar (with a land mass of nearly 600,000 sq. km. and 5,000 km. of coast), lies to the east of Africa in the Indian Ocean. The present population is approximately 10 million. Europeans first arrived in the sixteenth century but until the eighteenth it was used as nothing more than a staging-post on the route to India. During this period the island was divided into a number of kingdoms: the Betsileos in the south, the Betsimisarakas on the east coast, the Sakalavas in the north west and the Merinas in the centre of the country. Formal Anglo-Malagasy agreements were signed in the nineteenth century but as the Merina monarchy began to lose control so the French gained ground, gradually pushing out the English. In 1890 what had been a relatively surreptitious move turned into invasion. A French expeditionary force arrived and conquered one town after another. In 1895 the capital Tananarive was taken and rebellion broke out. The French general in charge, Gallieni, responded by having two ministers and ten dignitaries shot and by exiling the last Queen of Madagascar. Insurrections and revolts continued. The repression of 1915 was particularly brutal. So too was that of 1947 in which so many were killed.

Philibert Tsiranana became president in 1960 when the island assumed its independence. Popular pressure forced him to cede power to General Ramanantsoa in 1972 who, in his turn, was forced to resign his place to Colonel Ratsimandrava in 1975, assassinated that same year. A military *directoire* of nineteen men took over until the end of the year when in December 1975 Captain Didier Ratsiraka became head of State.

The literary history of the island differs from that of most francophone areas because of the linguistic unity of the island's first language, Malagasy. Classified within the Malayo-Polynesian family, its written history dates back several centuries. An essentially Arabic alphabet was replaced at the beginning of the nineteenth century by a Latin alphabet. In 1823 King Radama I standardized Malagasy orthography. The status of written Malagasy was further guaranteed by translations of the Bible, other printed texts, an improved educational system, and a Malagasy press. By the end of the nineteenth century, before the French took control in 1895, there already existed a sizeable body of works in Malagasy mainly consisting of memoires, scholarly works, religious texts, transcriptions from the oral tradition, and poems. These last were written in imitation of the canticles and introduced the principle of rhythm into Malagasy writing.

Colonial rule imposed French as the 'civilized' language, transforming Malagasy into the language of resistance. Ny Avana Ramanantoanina (exiled from the island in 1916 for his alleged participation in the 1915 uprising) and, more recently, Dox, are two poets who have attracted considerable readerships. Between the wars literary groups formed on the island encouraged by figures

such as Pierre Camo, the French 'fantaisiste' poet and, later, Octave
Mannoni who was, with Frantz Fanon, to become one of the two
major writers on the psychology of colonialism. In addition to the
official *Revue de Madagascar* which occasionally carried literary articles, the journals *18 Latitude Sud* (1923–7), *Capricorne* (1930–1), were
all published on the island. Most of the French texts by Malagasy
writers which appeared in these journals were translations of traditional Malagasy forms.

The most important Malagasy genre is the *hain teny*. The French
writer Jean Paulhan was to make the form known to a French public
when, in 1913, he published *Les Hain teny merina: poésies populaires
malgaches recueillies et traduites par Jean Paulhan* in Paris. Paulhan had
learnt Malagasy and collected documents for research on Malagasy
proverbs, a project on which he continued to work until 1936. In
1939 he published a less scholarly version of his earlier work without
the Malagasy texts. This was to attract the fascinated attention of a
number of French writers including Apollinaire, Max Jacob, and
Paul Éluard.

Translated literally, *hain teny* means 'linguistic science' or 'science
of words'. Distinct from, but related to, other Malagasy forms,
ohabolana (proverb or aphorism), *kabany* (public oratory), and
angano (folktale), the distinctive features of the *hain teny* relate to its
original function as a means of resolving disputes. The two oppo-
nents of the litigation improvised a dialogue based on proverbial,
aphoristic statements (*ohabolana*). Often under the disguise of a
love quarrel, the *hain teny* progresses by means of antitheses,
parallelisms, oppositions, and reversals.

Divorced from their context of performance and social purpose,
fixed in a written form and translated into a European language,
Paulhan's *hain teny* are necessarily more gnomic and cryptic than
their origin or source. They have passed through a series of transi-
tions which bring them close to a form such as the *chant alterné*. The
study of the *hain teny* was further encouraged by the discovery of
mid-nineteenth-century manuscripts. A colossal study of these
manuscripts, *Du Ohabolana au hain teny: langue, littérature et politique
à Madagascar*, was published in Paris in 1983.

Comparisons between different French translations of what are in
essence the same *hain teny* (material in the oral tradition is never
word-for-word the same) reveal the polysemy, plurality, ambiguity,
and cryptic quality of the genre where different translations represent different sense—itineraries through the same linguistic net-

work. In addition to attracting the attention of the surrealist poets mentioned above, Paulhan's project was to influence the work of a number of young Malagasy poets writing in French, most importantly Jean-Joseph Rabearivelo and Flavien Ranaivo.

Rabearivelo's early poetry, however, constructs a symbolist aesthetic. There are echoes of the early Mallarmé, Heredia, Laforgue, Jammes, Leon Deubel, and above all Baudelaire, whom Rabearivelo considered to be the greatest French poet. The term 'imitative' has invariably been used to describe Rabearivelo's early poetry and it is certainly true that the reader well versed in French poetry can easily identify his 'influences'. But within a largely oral literary culture, the question of influence has to be entirely reconsidered. As Rabearivelo's contribution is a written one, however, it may be that Valéry's contention in his 'Lettre sur Mallarmé' is valid:

Nous disons qu'un auteur est *original* quand nous sommes dans l'ignorance des transformations cachées qui changèrent les autres en lui; nous voulons dire que la dépendance de *ce qu'il fait* à l'égard de *ce qui fut fait* est excessivement complex et irrégulière. Il y a des œuvres qui sont semblables à d'autres œuvres; il en est qui n'en sont que les inverses; il en est d'une relation si composée avec des productions antérieures, que nous nous y perdons et le faisons venir directement des dieux.[1]

In Rabearivelo's later poetry it is frequently the Malagasy gods who speak, the voices of the ancestors with whom Rabearivelo sought to communicate in his search for Malagasy identity. His two mature collections, *Presque Songes* (1934) and *Traduit de la nuit* (1935) were subtitled 'traduit du hova par l'auteur' and 'traduit par l'auteur du malgache'. How this should be understood is uncertain but relates to a problem central to francophone writing: the extent to which translation into French from another language constitutes French writing.

Some commentators explain Rabearivelo's description as justification for having abandoned fixed forms in favour of free verse, the poet assuming a hostile reaction to this innovation. It seems likely that the move to freer forms was influenced by a similar move within French poetry. This is further suggested by Rabearivelo's use of quotations from Jules Supervielle as epigraphs to certain poems.

That the mature poetry draws on the Malagasy tradition is clear. Throughout his poetic career he had translated, rewritten, and

---

[1] Paul Valéry, *Œuvres I* (1957–60), 633–43 (pp. 634–5).

adapted Malagasy texts. His relationship with the French tradition is equally clear. So too is the way in which many of his texts dramatize this confrontation of language, culture, and race. 'Influences' from the early collection *Sylves* (1927), is explicit:

> Mon chant est imprégné de ta lumière vive
> et son âme a subi, dès longtemps, l'influence
> de la mobilité du son et des nuances
> de ton horizon bleu, vaste ciel d'Iarive!
> Mais que sa courbe épouse plus ta rive
> . . . et sa souplesse aura la suprême élégance
> . . .
> Afin d'honorer mieux cette langue étrangère
> qui sait tant à mon âme intuitive plaire
> et que j'adopte sans éprouver nul remords
>
> quand j'apaise mon cœur sur les hautes terrasses
> où, d'un regard ému, je dénombre les grâces
> de ta beauté finie, ô terre de mes morts![2]

In a later poem, 'Tu viens de relire *Virgile*' (*Traduit de la nuit*), pastoral images of Imerinan life are conflated with Virgilian images:

> Tu viens de relire Virgile,
> tu viens aussi d'écouter les enfants
> qui saluent la néoménie,
> et les contes et les fables de ceux qui ne sont plus.[3]

More mysterious is a cryptic or suggested symbolism within the dense poetic fabric of his texts. In a poem such as 'Zébu' (*Presque-songes*, 1934), the bull is the active subject of the poem. He is associated (through metaphor) with Imerina:

> Voûté comme les cités d'Imerina
> en évidence sur les collines
> ou taillées à même des rochers;
> bossu comme les pignons
> que la lune sculpte sur le soi,
> voici le taureau puissant
> pourpre comme la couleur de son sang.

The flora and fauna of the poem, the reference to ritual sacrifice and the suggestion of a historical perspective locate the poem within a specifically Malagasy landscape:

---

[2] Jean-Joseph Rabearivelo, 'Influences', *Sylves* (1927), 22.
[3] Rabearivelo, 'Tu viens de relire *Virgile*' (*Traduit de la nuit*), *Poèmes* (1990), 165.

Désert, désert,
désert devant le taureau puissant [. . .]
qu'évoques-tu dans son demi-sommeil?
[. . .]
[. . .] ses aïeux qu'engraissaient les paysans
et qu'ils amenaient en ville, parés d'oranges mûres,
pour être abattus en l'honneur du Roi?'[4]

The Malagasy landscape is also a Malagasy 'landscape of the mind' and suggests a network of symbols associated with the ways of that place. The poem also refers to the future, prophesying the bull's death, 'lui qui mourra sans gloire'. But the *significance* of the bull, his symbolic meaning, and the allegory which is the extension of his symbolic status—if he is a symbol of something then the sequence of actions which he performs becomes allegorical or at least suggest allegory—remains mysterious. But both the bull and the story fail to achieve the true status of symbol and allegory if their significance remains mysterious or cryptic. What is true of much modern French poetry takes on a new dimension where a *context* is suggested, particularly one which *if the reader were familiar with it*, might explain the mystery. The poem becomes a linguistic analogue for a psychological state: one of cultural alienation. The locus of the poem is foreign to the poem's language (*langue*, 'tongue') but this in turn suggests that the *meaning* of the language (*langage*, 'system') will remain foreign and therefore allusive.

In the early collections the prominence of death is associated with the symbolist aesthetic. It is gradually transformed and becomes part of a preoccupation with the Malagasy identity, intimately bound up with communication with ancestral voices. Identity and its psychological concomitants and language (*langue* and *langage*) and meaning, become the focus of his work. The poetic tropes associated with these are antitheses, and also moments of uncertainty and transition, such as those between night and day, sleep, dreaming, and wakefulness.

It was Léopold Sédar Senghor's *Anthologie de la nouvelle poésie nègre et malgache* (1948) which was to make Rabearivelo's poetry known to a wider audience. This was equally the case for the poetry of Jacques Rabemananjara. Both his life and work have been dominated by politics. His first two works, *Ansta* (Malagasy for hymn or eulogy) and *Lamba* (Malagasy for the traditional strip of cloth worn

---

[4] Rabearivelo, 'Zébu', ibid. 79.

as clothing), were published in 1956, the year of his release from prison and move to France. In 1959 he published *Nationalisme et problèmes malgaches*, an influential essay, and the following year, the year of the country's Independence, he returned first as Deputy, then Minister, and finally Vice-President of the Republic.

His poems are often long and dense with violent images; both *Ansta* and *Lamba* enact births: in the first case the island's birth and liberation, and in the second, the delivery of a fictional continent. The importance of origins is part of a nostalgic longing for a return to a primordial innocence and coherence, symbolic of a pre-colonial time. *Antidote*, written during a period of considerable political instability and violence, is more overtly militant. Whilst these poems belong within the 'protest' tradition, they are, simultaneously, difficult and complex. Rabemananjara's three plays, *Les Dieux malgaches* (1942), *Boutriers de l'aurore* (1957), and *Les Agapes des dieux* (1962), are concerned with history and the human relationship with the environment. His *Œuvres complètes* were published in 1978.

Four small collections of poetry (*L'Ombre et le vent* (1947), *Mes chansons de toujours* (1955), *Le Retour au bercail* (1962), and *Hain teny* (1975), have been sufficient to confirm Flavien Ranaivo's status as one of the three major Malagasy poets writing in French. His poetics is a poetics of translation where the transposition from Malagasy tradition to French constitutes the generative, creative moment. Certain poetic tropes (ellipses, literal translation of Malagasy compounds) and poetic subjects (love and a fascination with the wistful 'Pays Imerina') are the most obvious features common to Malagasy forms and Ranaivo's texts.

Various less well-known poets have contributed to the francophone Malagasy tradition: Élie Charles Abraham (*Les Saisons de mon cœur*, 1940), Randriamarozaka (*Illusoire ambiance*, 1947), P. Nomyard (*Souffles du printemps*, 1947), Regis Rajemisa-Raolison (*Les Fleurs de l'île rouge*, 1947), Paul Razafimahazo (*Une Gerbe oubliée*, 1947), Louis Sumski, Michel-François Robinary, Jean-Louis Ranaivoson, Fidelis-Justin Rabetsimandranto, and Paul Rakotonirina.

After Independence both Rabemananjara and Ranaivo went into political exile in France: the atmosphere on the island did not encourage literary activity. It was during this period that the first Malagasy novel in French was published, Rabearison's moralizing *Les Voleurs de bœufs* (1965). Equally moralizing but less politically motivated are the stories by Aimée Andria, *Brouillard* (1967) and

Esquif (1968). The process of *malgachisation* which followed the change of leadership in 1973 has discouraged writing in French, but a number of short-story writers including Patrick Andriamangatiana and Tsilavina Ralaindimby have been awarded major prizes for their work. A number of texts, Pélandrova Dreo's autobiographical novel, *Pélandrova* (1975), Michèle Rakotoson's plays, *Sambancy*, one of the winners in the Concours théâtral interafricain in 1980, and *Histoire de Koto*, one of the winners in the same competition in 1982, and Jocelyne Trime's albeit slim collection of poems entitled *Moïka* (1984), testify to the continuing tradition of francophone Malagasy writing suggesting, however marginal it might be, the continuing existence of a body of texts to which new material will be added.

Guide to Further Reading

Novels

Among the most widely known novelists (and novels) of the period before Independence are: Mongo Beti (*Le Pauvre Christ de Bomba*, 1956), Camara Laye (*L'Enfant noir*, 1953), Ferdinand Oyono (*Une Vie de boy*, 1956), and Ousmane Sembène (*Les Bouts de bois de Dieu*, 1960).

After Independence Ahmadou Kourouma's *Les Soleils des indépendances* (1968) is a major literary landmark. Yambo Ouologuem's *Le Devoir de violence* (1968), is, as its title suggests, a controversial publication. V. Y. Mudimbé's *Entre les eaux* (1973) and Jean-Baptiste Tati-Loutard's *Les Chroniques congolaises* (1974) are also major publications of the period.

During the 1980s Henri Lopès's *Le Pleurer-Rire* (1982) is notable particularly for its linguistic and formal innovation. Tchicaya U Tam'si's trilogy (*Les Cancrelats*, 1980; *Les Méduses ou les orties de la mer*, 1982; and *Les Phalènes*, 1984) are also important. Other major novelists of the period include: Mariama Bâ (*Une si longue lettre*, 1979), Nafissatou Diallo (*Le Fort maudit*, 1980), Werewere Liking (*Elle sera de jaspe et de corail*, 1984, a *chant-roman*), M. a M. Ngal (*L'Errance*, 1979), Sony Labou Tansi (*La Vie et demie*, 1979), Aminata Sow Fall (*La Grève des battus*, 1979), Marie Ndiaye (*Comédie classique*, 1986, and *En famille*, 1990).

Poetry

The most famous of the major poets of the first generation is Léopold Sédar Senghor beginning with *Chants d'ombre* (1945). His complete (to that date) *Œuvre poétique* was published in 1990. David Diop, whose work belongs within the protest tradition (*Coups de Pilon*, 1961) and Birago Diop, whose work is more preoccupied with traditional Africa (*Leurres et lueurs* (1960), are also important.

The two major poets of the second generation are Tchicaya U Tam'si, beginning with *Le Mauvais sang* (1955) and Jean-Baptiste Tati-Loutard, beginning with *Poèmes de la mer* (1968).

More recently, important collections have been published by Paul Dakeyo (*D'Éclairs et de foudres*, 1980), Véronique Tadjo (*Latérite*, 1984), and Pascale Quao-Gaudens (*Et . . . sens*, 1988).

Madagascar's outstanding writers have all been poets: Jean-Joseph Rabearivelo (beginning with *La Coupe de songes*, 1924), Flavien Ranaivo (*L'Ombre et le vent*, 1947, is his first collection), and Jacques Rabemananjara (*Œuvres complètes (Poésie)*, 1978). Rabemananjara has also contributed a number of important essays (for example *Nationalisme et problèmes malgaches*, 1959).

Tales

Among the early publications of traditional tales is Léopold Sédar Senghor and Abdoulaye Sadji, *La Belle histoire de Leuk le lièvre* (1953). Tchicaya U Tam'si's *Légendes africaines* (1968) is also important. More recently, and written to connect with the contemporary, Francis Bebey's *La Lune dans un seau tout rouge* (1990) and Guy Menga's *Moni Mambou: retrouvailles* (1991) are notable.

Theatre

Early plays include those by Guillaume Oyono-Mbia (*Trois prétendants, un mari*, 1966) and Bernard Dadié (*Monsieur Thogo-Gnini*, 1970). Two African playwrights stand out both in terms of the amount they have produced and for their contribution to the animation of African theatre. They are Tchicaya U Tam'si (most famously, *Le Bal de Ndinga*, 1987) and Sony Labou Tansi (most controversially, *Qui a mangé Madame d'Avoine Bergotha?*, 1989).

Secondary Material

Among the most useful bibliographies is that published in the *Notre Librairie*, 94, a Special Number listing 2,500 titles by genre and author (alphabetically). Bernard Magnier, *Littératures d'Afrique noire* (1991) is a smaller select, descriptive bibliography of both primary and secondary material.

Studies of African Literature

The seminal introduction is Lilyan Kesteloot, *Les Écrivains noirs de langue française: naissance d'une littérature*, first published in 1963 (most recent translation, *Black Writers in French: A Literary History of Negritude* (Washington, DC, 1991). Other studies include: Dorothy Blair, *African Literature in French* (Cambridge, 1975), Jacques Chevrier, *Littérature nègre* (1974), Robert Cornevin, *Littérature d'Afrique noire de langue française* (1976) and Bernard Mouralis, *Littérature et développement* (1984), a thorough study of the origins and development of writing in French from Africa. Cornevin is also author of *Le Théâtre en Afrique noire* (1970). More specialized and textually analytical is Michel Hausser, *Poétique de la négritude* (Lille, 1982). Pius Ngandu Nkashama, *La Littérature africaine écrite* (1979) is a major study. Mohammadou Kane, *Roman africain et tradition* (1982) is solely concerned with the novel.

The major textbook is Gérard Clavreuil and Alain Rouch, *Littératures nationales d'écriture française* (1986).

Studies of Malagasy writing

There are three particularly important studies of Madagascar's two major writers. Robert Boudry, *Jean-Joseph Rabearivelo et la mort* (1958), which is an early and largely biographical study, situates the writer at a particular moment in colonial history. The proceedings of a major international conference, *Jean-Joseph Rabearivelo, cet inconnu?*, Colloque international sur Jean-Joseph Rabearivelo (Marseille, 1990) contains a number of fine articles. Mukala Kadima-Nzuji, *Jacques Rabemananjara* (1981) is a sound introduction to the author.

Studies of a more theoretical kind and books and articles relevant not only to sub-Saharan Africa and Madagascar but to other areas also, are to be found in the Select Bibliography.

CONCLUSION

I T is principally within a pedagogical context that the question of
how to group cultural productions arises as both an epistemological and ideological problem. Within the field of literature (although
the degree to which the different arts can usefully be studied independently from one another is another major question), it is mainly
literary historians—but also critics—who are bound to propose
structures within which a group of texts is then discussed. The
degree to which context affects 'meaning' is a much-debated philosophical question, but there can be little doubt that what is
foregrounded in a discussion, what is brought to the reader's attention, will be affected by the 'group' into which it has been placed.
Senghor's poem 'Neige sur Paris', collected in an anthology of Senegalese poems, will emerge principally as a poem of exile, whereas
as part of an anthology of poetry about Paris it will offer one of
many constructions of the city.

While historians and critics play a major part in the business of
grouping texts, so too do publishers, producing series and lists
which also suggest fields. As an individual reader, of course, there
may be few constraints on the selection of texts which might be read
(although availability is a significant factor), but as a student of
literature a logic is proposed to explain, if not justify, the choice of
syllabus. Often, however, little discussion of this logic takes place
and there is a sense in which it is proposed as natural, a *donné*.

Historically it is the national perspective which has most persis-
tently explained the logic of the syllabus, and this approach to literature, at least in Europe, gained a virtual monopoly in the nineteenth
century, reaching its zenith at the height of Empire, when the literary traditions of the colonial powers formed the basis of the literary

education in the colonized countries. For the French, and indeed other colonial powers, literature was an important means of assimilation. As Gauri Viswanathan concludes: 'British colonial administrators, provoked by missionaries on the one hand and fears of native insubordination on the other, discovered an ally in English literature to support them in maintaining control of the natives under the guise of a liberal education' ('The Beginnings of English Literary Studies in India', *The Oxford Review*, 9/1-2, 1987).

This book has privileged national and regional groupings in its own organization in part because the newly independent nations which emerged largely in the 1960s just as Empires were dismantled, have themselves proposed national literatures with their own canons, anthologies, histories, and critical studies. There are, however, a number of other models which might, equally, have been chosen. There are the race-based models, most obviously the 'Black writing' model which seeks to map literary production by those of African descent living in all areas of the African diaspora and writing in French. A third model is provided by comparative approaches of various kinds which focus on similarities and differences between two or more francophone literatures, to cite an example from many. The fourth category of model, and the one which is rapidly gaining ground within the anglophone debate, posits characteristics such as hybridity and syncreticity as constituent features of all post-colonial literatures. Syncretism concerns the process which renders previously separate linguistic systems—and by extension, cultures—into a new whole.

This last model reacts against, even denies the possibility of, one of Imperialism's major concerns, which Edward Saïd describes as the 'consolidation of cultures'. A succinct example of the discourse associated with this consolidation is provided by Jean de Castellane's opening address for the 1931 Exposition Coloniale in Paris: 'Dans une pensée de solidarité patriotique et d'union fraternelle, les peuples viendront à Paris examiner, apprécier et aimer dans le riant décor de ce bois verdoyant, l'image véritable de la France intégrale, la France de cinq parties du monde.'[1] The notions of 'solidarity', 'union', and the 'integral' all illustrate Saïd's claim. It is in response to this 'consolidation of cultures' that post-colonial francophone literary projects react in what can—without

[1] 'Discours de M. Jean de Castellane', *Le Figaro* (7 May 1931), quoted by Adriano Moro, 'Paris, lieu de naissance de la négritude', *Paris et le phénomène des capitales littéraires* (2 vols., Paris, 1984), i., 307–12 (p. 307).

too great a risk of oversimplification—now be distinguished as a number of phases visible across the national and regional boundaries within which the literatures of the francophone areas have been discussed above.

During the first phase the educated élite, in the main settlers, who first write in the colonial language, identify with the perspective of that language and are, in most cases, representatives of the colonial power, writing largely with the vision of the outsider. Often the primary concern is to describe a foreign landscape, customs, and people.

During the second phase, although control of production—most importantly publishing—is still maintained by colonial institutions, colonial subjects, 'natives', are assimilated into an educated élite. The degree to which writers who are associated with this phase seek to write against the dominant colonial discourse varies enormously. Many writers of the first generation seek to demonstrate the degree to which they have been fully assimilated into the colonial culture rather than in any sense seeking to introduce anything new, whether in terms of ideology or literary practice. At another extreme is the example of René Maran whose preface to *Batouala* is relatively overt in its criticisms of French colonial policy in West Africa, while the text itself is much more ambiguous in terms of its ideology.

It is during the third phase that the 'Empire writes back' (to use Rushdie's expression), to the imperial centre, challenging the centre's authority, largely encoded in a set of simplistic antitheses: familiar/strange, civilization/primitivism, humanity/savagery, centre/periphery, and so on. In the case of French-Canadian writing it is in relation to both a French and English perspective that texts are written. In francophone North African writing the authority of Muslim fundamentalism may be challenged alongside that of the former colonial power (encoded above all in language). The most obvious manifestation of the periphery's questioning of the worldview which posits this structure involves the rewriting of canonical texts of the Western tradition in such a way as to restructure the European 'reality'. The literary *métissage* that results renders any notion of consolidation impossible, and in its place celebrates the plural, the hybrid, the heterogeneous. Thus, as Alain Baudot has argued: 'Se retournant contre ceux-là mêmes qui aimeraient y voir le triomphe de l'Identique (du Même) et donc de la domination, la francophonie se manifeste comme une stratégie de l'alterité, et se fait véritablement (pour parler comme Adorno), d'une meilleure pratique esthétique et sociale.'²

With the emergence of 'national' literatures (particularly in previously colonized areas but also in Quebec, which because of its political status is to some extent a case apart), the 'stratégie de l'alterité' (as Baudot defines it above) might have lost ground. In other words the rejection of the colonial identity in favour of a freewheeling 'otherness' might have been replaced simply with the affirmation of a new exclusive identity. To some extent this is true of the literature of Quebec, but the complexities of contemporary Quebec culture (there are large French-speaking immigrant communities from other francophone areas) have also encouraged a celebrating of *métissage*, for example. It is also true that 'issues of nationalism, nation and nationhood' have come to the forefront of recent debate in the wake of events in Eastern Europe and the Soviet Union. Christopher Miller argues that these happenings:

Have reminded us of what Renan said about unity in his famous essay 'What is a nation?': it always comes about brutally. In order for a unit to arise and take on the condition of nationhood, it is necessary for all the individuals within it to remember certain things; to remember what brings them together and forget what could tear them apart. The problem is, of course, in deciding whom and what to 'forget'.³

Literature is a major storehouse for a nation's 'remembering' and the gaps or silences may sometimes be read as traces of the forgotten. But what is important, in the context of this discussion, is to be reminded that 'national literatures' may be problematic (dissident voices may have been silenced), rather they may be necessary moments in a historical progression, *one* epistemological configuration among many. Where that progression will lead is a matter for conjecture.

What is unquestionable is the degree to which the growth of francophone literatures, and the complexity of the critical debates which accompany them, have fundamental consequences for French literature. The interactions between French literature and

---

² A. Baudot, 'Autonomie et autonymie des littératures francophones?', paper presented at the Modern Languages Association Conference, Los Angeles, 1982, quoted by D. Marx-Scouras, 'The Poetics of Maghrebine Illegitimacy', *L'Esprit Créateur*, 26 (1986), 3–10 (p. 4).

³ Christopher Miller, 'Nationalism as Resistance and Resistance to Nationalism in the Literature of Francophone Africa', *Yale French Studies* 82/1 (1993), 62–100 (p. 62).

francophone literatures are complex and cannot be accounted for simply in terms of notions of continuation or adaptation. Post-colonial francophone discourse questions European discourse from a position within (in linguistic terms) and outside (in terms of place and from the perspective of multilingualism). French fictional and historical accounts are reread and rewritten. These *subversions*—encoded in the/a French—as the term suggests, disturb the French account. Each must take the other into consideration. It is this dialectical relationship between the colonial and the post-colonial which is the most important characteristic of francophone writing, rather than an 'independent' recovery and reconstruction of a pure and *original* national or regional identity.

An interesting response to the question is provided by Édouard Glissant:

On ne peut pas être prophète. Je crois que le destin des langues est lié au rapport entre oralité et écriture. Peut-être que le livre va mourir, en tant que forme concrète de la connaissance de nos sociétés. Il est fort possible que le livre meure et que dans trente ans les lecteurs des livres se constitu-ent en sectes des catacombes, réprouvés par la morale publique. Il est possible que, dans cette perspective, les livres soient des réceptacles, à peu près clandestins de l'organicité des langues et que la publicité des langues, ce soit une publicité de codes, un peu comme le code de la route, le code gastronomique, etc. Les langues s'appauvrissent. Mon espoir, c'est que cette espèce de fragrance, de variances, d'infinie multiplicité des contacts, des conflits de langues, va donner naissance à un nouvel imaginaire de la parole humaine qui va peut-être transcender les langues. Je ne veux pas être prophète, mais je pense qu'un jour la sensibilité humaine va aller vers des langages qui vont dépasser les langues, qui vont intégrer toutes sortes de dimensions, de formes, de silences, de représentations, qui seront autant de nouveaux éléments de langue.[4]

[4] Lise Gauvin, 'L'imaginaire des langues: Entretien avec Édouard Glissant', *Études françaises*, 28/2–3 (1992–3), 11–22 (p. 22).

Select Bibliography

A selection of major works concerned with the theory of francophone literatures or two or more of them.

AZIM, F., *The Colonial Rise of the Novel* (London, 1993).

BURTON, P., DYSON, K. K., ARDENER, S. (eds.), *Bilingual Women: Anthropological Approaches to Second Language Use* (Oxford, 1994).

CHEYFITZ, E., *The Poetics of Imperialism: Translation and Colonization from The Tempest to Tarzan* (New York, 1991).

GATES, JR., HENRY LOUIS (ed.), *Black Literature and Literary Theory* (New York, 1984).

——(ed.), *'Race', Writing and Difference* (Chicago, 1986).

HAMERS, J. F., and BLANC, M. H. A., *Bilinguality and Bilingualism* (Cambridge, 1989), originally published in French as *Bilingualité et bilinguisme* (Brussels, 1983).

HARASYM, S. (ed.), *Gayatri Chakravorty Spivak: The Post-Colonial Critic; Interviews, Strategies, Dialogues* (New York, 1990).

Itineraires et contacts de cultures, 1, 'L'Écrit et l'oral' (1982).

——7, 'Le Roman colonial' (1987).

JOUBERT, J.-L., LECARME, J., TABONE, E., VERCIER, B., *Les Littératures francophones depuis 1945* (1986).

KHATIBI, A. (ed.), *Du bilinguisme* (1985).

LEINER, J., *Imaginaire langage—Identité culturelle Négritude* (Tübingen, 1980).

MILLER, L. M., *Blank Darkness: Africanist Discourse in French* (Chicago, 1985).

Œuvres et Critiques, 3/2, 4/1 'Littérature africaine et antillaise' (1979).

ROUCH, A., and CLAVREUIL, G., *Littératures nationales d'écriture française: Histoire littéraire et anthologie* (1986).

SAID, E., *Orientalism* (London, 1978).

——*Culture and Imperialism* (London, 1993).

VIATTE, A., *Histoire comparée des littératures francophones* (1980).

WALL, C. A. (ed.), *Changing Our Own Words: Essays on Criticism, Theory, and Writing by Black Women* (New Brunswick, NJ, 1989).

WILLIAMS, P., and CHRISMAN, L. (eds.), *Colonial Discourse and Post-Colonial Theory: A Reader* (Hemel Hempstead, 1993).

Yale French Studies, 82 and 83, 'Post/Colonial Conditions: Exiles, Migrations, and Nomadisms' (New Haven, 1993).

Index